AF335429

JOURNEY THROUGH GRIEF

A Sephardic Manual for the Bereaved
and Their Community

JOURNEY THROUGH GRIEF

A Sephardic Manual for the Bereaved
and Their Community

by
RABBI YAMIN LEVY

Library of Congress Cataloging-in-Publication Data

Levy, Yamin.
  Journey through grief : a Sephardic manual for the bereaved and their community / Yamin Levy.
      p. cm.
  ISBN 0-88125-802-4
  1. Jewish mourning customs. 2. Funeral rites and ceremonies, Jewish.
3. Death--Religious aspects--Judaism. 4. Judaism--Sephardic rite. I. Title.
  BM712.L49 2003
  296.4'45--dc21

                          2003007660

Manufactured in the United States of America
Typeset by Raphael Freeman, Jerusalem Typesetting

Published by
KTAV Publishing House, Inc.
930 Newark Avenue
Jersey City, NJ 07306
Email: info@ktav.com
www.ktav.com
(201) 963-9524
Fax (201) 963-0102

CONTENTS

This project was made possible
By a grant from Fran and Morris Gad

In Memory of
David Ben Nissan Gad ז"ל
May his memory be a blessing to all

PREFACE

The *raison d'etre* of this book has been clear to me ever since I became a conscious member of the Sephardic community. It was conceived in my early years as a Rabbinical student at Yeshiva University under the tutelage of Haham Solomon Gaon (see author's dedication below) and began taking shape after the publication of my first book *Confronting the Loss of a Baby: A Personal and Jewish Perspective*.

Over the years I have participated and officiated at countless funerals and observed time and again the bereaved seeking guidance. No matter the educational or religious background – with the death of a loved one come feelings of guilt, regret and fear. Our *hakhmim* of blessed memory offer a penetrating insight into the psyche of the bereaved by suggesting a prayer that may be recited by the *onen*:

> …And he accepts upon himself [herself] the divine decree. And what does he say? "Master of the universe! I have sinned before you. Few of my obligations have I wiped clean and am I not fit for more [punishment]? May it be your will to repair our breaches and comfort us." (*Masechet Semahot* chapter 10)

The simplicity of this short prayer suggests an almost universal quality of the nature of reflection the bereaved might experience. I have yet to meet mourners who do not want to meticulously observe the ritual as prescribed by tradition. This work is, therefore, intended to be a guide, as the title suggests, and not a code or record of the laws, traditions and observances. It is my hope that it will be useful to both the bereaved and their community.

There are other books (in English) in the market place on mourning and bereavement. I occasionally make reference to them primarily the pioneering work of Maurice Lamm, *The Jewish Way in Death and Mourning*, Abner Wiess's book *Death and Bereavement: A Halachik Guide*, and Rabbi Chaim Binyamin Goldberg's *Mourning in Halacha*. While each of these works make important contributions on the subject of mourning none afford the Sephardic bereaved a comprehensive guide for his or her grief. Dr. Herbert C. Dobrinsky's book *A Treasury of Sephardic Laws and Customs* has a series of chapters on the subject that have been instructive on multiple levels. Recently Abraham Sutton of the Syrian community of Brooklyn published a short book called *Meir Or*, which guides the bereaved through the Syrian Sephardic rituals of mourning. The book you are now holding incorporates the Syrian traditions as well as affords the reader the benefit of my personal experience in the rabbinate, pastoral guidance, and a broad range of topics.

I humbly submit this book for publication and pray that the principles of *Hesed* presented within its covers correctly reflect the wisdom of our Torah and of our sages of blessed memory, and be a guide for those who wish to bring a degree of healing to a world in need.

ACKNOWLEDGEMENTS

Before I acknowledge the many who have helped along the way I will continue an old yet scarce tradition of stating: Odeh Hashem Bekhol Levav – I thank the almighty with a full heart for His countless blessings including the opportunity to bring this book out to light.

With the passage of time, maturity and experience comes a profound recognition and deep sense of appreciation for those who pointed the way, offered boundless love and support, and made courageous sacrifices. In this spirit I acknowledge my dear parents Mimon and Esther Levy.

This book has gone through numerous incarnations. The first of which were carefully read and gently commented on by Frances Israel of Seattle. Its later version incorporates comments by Allan Beyda and Evan Hoffman of Great Neck. David and Vicki Angel have been involved with this project from its inception. Their support and friendship continues to enrich me intellectually and spiritually.

A special thank you goes to Fran and Morris Gad, for their trust and support of this project. This book is dedicated in memory of David Gad who remains an inspiration to all who new him and those who benefited from his kindness and generosity. I also thank Marcos Benzaquen and Maurice Setton for their commitment and support of this project. A warm thank you to Laura Tammero for her help and assistance. I acknowledge the leadership and membership of Congregation Shaare Zion of Great Neck for affording me a base to do that which I do.

This project is in no small measure a continuation of the work begun approximately 20 years ago by Yeshiva University's Dr. Herbert C. Dobrinsky, Vice President for University Affairs and co-founder and consultant of the Sephardic Studies program. I am indebted to him on a personal level for his support and friendship over the years. I express a *Hakarat HaTov* to Rabbi Dr. Michael D. Schmidman, Dean of undergraduate Jewish Studies at Yeshiva University for his guidance and friendship.

Thank you to Mr. Bernard Scharfstein at Ktav Publishing for his enthusiasm and personal attention he gave this book from start to finish. Raphaël Freeman who did the typesetting exercised incredible patience and kindness towards me and for that I am grateful.

It is with great humility and immeasurable gratitude that I thank Rabbi Shalom Carmy for his majestic example of what it means to love learning, teaching and *Yirath Shamayim*.

My in-laws Dr. Mel and Goldie Isaacs are a constant source of support and encouragement offering generously their wisdom and eternal optimism. My children Amichai, Yedidya, Hananel, Shira and Eliyahu are each in their very own way an incredible source of joy and Nachat.

This book is as much a result of my wife Dvorah's work as it is mine. She is truly a partner in our shared mission in *Olam Hazeh*. Words of gratitude would only be a pale expression of my profound indebtedness to her. Her strength, wisdom, and sensitivity are both humbling and inspiring.

I dedicate this book to the memory of *Haham* Solomon Gaon *Alav Hashalom*. *Haham* Gaon held the Maxwell R. Maybaum Memorial Chair in Talmud and Sephardic Codes (Halakhah) at Rabbi Isaac Elchanan Theological Seminary, an affiliate of Yeshiva University from the late 1960s until the mid-90s when he passed away. *Haham* Gaon was a dedicated communal leader and gentle teacher. I was the beneficiary of his attention and warmth.

INTRODUCTION

If life is a pilgrimage, death is an arrival, a celebration. The last word should be neither craving nor bitterness, but peace, gratitude.

– Abraham Joshua Heschel[1]

If you are reading this book because you are a mourner, I pray: *Min hashamayim tenuhamu*, "May you be comforted from the heavens above." Indeed, the death of a loved one, no matter how prepared we may be, is a very profound sorrow. The grief associated with such a loss affects us in so many different ways. Every aspect of our life is thrown out of balance. Our emotions, our physical bodies, and our day-to-day living are all touched by our grief. Grief affects almost every human being, and yet we are so ill prepared for the confrontation with the loss of a loved one.

Our entire life is spent learning how to acquire "things" and accumulate "stuff." Bookstores are stocked with practical guides, manuals, many of them best-sellers, on "How to Get What You Want," while little attention is given to the learning process of letting go of something we once had. Let us think about it for a moment: during our formative years the emphasis was always placed on learning how to acquire. Getting what we want is such a central part of our lives, be it praise and approval, which is something we sought as children and continue to seek as adults, or happiness through the acquisition of gifts, money, and other material goods. This frame of mind makes learning how to accept loss, heal its trauma, and get on with life that much more difficult.

Grief is confusing precisely because of what we have learned about acquiring. Western culture has trained us to believe that only through the acquisition of "things" and by accumulating more will we find happiness. Yet the reality of life is that we are always experiencing loss. So what happens to us when a core value of our culture clashes with the reality of our lives? Tragically, the answer is usually confusion and denial. Oftentimes those who are bereaved withdraw into themselves, not knowing how to feel or how to act. Society oftentimes helps to isolate the bereaved by stigmatizing them or by making mourners feel like a burden. Both as individuals and as a community, we must learn how to grapple with loss appropriately. By learning how to grieve in a safe and structured environment, we can make a painful experience a magnificent process of transformation and growth. Our Jewish tradition affords the mourner precisely that: a safe and structured environment, as well as a guide on how to travel the difficult journey through grief and bereavement.

The scope of this book goes beyond the laws and customs on grief and mourning for the Sephardic mourner. This book is about recovery and resolution. To recover we must recognize that grief, like a wound, requires appropriate attention in order to heal. Recovery involves a confrontation with the tragedy of death and an expression of the intense feelings of sadness associated with the loss of a loved one. The Jewish laws associated with mourning and the various traditions that have developed throughout the ages afford the bereaved precisely that kind of spiritual response. The rituals reflect the horror and tragedy of death, and at the same time they facilitate the expression of emotions.

It is through knowledge and understanding of our laws and traditions that these rituals will have meaning for the mourner and will ultimately bring a degree of comfort for the loss entailed by death. Our sages of blessed memory saw mizvot (commandments) as much more than just religious practice. Their perspective is described in the Midrash as follows:

[Someone on a ship] has been thrown [overboard] into the water. The captain stretches out a rope and says to him: "Take hold of this rope with your hand and do not let go, for if you do, you will lose your life!" Similarly, the Holy One, blessed be He, said to Israel: Adhere to the commandments, then, "Ye that cleave unto the Lord your God are alive, every one of you, this day."[2]

We are not used to thinking of law and commandments in this way, yet Judaism insists that law offers a powerful way of giving meaning to human life. This is especially clear within the framework of the laws of *Avelut* (mourning). The law affords the bereaved guidance and gives structure to the grieving process.[3] An appropriate response to the loss of a loved one is *critical* to one's emotional and physical recovery. Some people repress their grief, unable to display emotion. Studies have shown that such a response can be harmful, both physically and emotionally. Others grieve too intensely; they cannot put their loss within a framework of reality. This too, is harmful to the bereaved. The Talmud understood the need for a structured response to grief, as illustrated in the following story:

A certain woman was in the neighborhood of Rabbi Huna. She had seven sons. One of them died. She wept over him too much. Rabbi Huna said to her: "Do not do thus!" She paid no heed to him. He said to her: "If you heed me, good; if not, prepare more shrouds."[4]

The story concludes with a tragic ending. The woman does not resolve her grief and dies of a broken heart.

But the questions arise: How much should one mourn? How much is too much? How little is enough? The answers lie within the structure that our rituals afford us. By observing the prescribed rituals, we need not ever reflect on whether we have grieved enough or too much. The structure has been tested by time and is the means through which a complete healing can occur.

A subtle, yet critical idea found within the laws of *Avelut* is the constant reminder that you are not alone in your grief. You are now a part of the not-so-exclusive club of mourners who have preceded you, who grieve with you, and who will come after you, and of all who mourn for Zion and Jerusalem – all of whom have used the rituals and traditions as an anchor and support on their journey through grief toward comfort and resolution.

Since mourning is a communal activity, we are required to study the laws of *Avelut* even though we ourselves are not bereaved. These laws are a fundamental part of *gemilut hassadim* (acts of love and kindness), one of the three pillars of our faith. Shimon the Righteous states in Pirke Avot (Ethics of Our Fathers):

> The world stands on three pillars; Torah, worship, and acts of love and kindness. Rabbi Yehudah further states that one who denies acts of *gemilut hassadim* is as if he denies God.[5]

Nihum aveilim (comforting the mourner) – being present and supportive for a relative, friend, or member of the community who is confronted with loss – is an act of great love and compassion. In order to fulfill this *mizvah* correctly, one must be educated in all the aspects of the law.

Furthermore, the study of the laws of *Avelut*, the laws of mourning, involves a great deal more than simply a code of laws. In particular, these laws are actually a study about life and living. They afford us an important reminder – namely, that we are all destined to die; that dying is the most natural reality of our existence. Death is one of the only certainties in our lives, and yet we act as if it is something that happens only to others. A few years ago, in the adult education classes I teach, I did a series on death and dying. Two-thirds of my regular participants did not show up. A few of them were honest and said they did not want to think about death. We spend our entire lives in complete denial of the reality of death – it is something that you see on television or read about in the papers, but not something relevant to "me." I have personally encountered people who actually believe that if they do not talk about it, it will go away and never occur.

Our society is notorious for its denial of death. Our obsession with the search for the fountain of youth has given birth to the philosophy that one should not even consider the possibility of mortality, for doing so brings one's own death closer. I often caution those who share this point of view. You cannot go through life trying to avoid dying. It just doesn't work. By recognizing the existence of death, we naturally concentrate on living and loving, on being present in the here-and-now.

And then there are those who do not deny death, and have a healthy respect for the idea that our time in this world is limited, but live in constant fear of it. Fear of death and fear of the aging process can be all-consuming and debilitating. People spend inordinate amounts of time making themselves miserable over the inevitable. How strange, I often wonder, that people expend so much energy on their fear of death when in reality our energies should be spent on how we live and the quality of life we set for ourselves.

I have learned from death and the reality of its existence some fundamental attitudes on how life should be conducted. Learning to cope with the fear of death and being able to talk comfortably about its inevitability makes for a more meaningful existence and an appreciation of every moment of life. The psychiatrist Viktor Frankl put it beautifully: "The meaning of human existence is based on its irreversible quality."[6] Living with the awareness that today may be our last day heightens our level of existence and inspires more noble living. It provides urgency for those things that are important and can no longer be put off until sometime in the future. Hillel the elder stated: *Im lo akhshav ematay*[7]? "If not now, when?" Indeed, a healthy understanding and awareness of our own mortality is not a sign of giving up but rather the seal of courage and wisdom. It is the mark of one who lives life fully, nobly, generously, creatively, and cherishes every moment. While there is a limit to how long we will ultimately live, it is we alone who determine the depth and the quality of our lives. Joshua Liebman writes: "We must make up for the brevity of life by heightening the intensity of life."[8] So often I am called upon to comfort mourners whose loved one died completely unexpectedly. "Just yesterday he was fine" are the words I hear. Recall what our sages advise us: "A man cannot say to the Angel of Death: 'I wish to arrange my affairs before I die.'"[9] Imagine living every moment of our lives with the consciousness of the psalmist: "Teach us to number our days that we obtain a heart of wisdom."[10]

In Jewish thought, one can choose life over death. "I shall not die, for I will live" are the words of King David. The righteous, the Talmud teaches, are alive even after their physical death.[11] And, just as there is life after death, there is also death even while alive, the walking dead, those whose lives lack a dynamic, life-affirming energy. Taking even one's breath for granted is to strip existence of meaning!

Learning to live within the framework that life is only temporary is not a depressing idea but a truly enriching experience. Awareness of our own mortality heightens our sensitivities. We learn to deepen our relationship with the familiar and appreciate more fully the new. The things we see we really *see*; and we really listen to the things we hear. Because we shall not always be together, we grow closer to our family and friends. We resolve to mend broken relationships and forget petty differences. We learn to forgive not only those who have hurt us, but also ourselves.

When our focus is on living, meaningful living becomes a priority. Uncovering a sense of life's patterns, coherence, and purpose becomes a part of our consciousness. We realize that "today is indeed the first day of the rest of my life." *Lo amut ki ehyeh va'asaper ma'aseh Yah* – "I shall not die, rather I shall live and relate the wonders of God" – is our motto.

Our tradition provides us with a complete and perfect religious response to death. It provides us with a means of accepting death, of mourning and grieving, and of living again fully. In this book I hope to provide mourners with a concise and clear guide to the laws and rituals of mourning in the Sephardic tradition. Along the way I pray that this book will also educate our communities on the *mizvah* of *nihum aveilim* and help to create an environment where people will develop a renewed respect for life, love, caring, and compassion.

It is my heartfelt prayer that one day we will merit to see the fulfillment of Isaiah's prophecy:

Bila hamavet lanetzah umaha Hashem dima me'al kol panim; veherpat amo yasir me'al kol ha'aretz.
May death be swallowed up forever, and may the Lord God wipe

away tears from every face and remove the mocking of God's people from throughout the world.[12]

Endnotes

1   Abraham J. Heschel, "Death as Homecoming," in *Jewish Reflections on Death*, ed. Jack Riemer (New York: Schocken Books, 1979), p. 72.
2   Midrash Rabbah, Shelah Lekha 27:6.
3   See Phyllis Plague, "The Socio-Cultural Expressions and Implications of Death, Mourning and Bereavement Arising Out of the War Situation in Israel," Israel Annals of Psychiatry and Related Disciplines 2, no. 4 (December 1972): 300–330; Victor Solomon, Psychodynamics of Grief Management in Jewish Law and Tradition. PhD. diss. New York University (University Microfilms International, 1981).
4   TB Moed Katan 27b
5   Ecclesiastes Rabbah 7:1.
6   Viktor Frankl, *Man's Search for Meaning* (New York: Washington Square Press, 1965).
7   Ethics of Our Fathers 1:14
8   Joshua Loth Liebman, *Peace of Mind* (New York: Simon & Shuster, 1946) p. 93.
9   Deuteronomy Rabbah 9:3.
10 Psalms 118:17
11 TB Berakhot 18a–18b.
12 Isaiah 25:8

CHAPTER 1
Viduy: Gateway to Healing

Thus says the Lord: Let not the wise man glory in his wisdom, neither let the mighty man glory in his might, let not the rich man glory in his riches; but let him that glorieth glory in this, that he understands and knows Me, that I am the Lord who exercises loving-kindness, judgment, and righteousness on earth; for in these things I delight, says the Lord.

– Jeremiah 9:22–23

While the pain of watching a loved one in the throes of death is great, it is important to remember that mourning begins only after death[1]. Receiving the news that a loved one has a terminal illness is devastating. Yet we know that we are all mortal, and at moments like these we pray that death will come later rather than sooner, and that until that time we will be spared further pain and suffering. The Jewish response to terminal illness is proactive and has always included both prayer and *teshuvah* (repentance).

Our tradition provides us with a formal response to terminal illness, namely the *Viduy*. The word *viduy* means "confession," and it is through the formal text of this response that the process of *teshuvah* and prayer is achieved. In fact, this process is not exclusively associated with death, for it is as relevant, if not more so, in life. The Talmud relates the lesson Rabbi Eliezer taught his students:

> "Repent one day before your death." His students asked him, "How are we supposed to know when we will die?" "All the more reason to repent today," replied the teacher, "lest you die tomorrow; and if you repent today, your entire life will be spent in repentance."[2]

The primary purpose of the *Viduy* is to help us find a sense of peace and equanimity in order to complete any unfinished business, especially if death is imminent. *Viduy* requires serious attention and should be facilitated by an experienced rabbi or member of the *hevra kadisha* (burial society).[3]

In the strict halakhic sense, *Viduy* is a confessional that is recited immediately prior to death. Regarding its recitation *Maran*,[4] author of the *Shulhan Arukh,* the classical code of Jewish law, suggests that is should be presented in a gentle and cautious manner "lest the dying person be distressed by the suggestion of his imminent death." Rabbi Yosef Karo further recommends what one should say to the sick person before the *Viduy* is recited in order to soften the shock and alleviate some of the fear. The text is as follows:

> Many have confessed but have not died; and many who have not confessed died. And many who are walking outside in the marketplace confess. By the merit of your confession, you shall live. And all who confess have a place in the world-to-come.[5]

Recitation of the Viduy

Since the actual text of the *Viduy* is a confrontation with the life one has led, the words should be recited not only in the Hebrew but also in a language that the sick person can understand. If, tragically, it is already too late and the sick person is unconscious or too weak to read the text or even understand what is taking place, the *Viduy* can be recited on the person's behalf by the rabbi or a family member. A suitable text follows. The Hebrew version can be found in the appendix.

TO BE RECITED WITH A TERMINALLY ILL PERSON
A Paraphrase of the *Viduy*

Ruler of the worlds, Master of forgiveness and mercy, may it be Your will, Lord, my God and God of my fathers, that I be remembered for good before Your throne of glory. Look upon my suffering, for there is no unblemished place in my flesh because of Your anger; no peace in my bones because of my sins. And now, God of forgiveness, turn Your kindness toward me, and do not enter into judgment against Your servant. If the time is drawing near for me to die, Your unity will never depart from my mouth, as it is written in Your Torah: "Hear, O Israel, the Lord is our God the Lord is one." Blessed is the Name of His glorious kingdom for all eternity. I acknowledge before You, Lord my God and God of my fathers and God of the spirits of all flesh, that my recovery is in Your hands and all the events of my life are in Your hands. May it be Your will to heal me completely. And may I be remembered by You, and may my prayers be remembered in front of You like the prayer of Hezekiah when he was ill. But if the time has drawn near for me to die, may my death be an atonement for all the mistakes, sins, and rebellions I have erred, sinned, and rebelled before You, from the day I came into being on this earth until this moment. Grant that my portion be in Gan Eden; may I merit the world-to-come, which awaits the righteous. Cause me to know the path of life, satiety of joys with Your countenance, pleasantness in Your right hand forever. Blessed is the One who hears prayer.

We beg You! With the strength of Your right hand's greatness, untie the bundled sins. Accept the prayer of Your nation; strengthen us, purify us, O Awesome one. Please, O Strong One – those who foster Your oneness, guard them like the pupil of the eye. Bless them, purify them, show them pity. May Your righteousness always recompense them. Powerful Holy One, with Your abundant goodness, guide Your congregation. One and only Exalted One, turn to Your nation which proclaims

Your holiness. Accept our entreaty and hear our cry, O Knower of mysteries. Blessed is the Name of His glorious kingdom for all eternity.

May the pleasantness of my Lord, our God, be upon us – may He establish our handiwork for us; our handiwork may He establish.

"And it came to pass, in the thirteenth year, on the fifth of the fourth month when I was in the midst of exile, on the river Chebar, the heavens were opened and I saw divine visions" (Ezekiel 1:1). "In the year of the death of King Uzziah, I saw the Lord sitting on a high and exalted throne, and its lower emanations filled the Temple. Fiery angels were standing above Him. Each one had six wings. With two he would cover his face. With two he would cover his feet. And with two he would fly. Each one called to the other and declared: 'Holy, holy, holy is the Lord, of hosts, His glory fills all the earth'" (Isaiah 6:1).

Hear, O Israel, the Lord is our God, the Lord is one.

The Lord is God. The Lord is God.

The Lord reigns, the Lord reigned, the Lord will reign forever and ever.

Moses is true and his Torah is true. I hope for Your salvation, Lord.

May the soul of Your servant rejoice, for I lift up my soul to You, Lord.

Into Your hand I entrust my spirit. You have redeemed me, Lord, the true God. May the words of my mouth and the thoughts of my heart find favor before You, my rock and my redeemer.[6]

While the recitation of the *Viduy* is formal and its words carefully measured, there is room in this process for a more spontaneous and personal component. I maintain that *Viduy* should be a process whose scope is much greater than simply the recitation of the words given above. In order to be complete, the *Viduy* should include three aspects.

The first involves personal transformation and the recognition that life is not only about physical health but also about spiritual and emotional well-being. I call this *redemptive healing*.

I have been asked a certain question time and time again, but never as poignantly as when Aaron asked it. Aaron, a young man, was living with a painful and terminal skin cancer. After services one week, exhausted from the chemotherapy and emotionally a wreck, he asked, "Rabbi, what for, the prayers and the *tehillim* (psalms), do you really think my cancer is going to be cured?" His words lingered for a moment. I embraced him, looked him in the eyes. and responded in as confident a voice as I could produce, "Yes, our prayers have purpose." We pray, and will continue to pray, for a complete physical recovery. Indeed, we cannot fathom the scope of God's wonders. We will never lose hope. Our sages have stated, "Even when a sharp sword is placed right on a person's throat, one should not desist from imploring the Almighty for mercy."[7] *Ein ye'ush*, we cannot allow ourselves to despair or give up.

Ours is a tradition that has always sought ways to inspire hope and faith even under the most difficult circumstances. Rabbi Marc Angel, in his classic work *The Rhythms of Jewish Living: A Sephardic Approach*, offers a penetrating insight into the text of the *Viduy*. "The confession," Rabbi Angel writes, "indicates a tenacity to life. Even when it appears obvious that one will die, he first asks God to heal him."[8] "Aaron," I implored: "Never, *never* give up praying for a complete and speedy recovery."

I continued to explain to Aaron that while we must do everything in our power to seek physical health, we must also learn to heal our emotional and spiritual selves. Praying, I said, is not simply about asking God to relieve the physical pain or disease from the body; we also pray so that our hearts will open into a realm of love and understanding[9]. Healing is the clarity we seek in order to grow, transform, and gain wisdom about ourselves and the world around us. This happens when we enter the unexplored territory of the mind and body – the vast indefinable spaciousness of our very being. This process goes beyond life and beyond death. Thus begins the process of letting go of those things that block the heart and clog our emotional arteries. Learning to dissolve the dark fog of anger, fear, forgetfulness, and unkindness that surrounds us at any given moment is a magnificent gift. Through prayer we learn to open the channels of love and compassion for ourselves and those around us.

"Our prayers," I told Aaron, "are not complete if they do not include this element of redemptive *refuah* (healing). And this too is what we pray for."

The second aspect of the *Viduy* includes a close introspective regarding the life we have led vis-à-vis God. In my experience with the terminally ill, I have yet to encounter an individual who does not welcome the opportunity to make peace with God.[10] Take Harriette, for example. I knew her for two years before she passed away. She was a woman who never made time for religion and seldom considered God in her day-to-day life. Her life was dominated by her concerns for her family and her business. When death was imminent and I introduced God into her consciousness, she was completely receptive. She was not, as some people suspected, cynical or derogatory. Prayer became a priority, as did the study of Torah and the observance of ritual. The last words she uttered we said together; they were the words of the *Shema,* which she recited with unique peacefulness.

Finally, for the *Viduy* to be complete, it must include an introspective regarding the life one has led vis-à-vis other people. There cannot be a true *teshuvah*, a real transformation, if we do not attempt to make peace with those whom we have had personal contact during our lifetime.

The terminally ill may at times feel hopeless; however, they are far from helpless. Death does not have to be accepted passively. This is the time to heal the soul and the spirit through our personal relationships. Indeed, this is the time to let go of past anger, fears, and disputes and focus all energies on mending relationships and correcting wrongs. *Viduy* is not complete if it does not include the component that brings healing and peace in one's personal life.

In the summer of 1991, I was asked to visit a fifty-year-old woman who was living with terminal cancer. The doctors had given her three to six months to live after finding fifteen tumors in her brain. She wasted no time. The minute I arrived she insisted on getting right to work. There were people she wanted to speak with, some of whom she had not spoken with in ten or fifteen years. I helped facilitate the contacts. There were decisions that she needed to make that would affect other people in different ways. I was there to offer my support for the decisions she made and to help the survivors understand her perspective. She was very excited when I suggested that she write a message to her recently born grandchild whom she would probably never get to know. The entire experience brought about incredible change and transformation, not only for her, but also for her family, her friends, and for me.

Again, I have yet to meet a terminally ill person who is not willing to resolve personal issues. Illness and the nearness of death have already altered their perspective. Oftentimes the resistance comes from the alienated family member. This is quite tragic. Studies have shown that unfinished business with the deceased does not get buried with them. If it does not surface shortly after death, it most certainly surfaces at a later time in life. The pain begins when feelings of guilt – "I should haves" and "If onlys" – creep into the psyche, haunting and tormenting the estranged mourner for years and years. No one wants to live with that burden, and now is the opportunity to lighten the weight, to let go of the ugly past and heal the present.

Death is the opportunity for parents and children, siblings, spouses, and extended-family members to come together and put an unpleasant past behind them. The same rules of day-to-day life do not apply when a family is confronted with death. "Death trumps all."[11] Letting go is the process by which we lighten our burden of anger and heal the pain of relationships that have been neglected or estranged. As a rabbi, I have witnessed the awful pain involved when people go to their grave without having resolved issues with family and friends. There comes a time when one must say "What was, was, and now it is over."

Practical Things That Can Be Done

It is important to remember that dying is actually about living. Don't mourn before death. Use the time to deepen and enrich your life and the life of your loved one who is living with a terminal disease. As Jews, we never give up hope and continue to pray until the end for a complete healing. Yet a cure is not necessarily all there is. Perhaps the journey is more important than the goal. The faith, the prayer, and the rise of the human spirit are ultimately the purpose of human existence. The last months, weeks, days, or even moments with a loved one can actually be the beginning of a search for harmony, meaning, and spiritual altitude. Here are some suggestions to help facilitate life in the face of death:

1. As we approach the end of life, many of us like to tell the story of our lives: who we were and what we did with our lives. Encourage the terminally ill to talk about their life story by asking them questions:
   - What was your greatest accomplishment?
   - What was your greatest failure?
   - How do you rate yourself in life?
   - What have you left undone?
   - What fears are you experiencing?

2. Help the dying person identify any practical tasks that should be done.
   - Drawing up a will.
   - Delegating power of attorney to a spouse or child who can make decisions regarding medical treatment.
   - Evaluating a medical directive or a "living will."
   - Checking insurance coverage and reviewing financial status.

3. Use this time to deepen and enrich relationships. Give the dying person the opportunity to share some personal thoughts with different members of the family and close personal friends.
   - Have each member of the family go in to see the dying person alone.
   - Hold the hand of the dying person.
   - Tell the dying person what meaning he or she has given to your life.

4. In a lifetime we are bound to make mistakes related to parents, co-workers, and friends. Occasionally we lie, cheat, or hurt another person's feelings. This is the time to reach out and ask for forgiveness.
   - Ask the dying person if you can help make contact with anyone he or she would like to reach out to.
   - Is there any unfinished business that has to be resolved?
   - Has anyone been hurt as a result of the dying person's actions?

Ethical Will

Illness, and especially terminal illness, causes us to confront our deepest recesses of faith and feelings. It is in this place of inner serenity that one finds clarity and perspective on life and living. The most beautiful moments I have shared with the terminally ill have been the times they tap into that clarity and share something meaningful with me, or with their family or their friends. Moving beyond the illness and transcending the body in order to share a quality moment with someone special is to give an incredible gift. As the English poet Thomas Campbell wrote, "To live in hearts we leave behind / Is not to die."[12]

The Torah records that when our forefather Jacob felt he was close to death, he called all his children and grandchildren in to see him and blessed them with the words: "The angel that redeemed me from all evil bless these children; may they carry my name and the name of my parents Abraham and Isaac; and may they grow into a multitude on earth."[13]

Parents and grandparents are encouraged to express their hopes and desires for the future of their children and grandchildren. They have the opportunity to articulate the values they cherished and the wisdom of their lives. Most important, this opportunity should be used to express words of love and admiration for their children and grandchildren. If this cannot be done in person, an effort should be made to put one's thoughts in writing or by speaking into a tape recorder or a video camera.

The healing potential through this process is incredibly profound and dramatic. It is a healing that prepares us for death. This kind of personal preparation and acceptance of the inevitability of death makes the dying process that much more peaceful.

This entire process has to be seen as an affirmation of life. Life in this world is not to be taken for granted, nor are the enjoyments and relationships formed in life. The *Viduy* process forces not only the terminally ill, but also the survivors to give meaning to the death process. I once read a powerful and insightful statement, I don't remember who said it, but I believe it goes as follows: "Our lives receive meaning from the meaning we give to death." Death is not something we should fear; rather we should learn to embrace and use it as a means to bring meaning into our lives.

Endnotes

1   See *Shulhan Arukh* YD 339:1 for a list of funeral preparations forbidden while the sick are still alive.

2   TB Shabbat 153a.

3   The *Shulhan Arukh,* YD 338:1, recommends that there be a certain emotional climate when facilitating the *Viduy,* and that is why I suggest this be done by an experienced professional.

4   *Maran* means "our teacher" and refers to Rabbi Yosef Karo (1488–1575). He authored a commentary (*kesef Mishneh*) to the work of Maimonides and an extensive commentary (*Bet Yosef*) to the *Tur,* which was later abridged and became the *Shulhan Arukh.* The *Shulhan Arukh* is the authoritative Code of Jewish Law.

5   *Shulhan Arukh,* YD 338:1 recommends that a sick person should not be made to confess unless obviously about to die, because the confession may cause him great distress.

6   There are several versions of the *Viduy.* See *Siddur Bet Oved.* Also *Tur,* YD 338.

7   TB Berakhot 10a.

8   Marc Angel, *The Rhythms of Jewish Living: A Sephardic Approach* (New York: Sepher-Hermon Press, 1986), p. 137.

9   Soloveichik Rabbi Joseph B. "Redemption, Prayer, Talmud Torah" *Tradition,* 17, no. 2, 55–73. Rabbi Soloveichik (1903–1993) was the leading Orthodox rabbinic thinker in the 20th century America. For half a century he served as Rosh Yeshiva of Yeshiva University. See Also Shalom Carmy, "Destiny, Freedom, and Logic of Petition." *Tradition,* 24, no. 2, 17–37.

10   Elisabeth Kübler-Ross makes this point in her book *Death: The Final Stage of Growth* (Englewood Cliffs, N.J.: Prentice-Hall, 1975).

11   I owe this expression to my dear friend Allan Alhadeff, whose wisdom permeates this book.

12   Thomas Campbell, *Hallowed Ground,* stanza 6.

CHAPTER 2

Creating a Caring Community

Nothing can take the place of a caring and supportive community. This is where Judaism stands apart from other religions and makes all the difference in our personal and communal lives. The community is an essential component in our quest for spirituality and self-actualization. Our sages of blessed memory spared no language in extolling acts of love and kindness. The path of spirituality is paved, according to our sages, with acts of *hesed* (kindness).[1] Deuteronomy 13:5 says:

> You shall follow the Lord your God, and Him you shall fear; His commandments you shall observe; His voice shall you hearken to; Him shall you serve; and to Him shall you cleave.

Commenting on this verse, Rashi paraphrases the Midrash and writes as follows:

> "His commandments" [refers to] the law of Moses; "His voice" [refers to] the voice of the prophets; "Him you shall serve" [refers to] the Temple; "Unto Him you shall cleave" [means] Cleave to His ways by doing acts of love and kindness, bury the dead, visit the sick, comfort the mourner, as does the Holy One, blessed be He.

Two fundamental principles of Judaism overlap when we speak of *gemilut hasadim*, acts of love and kindness. The principle of *imitatio Dei*, being God-like, and *V'ahavta lereiakha kamokha*, love your neighbor as yourself, merge into one, as our sages of blessed memory state:

> Said Rabbi Hama bar Hanina: "What is the meaning of the verse, After the Lord thy God ye shall walk (Deuteronomy 13:5)? Is it possible for a man to walk after the *Shekhinah* [Divine Presence]? Has it not been said: "The Lord thy God is a devouring fire" (Deuteronomy 4:24)? Rather, walk after the attributes of the Lord, blessed be He. He clothes the naked, as it is written: "And the Lord God made for Adam and for his wife garments of skin, and clothed them" (Genesis 3:21); so you clothe the naked! The Holy One, blessed be He, visited the sick, as it is written: "And the Lord appeared unto Abraham [who was recovering from his circumcision] by the terebinths of Mamre'" (Genesis 18:1); so too you visit the sick! The Holy One, blessed be He, comforted mourners, as it is written: "And it came to pass after the death of Abraham that God blessed Isaac his son" (Genesis 25:11); so you comfort the mourners! The Holy One, blessed be He, buried the dead, as it is written: "And He buried [Moses] in the valley" (Deuteronomy 34:6); so you bury the dead![2]

How do we achieve true union with our Creator? By being God-like. What does that mean? It simply means to act in ways that reflect compassion and love for other human beings.

In a caring community members are no longer individuals, for they coalesce with one another, to form a single entity that shares its pains and its joys. The community that is formed connects metaphysically with the larger community of Israel, past, present, and future. No individual member ever stands alone, especially at a time of sorrow and grief. The members of the community, with love, warmth, and sympathy, encircle the mourner.

Comforting the mourner, *nihum aveilim*, is at the heart of most of the laws and regulations, customs and restrictions that govern *Avelut*, mourning in a Jewish way. It is a *mizvah*, an opportunity that presents itself over and over for us. We are responsible to observe it at all times, not only when the bereaved is a relative or friend. Read the words of one person who received comfort during his time of need.

Dear Rabbi Levy,

Losing my father at such a young age was the most trying and difficult experience I have ever had. I will sorely miss him, his sense of humor, his attention, his kindness. I lost not only a father but a true soul mate. Yet when I think back on the entire experience I reflect on how fortunate I/we are to be part of a community that cares so very much about its members. My mother, my sister, and I would never have survived this trauma had it not been for the support, comfort, and care that was given to us. The food, the visits, the calls and the cards nourished us and gave us the strength to pick up the pieces and get on with life. Thank you.

I have heard the above sentiment expressed over and over again by bereaved persons who experienced their loss in the context of an educated and caring community. When the natural tendency of the mourner is to withdraw into loneliness, Jewish law, at precisely this time, calls upon the community to intervene.

This *mizvah,* our sages tell us, takes precedence over the *mizvah* of visiting the sick. Maimonides writes that this is so because comforting mourners is an act of kindness shown not only to the living but also to the dead.[3]

How to Help Others Through Their Grief

One consequence of the denial of death that is prevalent in our society is that we are often ignorant and unskilled in coping with loss, be it our own or another's. Most people, including those closest to the mourners, do not know what to say when making a condolence visit. A grieving friend or family member needs friendship and support to go through and complete the mourning process. The truth is that there is no purpose for words at this time. The most valuable thing we have to give is our presence. It is far more important than our knowledge or our advice. The companionship of family and friends is the greatest source of support and solace a mourner can receive. We can help our grieving friend most by sitting near, holding a hand, crying together, listening and sharing of feelings. In other words, what the bereaved need is an acknowledgment of their pain and sorrow. And both the bereaved and the comforter must realize that the pain cannot be erased.

The presence of others helps energize and renew strength for the mourner. Often mourners feel a drop in energy when guests depart; it is as if other people literally hold them up.

Making a Condolence Visit

Jewish law states that a mourner does not rise to greet anyone, even a great Torah scholar. In the house of mourning, the door is left ajar and people just come right in. Proper etiquette is not to greet the mourner upon entering but to sit next to the mourner or offer an embrace.[4]

Our sages recommend that one should not begin the conversation with the mourner[5]; rather, allow the "mourner to speak what is in his or her heart."[6] Being a caring presence and a good listener is more important than any words one might say. Above all, the bereaved need loving people to stand by them during their suffering. Not having to suffer alone is the greatest gift one can offer the bereaved. Being alone accentuates the despair and emptiness of loss.

Jewish law further suggests that if the mourner cannot say anything, then one should talk about the deceased.[7] No other subject is relevant at this time. The mourner is weeping, if not externally, then internally. Find a way to help the mourner express the feelings that are on his or her mind. Assist the mourner by showing genuine concern. At times, changing the subject sends the message that the mourner's pain is not important, or worse, that you don't care. Don't be afraid to ask questions, such as "Could you tell me about it?" "What happened?" "How did you find out?" "What was your relationship like?" Or you can simply say, "I'm sorry."

When helping others who are grieving, it is important to understand that people have different needs during the different phases of grief. In the initial period, immediately following the burial, the mourner is still experiencing shock, and practical help is what is most needed. Not only the meal of consolation, which is prepared by the community, but you can help coordinate people to prepare all the meals for the mourner during *Shivah*. What ordinarily are simple tasks can be extremely difficult for a mourner to handle during this time. Answering the phone, buying groceries, cleaning dishes or the house – all these are necessary tasks that usually go beyond the capability of those in mourning.

It is most important to be sensitive about how long one remains when visiting a mourner. Not knowing what to do, visitors sometimes stay too long, or engage in socializing with others in a lighthearted fashion. A house of mourning is not the place to catch up with old acquaintances; you are there to be helpful to the mourner, and if you cease to be helpful it is time to leave.

PRACTICAL THINGS THAT ARE HELPFUL TO THE BEREAVED

1. Organize the preparation of meals for the bereaved family for the entire week of *Shivah*.
2. Make sure the bereaved have everything they need for Shabbat.
3. Provide childcare for the children of the bereaved.
4. Do the grocery shopping.
5. Answer and return phone calls on behalf of the bereaved.

When Are Condolence Visits Appropriate?

There was a time when the Sephardic communities had a prescribed ritual that was followed when comforting mourners. Today that order is not observed, and it is customary and appropriate to extend a condolence visit immediately after burial. While a condolence visit is especially appropriate during the *Shivah,* it is also important to look after the well-being of the bereaved even after the *Shivah* within thirty days of the death.

Sephardic authorities permit condolence visits on Shabbat and holidays even though there is no public mourning on these days.[8]

Leaving the House of Mourning

Upon leaving the house of mourning, one does not extend the usual farewell to the mourner. Instead, one leaves the presence of the mourner by saying the following words:

מן השמים תנוחמו

From heaven above may you be comforted.

The following words are also appropriate:

המקום ינחם אתכם בתוך אבלי ציון וירושלים

May the Lord comfort you
among the mourners of Zion and Jerusalem.

When leaving the presence of the mourner, we are not called upon to offer advice or even words of encouragement. What we say is formal and prescribed. The individual does not speak as an individual. As individuals we have nothing to say. The wound is too deep, the pain too much to bear. Rather the individual retreats, is humbled, and invokes comfort from heaven.[9]

Confronting Intense Mourning

It is very painful to witness intense mourning. It is tempting to encourage mourners to stop crying, to deny their pain, or to rush them through the painful process of mourning. Accepting another's tears without interfering is a wonderful gift. So is listening without judging. Sometimes this means listening to the same thing over and over again. "Don't cry" is a cruel injunction for a bereaved person who has few options for expressing the intense feelings. The period of *Shivah, Sheloshim,* and the year of mourning is the appropriate time to confront the aspects of death and dying that will help the bereaved come to terms with their loss. Therefore, it is important to acknowledge the mourner's loss and the scope of its significance to the mourner. Mourners appreciate the sharing of memories and adding another's anecdotes to their expanding wealth of recollections. If you don't have a story or memory of the deceased, ask the mourner to share one with you. This kind of sharing brings the deceased alive once again in the eyes of the survivors.

It is clear that the bereaved need to be helped on many levels, whether by our presence, our energy, our sharing, our listening, our weeping together, or the many practical services we have to offer. Even our simplest acts may be of immeasurable value.

Endnotes

1 See Rashi on Deuteronomy 13:5; TB Shabbat 133b. Also Maimonides MT Yom Tov 6:21.
2 TB Sotah 14a.
3 Maimonides MT Avel 14:7. Rabbi Moses Maimonides (1135-1204) was one of the greatest rabbinic figures of all-time. He was born in Spain and spent most of his public life in Egypt. His *Halakhic* code the *Mishne Torah*, covers the entirety of Jewish law, including sections that are no longer applicabale in the contemporary period. *Mishne Torah* is one of the primary sources for Rabbi Karo's *Shulhan Arukh*.
4 *Shulhan Arukh*, YD 385:2.
5 TB Moed Katan 28b
6 *Shulhan Arukh* YD 376:1, also *Arukh HaShulhan*.
7 Ibid.
8 See *Mekor Hayim* 285:33; also see vol. 3, chapter 132:64.
9 For a beautiful discussion on this, see Joel B. Wolowelsky, "A Midrash on Jewish Mourning," *Judaism* 23, no. 2 (Spring 1974).

Points to Remember When Comforting Mourners
Nihum aveilim, the *mizvah* of comforting mourners, is more than simply a courtesy visit, it is an opportunity to afford the bereaved sensitivity and empathy. In essence, it is to do your share in healing a broken heart. The following are suggestions for making your visit to a house of mourning a successful one:

- Let the mourner begin to talk and set the tone of your conversation.

- Listen attentively. Remember it is better to be silent than talkative.

- Show concern for the mourner's emotional and physical well-being.

- Your conversation should be therapeutic and not distracting. It is not your job to get the mourner's mind off the loss. If there is going to be small talk, allow the mourner to take the lead.

- Levity may bring you relief, but it is inappropriate for the mourner. Anecdotes about the deceased that are humorous and said with respect are appropriate.

- Do not dwell on your own mourning experiences.

- Do not offer free psychological advice.

- Conclude your words of consolation with hope.

May you be comforted from heaven.
מן השמים תנוחמו

CHAPTER 3

Ani Ma'amin

A Belief System

A strong belief system is an important means of self-support. Whether or not our beliefs actually sustain us through a crisis is a personal matter. A well-formulated belief system does not necessarily cancel the urgency of tragedy, even for seriously religious people, and even if the belief ought to resolve certain issues, it does not always impress itself upon us with full vividness. Our perspective on life and our outlook on destiny very much affect how well we cope with loss and pain. There is not a bereavement that I share with the members of my congregation and friends where I am not asked about what Judaism has to say regarding the afterlife and the immortality of the soul. In our attempt to lessen the pain, we seek answers to these questions in hope that the loss can be given meaning. While we can generally cope with life without giving much thought to death, there is no denying its reality when confronted with the loss of a loved one. At such a time, death requires a spiritual context; otherwise the pain can become unbearable, and, worst of all, meaningless. I am not suggesting that a belief system will make the pain go away, because it will not. I am also not suggesting that a belief system will shorten the duration of the grief; it will not. The pain is real and must heal naturally. Yet, understanding what our tradition teaches regarding the body and soul, life and death, is not only important knowledge for every thinking

27

Jew, but it also affords the bereaved a context that will be an essential support through personal loss.

Body and Soul: Life and Afterlife

The Torah, the earliest Jewish text and certainly the most significant, says nothing at all explicitly about life after death or the nature of the soul. It seems that the Torah is exclusively concerned with the collective destiny of the Jewish people as a nation and the personal transformation of the individual. In fact there is no suggestion of the idea of a soul separate from the body.[1]

On exploring the biblical terrain, one finds conceptions of an afterlife emerging in the books of the prophets and in some of the psalms. Even then, the concern is primarily with the national destiny of the Jewish people, the messianic redemption, and the resurrection of the dead which remain fundamental to Judaism's worldview.[2]

While the Torah does not speak of a world-to-come for the soul, it does speak of death as a return to the company of one's ancestral family.[3] Of course this is not meant to be understood as a place in the afterlife where the family will gather, but rather as an expression meant to be interpreted either euphemistically or literally, as in the family tomb where other family members are buried.[4] This is the extent of the biblical interest in the afterlife.

The Bible does, however, warn against too much contact with the dead. Whenever a member of the priesthood came in contact with the dead, he was automatically disqualified from performing the service in the Temple. Students of the Torah immediately recognize the relationship between communion with the dead and the pagan and idolatrous practices that the Torah condemns. In Deuteronomy 18:10–11 you find the prohibitions of child sacrifice and communion with the dead side by side:

> Let no one be found among you who sacrifices his son or daughter in the fire, who practices divination or sorcery, interprets omens, engages in witchcraft, or casts spells, or who is a medium or spiritualist or who consults the dead.

The reason for such an attitude toward contact with the dead probably has to do with the fact that Judaism, from the earliest times, differentiated itself from the prevalent ancient Near Eastern practices of necromancy. Jewish monotheism condemns both physical and nonphysical forms of contact with the world of the dead. From the biblical standpoint, communion with the dead was not only a form of political and religious abuse[5] but was also regarded as a form of idolatry.

The World-to-Come

So how, then, does one understand the Jewish notion of *olam ha'ba,* the world-to-come? There is often confusion when we speak of *olam ha'ba* because Judaism distinguishes between the individual's personal eschatology and our national eschatology as a people. While the national eschatology is concerned with the fate of the Jewish people as a whole at the "end of days," the era of the Messiah, individual eschatology focuses on the fate of each individual after death.

It is no surprise that in Judaism the focus has always primarily been on the collective rather than the individual. We draw our greatest strength and worth as individuals from the covenantal community that we are a part of. We stood at the foot of Mount Sinai as a people. God engaged us as a nation. Therefore our tradition emphasizes national redemption as opposed to individual redemption. As individuals who share in the national destiny of our people, we do not ask "What will happen to me when I die?" but rather "What will happen to the nation of Israel in the future time when God transforms the world?"

Some of the sages of our tradition speak of an individual eschatology. For example: "My law will guide you in your path in this world; it will watch over you in your sleep, at the hour of death; and when you wake, it will converse with you in *olam ha'ba.*"[6] Other statements are not so clear, so it is hard to be certain whether they refer to individual or national eschatology. Take, for example, this often-quoted passage from the Mishnah:

All of Israel has a portion in the world-to-come, as it is said: "Thy people shall be all righteous, they shall inherit the land forever, the branch of My planting, the work of My hands, wherein I glory."[7]

Is this referring to a world-to-come that is each individual's destiny immediately after death or in the distant future, at the end of time, when the world will herald the messianic era?

Although the dominant stream in the Bible and early Rabbinic Judaism reflects a national eschatology, this does not mean that a belief in individual afterlife does not exist. In fact Maimonides, known as Rambam, affirms the existence of an immortal soul and *olam ha'ba*.[8] There are three specific texts in which Maimonides discusses *olam ha'ba*: in his commentary on the Mishnah in tractate Sanhedrin (*Perek Helek*), in his *Mishneh Torah* in the chapter in the laws of *teshuvah*, and in a lengthy essay on resurrection called *Ma'amar Tehiyat Hametim* (Treatise on Resurrection).

Rambam integrates the philosophical ideas of the immortal soul with the elaborate images described in the Talmud regarding the afterlife.[9] Related to the subject of the afterlife, Maimonides also explains fundamental issues of reward and punishment and the philosophical implications as related to life and death.

For Rambam the existence of a soul and a life after death is an absolute fact, but it is a subject beyond human comprehension. "As to the blissful taste of the soul in the world-to-come, there is no way on earth in which we can comprehend or know it."[10] There is an unbridgeable chasm between the world of the spirit and the world of the flesh.

For Maimonides the body and spirit exist in two separate and distinct realms, and the human beings are limited as to the extent that they can truly appreciate the realm of the spirit. This view is expressed in *Perek Helek* as follows:

Just as a blind man cannot perceive colors, nor a deaf man hear sounds, nor a eunuch feel sexual desire, so bodies [of human beings] cannot attain spiritual delights. And just as fish do not know the element of fire because they live in its opposite, so are the pleasures of the spiritual world unknown to this world of flesh.[11]

While human beings can never truly know the world of the spirit, Rambam envisioned that they could know the delights of the spiritual world after death through the process of intellectual contemplation of God and the infinite mysteries of the world. It is those who have lived properly, Rambam writes, who enjoy infinite life as a bodiless soul. Immortality of the soul is not an inherent property of the soul but a consequence of a virtuous life.

A Theory

Our need for a belief in the immortality of the soul is as great as any other human need. Yet we are suspicious of religious teachings that simply console us. We do not want to close our eyes to the harshness and tragedy of life in this world, but neither are we at peace with the idea that God might have created nothing beyond it.

Numerous attempts throughout the ages have been made to describe what life after death is like. Some are scandalous to reason, others embarrassing to those who believe in a reasonable theology. I include in this chapter one such attempt written by the late Rabbi Aryeh Kaplan, an influential popular writer of the twentieth century. His idea is discussed in a small booklet called *If You Were God*, published by the Orthodox Union. His presentation is clear and based solely on Jewish sources, and it represents one view on the issue at hand. The following excerpt from his book is relevant to our discussion on the immortality of the soul.

What happens then when a person dies?

We know that the body ceases to function. The brain becomes inert and the physical man is dead.

But what happens to the real you – the human personality? What happens to all this information – the memories, thought patterns and personality traits?

When a book is burned its contents are no longer available. When a computer is smashed the information within it is also destroyed. Does the same thing happen when a man dies? Is the mind and personality irretrievably lost?

We know that God is omniscient. He knows all and does

not forget. God knows every thought and memory that exists within our brains. There is no bit of information that escapes His knowledge.

What then happens when a man dies? God does not forget and therefore all of this information continues to exist, at least in God's memory.

We may think of something existing only in memory as being static and effectively dead. But God's memory is not a static thing. The sum total of a human personality may indeed exist in God's memory, but it can still maintain its self-identity and volition, and remain in an active state.

This sum total of the human personality existing in God's memory is what lives on even after man dies.

The concept of immortality of the soul may well be outside the realm of human comprehension. "No eye has seen it other than God." However, our limited understanding of both God and man can provide us with some degree of perception into our ultimate future.

To speak of a concept such as God's memory is indeed very difficult. It involves a deep discussion of the entire transcendental sphere. We therefore give it names that have meaning to us, such as *Gan Eden*, Paradise, the World-to-Come, the World of Souls, or the bond of eternal life. However, the Bible speaks of immortality as a return to God Himself (Eccl. 12:7): "The dust returns to the dust as it were, but the spirit returns to God who gave it."

Attitude Toward Death

Jewish tradition puts the seal of life on the chapters dealing with death. As Jews we believe that it is not death that has the last word, but life. The soul is eternal. Jewish tradition teaches us that the grave is not the end. The pain of parting is mitigated by our faith in divine providence, which permits no life to be utterly destroyed. The twelfth principle of faith of Maimonides states: "That the King Messiah will come, and that the dead are destined to be revived." When death robs us of our loved ones, we are comforted by our faith that the essence of our beloved lives on not only in our hearts and in our memories, but with the Creator of life.

I am constantly aware of the immense task of faith. The pain of remaining conscious is so extreme, and the presence of death is so ever-constant, that the belief in a life after death remains a profound truth of what I know about God. Do I presume to know exactly what lies ahead for us after death? The answer is no. Yet I know that my belief in God and a purposeful existence remains constant.

Samuel Hugo Bergmann, a twentieth-century philosopher, captured this idea on his eightieth birthday in 1963:

> [First] I believe in the Holy One, blessed be He, creator of heavens and the universe. Secondly, we know from this that the world is not subject to blindness…. Thirdly, I do not accept the reality or actuality of death. Our lives are possessed of significance entirely different from that which we usually ascribe to them…. I am saying here that people will live after death and will have to account for themselves…. Everything we do here on earth has an eternal, cosmic meaning.[12]

Personal Growth

Isaiah the prophet, while chastising the people of Israel, makes a remarkable statement: "I have purged you but nothing came of it, tested you in the furnace but all in vain." The prophet rebukes the people for learning nothing from the experience of being put through the furnace of affliction. The tragedy, according to Isaiah, is not the pain that was endured; rather, the tragedy is that the suffering was wasted, leaving the people no wiser and no better. We should expect of ourselves to do more than just accept pain. We must use adversity to learn and grow wiser in understanding. The poet Robert Browning Hamilton expressed this thought when he wrote:

> I walked a mile with Pleasure,
> She chattered all the way,
> But left me none the wiser
> For all she had to say.
>
> I walked a mile with Sorrow,

And ne'er a word said she;
But, oh, the things I learned from her
When Sorrow walked with me!

In our hour of sorrow and bereavement, our loss can teach us to live life at its highest level. All life is brief, and yet we determine its quality. Because of its brevity, we must be very discriminating as to how we live it. Rabbi Soloveitchik, of blessed memory, argued that instead of engaging in a futile search for explanations and reasons for evil, we should respond to suffering as a challenge and convert it into a source of some good that otherwise would never have been obtained.[13]

Rabbi Soloveitchik suggests that the entire grief experience is not only a "catharsis of sorrow, but also an experience of self-judgment and penitence."[14] He depicts two areas of penitence. The first is *teshuvah* vis-à-vis our fellow human beings, and the second, *teshuvah* vis-à-vis God.

Man, in Rabbi Soloveitchik's assessment, appreciates and values people and things in hindsight.

> In retrospect, man discovers the precise value of someone who was but is no longer with him. This delayed understanding and appreciation is painfully tragic. While the departed was near and we could communicate, we were only partially perceptive of his (her) identity. Our awareness of his special qualities, as someone vital and precious to us, comes at the very instant he departs and withdraws into a mist of remoteness. Only then do we inquire with painful longing, "Who was he who brightened my days? What did he mean to me? Why do I feel so bereft and disoriented?"

Rabbi Soloveitchik continues by stating that the *Avelut* experience plagues us with guilt. We realize how fragmentary our relationship with the deceased was. "Such ex post facto judgments are the saddest of life's experiences. Even those closest to us are elusive."

The mourner bemoans opportunities lost forever, and is inspired to intensify and renew relationships with those closest to him.

Vis-à-vis God

Avelut (mourning) is intrinsically an expression of *teshuvah* (penitence). "The aching heart" writes Rabbi Soloveitchik, "is a contrite heart and a contrite heart seeks atonement." *Shivah* and its restrictions are reminiscent of Yom Kippur, a day when Jews seek forgiveness and renew their relationship with God[15].

Teshuvah, the act of yearning for God, is similar to the mourner's yearning for the departed. "For the penitent also mourns the loss of a precious comradeship, the departure of divine closeness." The relationship, between God and the mourner, however, unlike the lost relationship between the mourner and the deceased, will be reconciled and renewed. The Torah assures us: "If you search for the Lord your God, you will find Him, as long as you seek Him with all your heart and soul."[16]

A Final Thought

The meanings we ascribe to life and death are often the keys to how well we restructure our lives after a loss. Living a life of meaning is much easier with spiritual values. The following is a statement on the subject by Rabbi Abraham Heschel:

> The deepest wisdom man can attain is to know that his destiny is to aid, to serve. We have to conquer in order to succumb; we have to acquire in order to give away; we have to triumph in order to be overwhelmed. Man has to understand in order to believe, to know in order to accept. The aspiration is to obtain; the perfection is to dispense. This is the meaning of death: the ultimate self-dedication to the divine. Death so understood will not be distorted by the craving of immortality, for this act of giving away is reciprocity on man's part for God's gift of life. For the pious man it is a privilege to die.[17]

That we can grieve and recover from a loss of this nature seems to be an amazing feat, yet human resilience is amazing. Just as a perennial garden that in the fall and winter looks desolate and run-down eventually springs back anew, we too can overcome grief, recover, and restore our lives.

Endnotes

1   For a discussion of the understanding of human consciousness during the biblical period, see Ken Wilber, *Back to Eden: A Transpersonal View of Human Evolution* (Garden City, N.Y.: Doubleday, 1981).

2   See R.H. Charles, *Eschatology: The Doctrine of a Future Life in Israel, Judaism and Christianity* (New York: Schocken Books, 1963).

3   For example, Genesis 25:8, 35:29, 49:29–31, 33; Numbers 27:13; 1 Kings 11:43.

4   Archaeological evidence indicates that the dead were laid to rest on rock shelves in family burial caves (e.g., the Cave of Machpelah). See Walter Eichrodt, *Theology of the Old Testament*, trans. J.A. Baker (London: SCM Press, 1967), vol. 2, p. 213.

5   See below, chapter IV.

6   Sifre on Leviticus 18:4.

7   Mishnah Sanhedrin 10:1.

8   As does Saadia Gaon, *Emunot VeDeot* 6:3 and 9:5.

9   See the article on eschatology in the *Encyclopaedia Judaica*.

10   *Mishneh Torah*, Book of Knowledge, Teshuva 8:6

11   Commentary on Mishnah Sanhedrin 10:3.

12   Eli Shai, "Samuel Hugo Bergmann: A Partial Portrait," in *Ariel* 57 (1984).

13   Joseph B. Soloveitchik, "Kol Dodi Dofek," in *Besod HaYahid VeHayahad*, ed. Pinchas Peli (Jerusalem: Orot, 1976).

14   The next few quotations from Rabbi Soloveitchik are all taken from the essay "Sitting *Shivah* Is Doing *Teshuvah*," in *Reflections of the Rav*, ed. Abraham Besdin, vol. 2, *Man of Faith in the Modern World* (Jerusalem: World Zionist Organization, 19).

15   With the exception of eating, all of the prohibitions of Yom Kippur apply during *shivah* (working, bathing, grooming, wearing leather shoes, and having conjugal relations).

16   Deuteronomy 4:20.

17   Abraham J. Heschel, "Death as a Homecoming," in *Jewish Reflections on Death*, ed. Jack Riemer (New York: Schocken Books, 1979).

CHAPTER 4

Kavod Hamet

Pain is hard to bear....
But with patience, day by day
Even this shall pass away

– Theodore Tilton

Kavod Hamet

No matter how expected the death of a loved one may be, the surviving relatives are always thrown into a state of shock and confusion. The deep sense of loss mixed with feelings of remorse and frustration make for a confusing and debilitating state of mind. Jewish tradition has always understood the value of confronting and accepting the reality of death. Our religious and theological consciousness has always been oriented toward, and rooted in, life-affirming beliefs and actions. Denial of the loss is the antithesis of the religious mourning experience. Only through a confrontation with the issue of death and a complete expression of the emotions associated with loss will there come a complete healing and resolve.[1] *Aninut,* the period between death and burial, affords the mourner the ritual structure necessary to confront the initial state immediately following the death of a loved one.

From the moment of death until the burial of the deceased there is one central and overriding principle that governs the mourner's every action. In Hebrew this principle is called *kavod hamet,* which means according the deceased appropriate respect and honor. A human corpse, according to Jewish tradition, is more than just a lifeless physical body which can be treated casually. Rather, a lifeless human body is compared to a *Sefer Torah* (Torah scroll) which has become unusable. Because the Torah scroll was once an item used for religious and holy purposes and still contains Holy Scripture, it must be treated with respect and reverently buried. So, too, the human being, whose essence in this world was for religious and holy purposes, whose life is imbued with holy sparks, and whose image, the image of God, no less, is an intrinsic part of his or her being, deserves reverent treatment even as a lifeless body.[2]

Today, because most deaths occur in hospitals or in nursing homes, and the caregivers or their staff notify the families, it is important to know that anything done to the corpse requires consent from the next of kin or custodian of the body. It is our obligation to exercise this right at all times.

When death occurs, those present at the time of death rend their clothes and recite the blessing *Dayan Ha'emet* (see Appendix 1). Rambam, in his *Mishneh Torah,* and Rabbi Yosef Karo, in his *Shulhan Arukh,* both codified the law in this way[3]. Later codifiers of Jewish law were concerned that people would not remain with the dying person because they would have to rend their clothes. Therefore they waived the requirement to rend one's clothing at the time of death so that people would continue to stay at the side of the dying while death occurs.[4]

Insist that the deceased not be left alone even for a short time. The eyes and mouth of the deceased should be shut, and if possible the body should be positioned in such a way that the feet are facing the doorway.[5]

In the presence of the deceased it is forbidden to pray, wear *tefillin,* and study Torah.[6] The recitation of psalms is permitted while in the presence of the deceased.[7] It is also not appropriate to eat or drink, smoke, or exchange greetings while in the presence of the deceased. In a large room one must distance oneself at least six and a half feet from the deceased in order to do any of the above.[8]

Shabbat and Holidays

On Shabbat or holidays, only a minimum of arrangements are made; specifically, those that are limited to the immediate needs and honor of the deceased. On Shabbat and holidays, one does not rend one's clothing[9], nor should any desecration of the Shabbat and holiday take place. The body is not moved or transported until after the Shabbat or holiday. The body should be covered, and someone should remain with it until the conclusion of the Shabbat or holiday. At that time the *hevra kadisha*, (burial society) is informed, and they will make the necessary arrangements. If the hospital or nursing home does not allow the body to remain on its premises until the end of Shabbat or the end of the holiday, a non-Jew should be asked to contact a funeral home that hires non-Jewish employees, to pick up the body. The body should remain with the non-Jewish caretakers until the conclusion of the Shabbat or holiday.

Onen

In our tradition, a person who has lost an immediate relative, such as a father, mother, spouse, son, daughter, sister, brother, half-sister, or half-brother,[10] is referred to as an *onen*. The term *onen* literally means "grief-stricken" or "oppressed."[11] A mourner is an *onen*, or in the state of *Aninut,* until the burial of the deceased. Until that time all energies are focused on preparing the final arrangements and funeral service in order to ensure *kavod hamet,* preserving the honor and dignity of the deceased. Our *hakhamim* (sages) were very much aware of the emotional and psychological distress of the bereaved, as shown by the following perceptive statement: "There is no one to carry his heavy burden."[12] In fact Jewish law makes no positive demands on one who is an *onen.*[13] Instead the law requires individuals in a state of *Aninut* to occupy themselves only with arrangements for the funeral that will reflect the tragedy of the loss of life and the dignity appropriate for the deceased. Our sages tell us that there is no virtue in performing commandments that one is exempt from at this time.[14] The Talmud states it clearly:

> One whose dead [relative] lies before him is exempt from the recital of the *Shema*, and from prayer, and from *tefillin* and from all precepts laid down in the Torah.[15]

The reason the law exempts the mourner from the performance of *mizvot* goes beyond the practical issue of having enough time to accomplish everything that has to get done before the funeral. It might have something to do with the psychological state of mind of the mourners and the context in which *mizvot* are to be performed.[16]

Preparation of the deceased for burial is considered to be a great *mizvah*. It is an act filled with religious meaning and significance. As was mentioned earlier, Jewish tradition mandates that the deceased be handled with great care, honor, and dignity. At a time like this, it becomes irrelevant whether or not the deceased was a religious person and whether or not the mourners are traditionally observant people.[17] As a people we have a three-thousand-year-old tradition on handling the deceased in a dignified and honorable fashion. It is the way in which our parents buried their loved ones and the generations before them buried their loved ones. We are the next link in following the traditions that have been handed down to us from previous generations.

Issues That May Arise Immediately After Death

Questions relating to autopsies, organ donations, and amputated limbs will probably arise at this time, and it is important that the family consult their rabbi before making decisions on these matters. Below is a brief examination of some of the issues relating to autopsies, organ donations, and amputated limbs.

AUTOPSIES

An autopsy is a careful examination of the internal tissues and organs of a dead body. There are several possible reasons for performing an autopsy. Among them are a desire to better understand the cause of death or to further the cause of medical research. The dissection of the human body for reasons that have no medical benefit is considered a desecration of the human body. The prohibition against desecrating dead bodies, and the correlation of showing respect and honor to dead bodies, are based on the principle that was stated earlier, *kavod hamet*, showing respect for the dead body.

The human being is the totality of body and soul.[18] In Judaism, the body, even soulless, has value and deserves appropriate dignity and respect. The physical body is regarded as having unique value. The fact that we perform *mizvot* with the body,[19] and that our body is a vehicle for the worship of God, reflects its everlasting worth. The operative legal principle is as follows: anything we would not do to a person while they were alive cannot be done to them after they are dead.

An extension of the principle of *kavod hamet* is the prohibition of *hana'ah min hamet* (deriving benefit from the dead body).[20] It is forbidden by Jewish law to benefit from another human being without the other person's consent. The body is more than just an object that can be used or abused. The human body *is* the person. The relationship to the human body, even a dead body, must be the same as the relationship to the living person. Therefore an autopsy cannot even be considered if the deceased did not consent to it before his or her death.[21]

Having made the case for prohibiting autopsies, it should be stated that there are extenuating circumstances in which an autopsy would not only be permitted, but required. If the argument could be made that there is a legitimate possibility of saving a human life by performing the autopsy, it would then be permitted. Two examples could include: (1) if the autopsy can reveal the cause of death and in turn save other lives; (2) when an autopsy may assist in the investigation of a murder and by doing so save the lives of other potential victims. Rabbi Yaakov Ruza, the chief *posek* for the Tel Aviv area *hevra kadisha* and coroner's office, shared with me an incredible story.

Some years ago a forty-eight-year-old man unexpectedly died of heart failure. His father had died the same way, and there was concern that this might be a congenital genetic disease. Rabbi Ruza was inclined to go along with the doctor's advice that an autopsy should be performed. Before he made such a decision he consulted some other leading halakhic authorities. Two of the three he consulted advised against an autopsy, but Chief Rabbi Mordechai Eliyahu insisted that an autopsy must be done. Rabbi Ruza followed Chief Rabbi Mordechai Eliyahu's ruling, and as a result twelve family members may have been saved from congenital heart disease.

When a doctor insists that an autopsy is necessary, it is important to know that alternatives to full autopsies can be explored. For example, in Israel specific-organ biopsy is a common procedure that often provides the same results as an autopsy.[22] In discussions with Dr. Harvey Shiller, chief pathologist at Providence Hospital in Seattle, I learned that similar options are available in the United States. The family of the deceased can request limited autopsy of certain organs, and/or biopsy of organs or tissues.

Other notable examples of when autopsies would be permitted are recorded in the responsa literature of the rabbinical authorities who deal with medical questions in Jewish hospitals in Israel.[23]

ORGAN DONATIONS

Jewish tradition has always recognized the supreme importance of *Pikuach Nefesh*, the obligation to save a human life if it is in our power to do so. This commandment is stated in the Torah both in the negative: "Do not stand idly by the blood of your neighbor" (Leviticus 19:16) and in the positive: "Return your neighbor's lost possession (his or her life) to your neighbor" (Deuteronomy 22:2). Thus, when the opportunity presents itself we must do everything in our ability to save a life provided our own life is not at risk.

With the increased success rate of organ transplants, contemporary Halakhic authorities have been discussing what might appear to be objections to organ donations in light of the great potential for *Pikuach Nefesh*.

The first and most obvious objection regards laws relating to *Kavod HaMet*, treatment of the body after death. As was mentioned earlier *Halakha* prohibits desecration of the body and gaining any benefit from the body. The potential to save another life, however, overrides any of these concerns. A secondary concern relating to the above issue might be the delay of burial. Once again if an organ of the deceased can save an immediate life or enhance another person's quality of life (e.g., eyesight), then delay of burial would not be a serious enough objection to withhold the donation of organs. The emphasis here is the immediacy issue. The organ must be used immediately and not frozen for future use or for experimentation.[24]

Another objection raised in the literature suggests that a dead person is not obligated to observe *mizvot* and thus not required to save anothers life. This of course is easily obviated if the deceased declared his or her desire to donate organs or if the "patient advocates" deemed that the deceased would have wanted to save another's life.

The more serious objection to organ donations in Jewish law regards assessing the time of death. Organs used for transplants must be taken while respiration and circulation is ongoing. The only time when this can happen is when brain death has been established and the organs are being perfused by external means. Rabbi Moshe Tendler, a leading Halakhic authority in the Orthodox community, Rosh Yeshiva and Biology professor at Yeshiva University, has ruled that Halakhic death is brain death.

Recently this issue has received significant attention in the Jewish media, most notably with the tragic death of Jonathan Joseph (J.J.) Greenberg, a talented young leader in the Jewish community, and Jonathan Jesner, a 19-year-old rabbinical student. They both died in Israel and their organs saved and enhanced the lives of others.

In 1986 Sephardic Chief Rabbi Ovadia Yoseph ruled that transplants were a *mizvah* for the living and though the dead are not obligated to perform *mizvot*, an organ donation was an honor for the dead. The Rabbinical Council of America, in 1991 approved organ donations and the acceptability of brain-stem death, which makes the donation of organs possible.[25]

AMPUTATED LIMBS

According to Jewish tradition the entire body is to be buried after death. Therefore if an individual dies with severed limbs, the limbs must be buried with the deceased. If a limb or limbs were amputated before death, they should be buried in the eventual grave of the individual. If the individual does not have a grave, the limbs should be buried in a Jewish cemetery. There is no special service associated with the burial of limbs.

Laws of *Aninut*

The following are some of the laws relating to the stage of *Aninut*:

- One whose father, mother, son, daughter, sister, brother, half-sister, or half-brother died is termed an *onen* from the time of death until interment.[26]
- An *onen* may not eat meat or drink wine or liquor.[27]

- An *onen* may not attend a festive meal or celebration.
- An *onen* is denied the luxuries of self-adornment, bathing for pleasure, shaving, and taking a haircut.[28]
- An *onen* may not indulge in conjugal relations.[29]
- An *onen* may not engage in work or business.[30]
- An *onen* is exempt from all the *mizvot asseh* (positive commandments) of the Torah and does not recite the *Hamosi* blessing or the *Birkat Hamazon* (Grace after the meal).[31]
- An *onen* does not recite the morning blessings. However, after burial, the morning blessings can be recited all day and all evening. In the evening, the blessing on the Torah is not recited.[32]
- An *onen* may not study Torah.[33]
- An *onen* is exempt from prayers and specific positive commandments. He must, however, observe all the negative commandments.[34]
- Hakham Ovadia Yosef holds that the *onen* may wear *sisit*, *talleth*, and *tefillin* but does not recite the blessings.[35] Many communities, however, follow the *Shulhan Arukh* and do not wear *talleth* and *tefillin*.

MEALS DURING THIS TIME

It is forbidden to eat in the presence of the deceased. This applies to both the mourners and anyone else. The *onen* is not permitted to eat a regular elaborate meal at a table with company, and should eat alone at a separate table.[36]

SHABBAT

- On Shabbat the *onen* may eat meat and drink wine and must observe all of the Shabbat commandments. The *onen* must abstain from matters of private enjoyment (e.g., conjugal relations and the study of Torah) even on Shabbat.[37]

HOLIDAYS

- On Sukkoth the *onen* eats and sleeps in the *sukkah* without reciting the blessing. If this is difficult, however, he is exempt from the *mizvah*.[38]
- On Pesah the *onen* must observe all the *mizvot* of the *Seder*. He does

not recite the blessings and must respond *Amen* to someone else's blessings. The same applies to the recitation of the Haggadah and the *Hallel*.[39]

- The *onen* must recline on the night of Pesah in order to fulfill the *mizvot* of the *Seder*.[40]
- An *onen* must observe all communal fast-days.[41]
- On Hanukkah an *onen* should have someone else light the *menorah* on his or her behalf.[42]
- During *Sefirat Ha'omer*, the counting of the *Omer*, the *onen* does not count the *Omer* in the evening prior to burial. On the next day, after the burial, the *onen* counts without a blessing and that evening continues to count with a blessing.[43] If the burial is postponed and the *onen* missed an entire day of counting, the remaining days of the *Omer* are counted without a blessing.
- The custom in some Sephardic communities is that the *onen* recites *Kaddish* with the hazan for the relative who has just passed away.[44]

Religious Support

One should call the rabbi immediately upon learning that a dear one has passed away. The rabbi will in turn notify the *hevra kadisha*, the community's burial society. The rabbi is a trained professional who knows how to deal with issues related to grief and loss. Consult with your rabbi on all matters that you may face at this time.

The rabbi will also want to spend some time with the mourners and close relatives to learn more about the deceased. The information he is provided will help the rabbi prepare for the funeral service. The bereaved should be honest and open with the rabbi. The different relationships with the deceased should be discussed, as well as both the good times and bad times. The mourners could share with the rabbi what they loved and admired about the deceased and what they found difficult about him or her. Meeting with one's rabbi at a time like this can be very helpful and comforting for the mourners and the others who share the grief. This is a time when the bereaved will need someone to talk to, a time for them to ask questions regarding death, life, the afterlife, and the rituals associated with death.

The rabbi will want to know the following information:

- The Hebrew name of the deceased.
- The Hebrew name of the deceased's mother and father.
- The exact time of death.

The Burial Society

The burial society, also known as the *hevra kadisha* or brotherhood, is a nonprofit organization of volunteers who are familiar with Jewish funerary traditions and are willing to help the mourners with all the burial preparations. In some Sephardic communities, the members of the *hevra kadisha* visit the critically ill and recite prayers for healing on their behalf. In these communities the *hevra kadisha* will make sure that one of its members is present at the time of death. From that moment on, they take care of all the necessary preparations.

The *hevra kadisha* is responsible for picking up the body, for the rituals of *Rehisah* and *Shemirah* (see below), and for transporting the body to the chapel for the service, and from the service to the cemetery.

The *hevra kadisha* has the responsibility of providing burial for all members of the community, rich and poor alike. It operates as an independent organization whose officers represent a cross-section of the larger community.

Ideally, the *hevra kadisha* consists of trained volunteers and professionals who act with great efficiency, dignity, and discretion. Members of the community should be encouraged to join the *hevra kadisha* or brotherhood as well as to support it financially.

The following are some questions you will be asked by the *hevra kadisha* before the deceased is picked up:

- Full legal name of the deceased, full Hebrew name of the deceased including Hebrew names of mother and father.
- Social Security number of the deceased.
- Family contact.
- Current location of the deceased.
- Synagogue affiliation.
- Has the death certificate been signed yet?
- Is there any intervention required by an official (e.g., autopsy)?
- *Talleth* of the deceased.

- Name of cemetery.
- Date and time of funeral service.
- Name of officiating rabbi.

Preparation of the Deceased for Burial

SHEMIRAH

Once again, *kavod hamet*, preserving the sacred dignity of human life and the reverence for the human body, is the governing principle for all the rituals and traditions we have when responding to death. Therefore, from the moment of death until the burial, the deceased may not be left alone. The family should make sure that someone remains at the side of the deceased at all times until a member of the burial society or the rabbi arrives. Once the burial society takes over, a *shomer* (watcher) is assigned to stay at the side of the deceased at all times. The *shomer* recites psalms and is forbidden to smoke or eat in the presence of the deceased.[45] The *shomer* remains awake throughout the entire night. While it is preferable that the *shomer* be a member of the family or a personal friend, this is not always possible.

TAHARAH

The *hevra kadisha* is responsible for preparing the deceased for burial. The preparation involves three parts: *Rehisah*, washing of the body; *Taharah*, a ritual cleansing; and *Halbashah*, dressing the deceased in the appropriate shrouds. While engaged in these three steps of preparation, those attending to the procedure recite the appropriate biblical verses or prayers. Experienced members of the *hevra kadisha* who have had the appropriate training should conduct these procedures. The only ones excluded from the performance of this *mizvah* are *kohanim* because of their religious prohibition of being in close contact with a dead body.

Rehisah, Taharah, and *Halbashah* for a man are done only by men, and for a woman by women. Under no circumstances should a man participate in the preparation of a woman.[46] Only under extenuating circumstances and after consultation with a rabbi may a woman participate in the preparation of a man. And under no circumstances can it be performed by a non-Jew.

These preparations should take place as close as possible to the time of the funeral service. Ideally, no more than three hours should elapse between the preparation of the deceased and the funeral service.

Throughout the preparation of the body, the utmost respect for and dignity of the deceased must be preserved. This is maintained by adhering to the following rules:

- The attendants are not permitted to eat, drink, or smoke while in the presence of the deceased.
- The attendants are not permitted to engage in idle conversation or matters that do not directly pertain to the preparations of the deceased.
- The body of the deceased is never exposed except for a very short time when a particular body part is being washed.
- The body of the deceased must be handled with the utmost care.
- The body of the deceased is never placed face-downward.

Throughout the washing of the body, various prayers and biblical verses are recited, depending on what part of the body is being cleansed. There are appropriate readings for the washing of the different body parts and for the dressing of the deceased. When the deceased is a man, the procedure concludes by placing his *talleth* (prayer shawl) into the coffin.

Shrouds

The Babylonian Talmud records that Rabban Gamliel, the preeminent leader of his generation and a wealthy man, instituted the practice that every Jew, rich or poor, must be buried in similar simple shrouds so as to prevent families from vying with each other in providing elaborate garments for the dead, and shaming those who could not afford elaborate garments.

At one time, funerals in Israel became so costly that the expense was harder for some relatives to bear than death itself. Some relatives even abandoned the corpse and ran away. Such desertions ended when Rabban Gamliel left orders that his body be carried to the grave in a simple linen garment. From then on, everyone followed Rabban Gamliel's example…. Said Rabbi

Papa: "And now it is a general practice to carry out the dead even in rough cloth worth only a *zuz*."[47]

The shrouds (*takhrikhim* in Hebrew) are handmade clean, white, garments.[48] They are usually made of cotton, linen, or muslin. They symbolize simplicity and purity. The High Priest also wore simple white linen garments when he entered the Holy of Holies on Yom Kippur. The lesson for us is quite penetrating: When we face our Creator, our posture must be humble and contrite. Before the Master of the Universe there is no wealth or status.

The shrouds have no pockets, possibly symbolic of the fact that there is nothing the deceased can take with himself or herself. Ultimately, we must realize that we must not spend our lives solely on the accumulation of wealth and material possessions. Ideally, the *takhrikhim* should be supplied by the *hevra kadisha* or by the community.

Talleth

It is the custom of most Sephardic communities outside of Israel to bury men wrapped in a *talleth* (prayer shawl).[49] In Israel the deceased is wrapped in his *talleth* until the burial, but immediately prior to the interment it is removed and returned to the family.

Interring the deceased with his *talleth* is a custom that can be traced back to the early Middle Ages and should be observed in the fashion that the Sepharadim have been doing it for centuries. The Sepharadim do not cut or remove the fringes of the *talleth* before burial. In fact the *Maran* in the *Shulhan Arukh* states: "The deceased is buried with a *talleth* that has *sisit*."[50]

At some point before the funeral, the family should make sure to supply the *hevra kadisha* with the *talleth* the deceased wore throughout his lifetime. If the deceased did not own a *talleth,* or it cannot be found before the funeral, the *hevra kadisha* will supply another *talleth* or a *talleth* can be purchased for this purpose.

Transportation of the Body / Embalming

Transporting the corpse a long distance for burial presents a problem. There is a legitimate concern on the part of state and government officials regarding the decomposition and odor of decaying human remains in airports and airplane cargo, especially if transported in wood caskets.

The common solution to this problem is embalming. In this procedure all the blood is drained from the body and replaced with a chemical. This, of course, is not permitted in Jewish law.

The alternative to embalming, when the body has to be transported, is using a sealed Ziegler case or a metal-lined container which is leak-proof and odor-resistant.

When the body is transported, care should be taken to make sure that it is always accompanied by a Jew.

Endnotes

1   This idea represents a unique Jewish epistemology regarding confrontation with crisis. While other cultures and societies resort to mythology and denial, the Jewish response is always confrontation.

2   This analogy is made by the Gemara in TB Shabbat 105b. See also Ramban in *Torat HaAdam*.

3   MT Avel 9:11; YD 340:5 applies this ruling to any dead Jew who was not known as a habitual sinner.

4   See *Yabia Omer* 4:38. Rabbi Ovadia Yoseph (1920–) is the former Chief Rabbi of Israel. His voluminous *Halakhic* works, including *Yabia Omer* and *Yalkuth Yoseph*, make him the leading Sephardic *Posek* of this era.

5   See Rambam, Avel 4:1 As a means of *kavod hamet*. Today, if the body is being refrigerated, it does not require *Shemirah*.

6   Rambam, Avel 4:6.

7   See *Yabia Omer*, vol. 6, pp. 103–104.

8   Ibid.

9   see YD 340:1 where Maran requires tearing one's clothing on Hol HaMoed; Yalkuth Yoseph Volume 7, 4:17. There is however, a custom among some Syrians not to tear clothing on Hol HaMoed.

10   The first seven relatives, with the qualification of half-sister from father, are considered by most commentaries as biblically ordained, while the half-brother and half-sister from mother are rabbinically ordained. See TB Moed Katan 14b; Maimonides, Avel 2:1; see also *Shulhan Arukh* YD 374:6 and *Yalkut Yosef* 8:1.

11   Marcus Jastrow, *Dictionary of Aramaic*.

12   Berakhot Yerushalmi; also Devarim Rabbah, VaYelekh.

13   The *onen* is still obligated in all *mizvot lo ta'aseh* (negative commandments).

14 *Shulhan Arukh,* YD 341:1; also see Rambam, Avel, chap. 4; Tosafot Moed Katan 23b and Rosh on same.

15 TB Berakhot 17b; also see TB Moed Katan 23b.

16 In *Jewish Reflections on Death*, Rabbi Joseph B. Soloveitchik of blessed memory describes this state of mind as follows: "*Aninut* represents the spontaneous human reaction to death. It is an outcry; a howl of horror. Man responds to his defeat at the hands of death with total resignation and black despair, beaten by the fiend, his prayers rejected, forsaken and lonely, man begins to question his singular worth."

17 For a list of rare exceptions, see YD 345

18 See TB Shabbat 105b, also Yehudah Landau, *Noda Bi'Yehudah*, pt. 2, YD no. 210.

19 *Sefer Mizvot Katan* classifies the *mizvot* according to the different parts of the body that perform them.

20 See YD 349. One canot derive benefit from items that touch the corpse or coffin if they were intended to be buried with the body.

21 According to Rabbi Benzion Uziel, former Sephardic chief rabbi of Israel, in his responsa *Mishpetei Uziel*, YD nos. 28, 29, there would be no objection to autopsies for medical and educational purposes in Israel if they were carried out with proper respect for the dead body and with prior consent from the deceased.

22 *Iggerot Moshe,* YD, vol. 2 , chap. 151 (end).

23 Ibid.

24 For a discussion of this issue, see Yosef, *Yabia Omer*, vol. 3, YD, chaps. 20–23; see also Immanuel Jakobovits, *Jewish Medical Ethics* (New York: Bloch, 1975).

25 For further study on this issue, see *Jewish Bioethics* edited by Fred Rosner and David J. Bleich in particular the essays by Nachum Rabinovitch pp. 383–389, and Fred Rosner pp. 389–409. Also see on the Web www.hods.org. Hods stands for Halakhic Organ Donor Society.

26 See TB Moed Katan 20b; *Shulhan Arukh,* YD 374:6; *Yalkut Yosef,* vol. 7, 8:1.

27 *Shulhan Arukh,* YD 341:1.

28 *Arukh HaShulhan,* YD 341:27–28; *Kaf HaHayim* 341.

29 Ibid. see also Rambam 4:6.

30 Ibid.

31 See TB Berakhot 17b, Mishnah and Gemara; also Rambam, loc. cit; *Yabia Omer,* vol. 4, YD 25:2.

32 See *Yehaveh Da'at* , vol. 4, chap. 4; *Yabia Omer,* vol. 5, chap. 10.

33 *Shulhan Arukh* and Rambam, loc. cit.

34 See Rambam, loc. cit.; *Minhat Shelomo* 91 on whether an *onen* is required to fulfill the *mizvah* of *tzedakah*, which includes the negative command of "not withholding."

35 See *Yalkut Yosef,* vol. 7, p. 50, fn. 3; *Yalkut Yosef* 3:9.

36 *Shulhan Arukh,* YD 341:1.

37 *Shulhan Arukh,* OH 71.
38 *Yabia Omer,* vol. 4, p. 297.
39 See *Hazon Ovadia,* vol. 2, p. 185 and fn.
40 See *Yalkut Yosef* 3:6.
41 *Yalkut Yosef* 3:7.
42 See *Kaf HaHayim* 341:103; *Gesher HaHayim,* vol. 1 chap. 18:16.
43 *Yalkut Yosef,* vol. 7, 3:14.
44 See *Yalkut Yosef,* vol. 7, 3:17 see also footnote 18.
45 Yosef, *Yabia Omer,* vol. 6, p. 103 (OH 30:6).
46 YD 352:3.
47 TB Moed Katan 27.
48 YD 352:2.
49 See *Gesher HaHayim,* chap. 10:5.
50 *Shulhan Arukh,* YD 350:2; see also *Tur* and *Bet Yosef,* YD 350, and Ramban, *Torah HaAdam.*

CHAPTER 5

Planning the Funeral Service

Scheduling the Funeral Service

It is regarded as a sign of great disrespect to the deceased if he or she is not buried immediately. Human beings are created in the image of God and must be accorded the utmost of respect. The importance of burying the dead immediately is reflected in numerous halakhot (laws) that mandate us to forgo whatever we may be doing at any given time in order to bury the dead even when the deceased is not a relative or an acquaintance. The importance of this *mizvah* is highlighted by the halakhah that even the High Priest, on his way to perform the service on Yom Kippur, the holiest of days, must defile himself and forgo performing the service in order to bury the dead. This comes under the heading of a *met mizvah she'en lo kovrim*, a corpse that is unburied and no one else is taking responsibility.[1]

Deuteronomy states as follows regarding the death sentence of a criminal: "His body shall not remain for the night on the gallows; rather you shall surely bury him on that day, for a hanging person is a curse of God."[2]

The Talmud deduces from this verse that if the Torah shows such consideration for a criminal, it should apply all the more to an innocent person.[3] Based on this interpretation of the verse, burial within twenty-four hours following death is the norm in Jewish tradition.[4]

Having said all this, there are exceptions to the rule of immediate burial. One exception has to do with *kavod hamet,* showing honor and respect to the deceased.[5] If, for example, the presence of a close relative or a rabbi will bring honor to the deceased, and that person needs to travel a long distance to take part in the service, and is doing everything possible to arrive as soon as possible, the funeral can be delayed. Other exceptions include legal delays in the funeral service due to government regulations and situations where the burial will take place overseas. The only other times burial is delayed is when death occurs immediately before Shabbat or on a holiday on which funerals are not permitted. In such a case, the burial is postponed until after the Shabbat or holiday.

Casket

Traditionally the Jewish people have always used a casket made entirely of wood so that the body, shroud, and coffin decompose at approximately the same rate. The interior of the casket should not be lined. In some communities it is the custom to drill holes in the bottom of the casket in order to fulfill the passage "From dust thou art, and unto dust thou shall return."[6] In the Syrian communities of Brooklyn, New York, and Deal, New Jersey, it is the custom to uncover the casket and fill it with earth.

Most communities offer one standard casket, suggesting that all are buried equally and with simplicity. In his autobiography, Ed Koch, former mayor of New York, describes his experience with finding an appropriate coffin for his mother.

> We needed to pick out a casket. We told the director we were looking for something in the Orthodox tradition and he ushered us into a room with a twenty-five hundred dollar casket…. He knew we were looking for something simple but he figured he'd work his hard sell on us just the same. He took us into several rooms and in each room the caskets cost less. He didn't skip a room. Probably he thought our resolve would weaken and we would be shamed into buying an expensive one.

Finally, he took us into the basement, where he showed us two pine boxes, which is what we had told him we wanted in the first place. My mother would not have appreciated an expensive casket …besides, an Orthodox funeral requires a simple wooden casket without nails or ornament…. Yet …even here in the basement, he wanted to sell us the more expensive of the pine caskets…. We were so humiliated by the ordeal that we said yes [to the more expensive one]. We could resist no further. I've never forgotten that. That man made us feel cheap and we succumbed.[7]

This passage illustrates the wisdom of our ancient traditions and customs. This is the time when we need the tradition to help us make decisions as to what will appropriately honor our loved ones.

Flowers

The impermanent beauty of flowers, another of God's creations, lends unique beauty to any occasion, whether it be one of joy or sorrow. While Sephardic custom permits the use of flowers to adorn and show respect to the deceased,[8] it has never been considered an ideal custom. The primary reasons that flowers are discouraged include: (1) floral tributes at funerals are primarily a non-Jewish custom, and it would not be appropriate to model our service on gentile services; (2) floral decorations are expensive, and since their ephemeral beauty is short-lived, a charitable donation to a worthy cause is regarded as more meaningful; (3) the Jewish funeral service is traditionally distinguished by its simplicity and modesty, and allowing the use of flowers would run the risk of turning the chapel into an ostentatious display of elaborate floral decorations that would not fit the spirit of the traditional service.

If floral decorations are displayed in good taste, there are solid halakhic grounds for permitting their use. Rabbi Ovadia Yosef, a contemporary Sephardic halakhic authority, writes:

Those who have the tradition to adorn the casket of the deceased with flowers … have a halakhic basis for their custom….

However, whenever possible, if the family will listen to their rabbis' advice, they should be discouraged from displaying flowers at the chapel or cemetery.[8]

In place of floral gifts, the family and friends of the deceased should be encouraged to pay tribute to the deceased by sending donations to a worthy charity in memory of the deceased. Charitable donations are a meaningful memorial and also benefit the living. If people insist on flowers, they do not have to be discouraged, and they can display the flowers at the service in a non-ostentatious fashion.

Viewing the Deceased

Placing the dead body of the person we loved on display does not constitute appropriate *kavod hamet* because it does not show respect and dignity for the dead. Jewish tradition places human value in the soul and personality of a human being; the mass of lifeless flesh represents the antithesis of *Zelem Elohim*, the image of God. No amount of cosmetics, mechanical devices, chemical injections, or fancy clothing can bring dignity to a dead body. This is why the body is covered with a sheet immediately after death occurs. It is forbidden to manipulate or beautify the dead body for cosmetic purposes.

In many Sephardic communities, the immediate family may see the deceased prior to burial. This is practiced in a very private fashion, and under no circumstances is the body manipulated or altered. In some communities, as a sign of love and respect, the sons and daughters of the deceased will kiss the hand of their father or mother prior to the funeral service.[9]

Cremation

Jewish law states that the body of the deceased must be buried in the earth. It is therefore forbidden under any circumstances to cremate the dead. Even if the deceased willed a cremation, the family must ignore the wish and observe the tradition of our forefathers that has been passed on from generation to generation. Cremated ashes cannot be buried in a Jewish cemetery.

Mausoleum

The requirement for burial refers specifically to burial in the earth. In certain cities, due to the dampness of the ground, a mausoleum is built around a plot of earth. This kind of mausoleum is permitted.

Mausoleums that are built above ground and not surrounded by earth are not permitted according to Jewish law. Even if the deceased willed such a burial, his or her will is denied. The only exception to this rule is when civil law requires burials above ground due to the unstable and shifting nature of the land.

Kohanim

The title of *kehunah*, meaning that one is a male *kohen*, a member of the priesthood, is passed down from father to son and is retained as long as the male adult is either single or married to a Jewish woman. Chapter 21 of Leviticus, also known as the Holiness Code, mandates the regulations governing the behavior of *kohanim*. It was designed to ensure the highest level of sanctity for the spiritual leaders of the Jewish people.

The Holiness Code prohibits the *kohen* from having contact with the dead, with the exception of certain members of his immediate family.[10] Therefore a *kohen* is not permitted to carry, move, or touch a dead body or a detached limb of a human being. He is also not permitted to be present under the same roof with a corpse or limb. Jewish law mandates that if death occurs while a *kohen* is in a house or building, he must immediately leave the premises.[11] At a funeral service, a male *kohen* may not enter the chapel or any of its rooms if the deceased is in the building. In order to pay respect to the deceased, a *kohen* must listen to the service from outside the chapel. Some chapels have a special room for *kohanim* which is adjacent to the room where the service is held but is actually not part of the building and has a completely separate entrance.

Similarly, a *kohen* cannot enter the cemetery grounds. It is the custom in most Jewish cemeteries to bury *kohanim* at the entrance of the cemetery so that the family can visit the grave without stepping on the cemetery grounds.

The biblical Holiness Code of the priestly family was a radical departure from ancient Near Eastern traditions that oftentimes involved elaborate rituals around death, at which time the pagan priests would exploit the vulnerable mourners. As a result, the Torah mandates that the *kohen* completely disassociate himself and his office from death and its rituals. By doing so, the Torah redirects the function of the *kohen* and focuses on his role as teacher and spiritual guide.

The exception to the Holiness Code is when the deceased is an immediate relative of the *kohen*,[12] such as his wife,[13] mother, father, son, daughter, brother, or unmarried sister. In such instances the Torah obligates the *kohen* to participate in the *mizvah* of burying his relative. The only other time a *kohen* may defile himself by participating in a funeral service is in an emergency situation when there is no one else to attend to the dead person. This is called *met mizvah*, and it is deduced from the verse *lenefesh lo yitamah be'amav*, "he shall not defile himself amongst his people." The clause "amongst his people" is understood to mean only when he is among his people is he forbidden to defile himself. But when there is no one else available to attend to the corpse, he must defile himself and bury the body in order to preserve *kavod hamet*, the dignity and honor of the deceased.

LAWS RELATING TO *KOHANIM*

- A *kohen*, even under the age of thirteen, should follow the restrictions of the Holiness Code.[14]
- A *kohen* may not enter any area that is under the same roof as a Jewish dead body. If a *kohen* is informed that a Jew has died in his apartment building or office building, he should leave the premises immediately.[15]
- A *kohen* may not touch or carry a corpse or even the smallest part of a lifeless body or limb.
- A *kohen* may participate in the burial of the following relatives: wife, mother, father, son, daughter, brother, unmarried sister.[16]
- When a *kohen* enters the cemetery grounds for the burial of an immediate relative, he must leave the cemetery grounds immediately following the interment.[17]

Suicide

Because of the absolute sanctity of human life, it is strictly forbidden to take one's own life. As Jews we are charged with preserving life and with sanctifying God's name throughout our lifetime by the manner in which we live. The right to choose to die is not in our hands. Only God can exercise such a right. When one defiantly rejects God's will and takes one's own life, death not only loses its atoning qualities but is regarded as a serious transgression. Pirke Avot (Ethics of the Fathers) makes this point in absolute terms:

> Do not allow your natural impulse to convince you that the grave is a refuge for perforce you were formed; perforce you were born; perforce do you live; perforce you shall die; and perforce are you destined to give an account and reckoning before the Supreme King of Kings the Holy One, blessed be He.[18]

No matter how noble one may view the act of suicide, it can never be condoned. Active euthanasia, even intended solely for the purpose of ending suffering, is categorically forbidden. On some level, Judaism considers suicide to be more heinous than murder. Rabbi Bahya Ibn Pakuda writes in his seminal work *Duties of the Heart*: "The closer the relationship between the killer and the killed, the more heinous the crime, and man is closest to himself."[19]

Because suicide is considered to be a denial of God's supreme will over His creations, the bereaved are generally required to follow a different pattern of mourning for a person who commits suicide. The general principle is that *kavod hamet*, the usual honor afforded the deceased is denied to a person who commits suicide because of the nature of this crime. While honor to the deceased is denied, all the rituals that show honor to the bereaved are observed.

A person who commits suicide, God forbid, is buried away from all other Jewish graves. Most cemeteries reserve a row at the end of the cemetery along the fence for suicides. Under these circumstances, no formal eulogy is delivered, and *Keriah* and *Shivah* are not observed.[20]

Kaddish and *Hashkavah* are, however, recited for one who commits suicide. Relatives should also observe *Hazkarot* (memorial services) in memory of the deceased.[21]

WHAT IS A HALAKHIC SUICIDE?

The above laws take effect if it has been determined that the deceased did, in fact, commit suicide. Jewish law has its own criteria for determining whether a death was a suicide, independent of police records or court rulings. Some of the factors involved in such determinations according to Jewish law include:

- Can it be ascertained without a doubt that the death was in fact a suicide? If there is any doubt at all, we do not assume suicide.[22]
- Might the deceased have been insane to any degree, even temporarily, while committing suicide? If that is the case, the above laws do not apply.
- Was the deceased under the influence of drugs, alcohol, or any substance? Once again, if it can be determined that the deceased was under the influence of some drugs or substance, then the death is not considered to be a halakhic suicide.
- Was the deceased motivated by extreme pain, suffering, or anxiety? If so, we assume that the deceased had no control over his or her actions and thus the death was not, in fact, an actual suicide.[23]
- Was the death instantaneous, or was it lingering, during which time the deceased may have tried to alter the course of events or repent?[24] If so, we assume that the *teshuvah* (repentance) was sincere, and even though he or she died, we regard the deceased as a *ba'al teshuvah*, a person who has repented.
- Is it possible that the deceased committed suicide as a means of repentance? If this is true, we mourn his or her death even though the act is not condoned.[25]

Based on the above information, the rabbi decides whether or not this is a case of suicide. As was mentioned earlier, the rabbinical decision is independent of any police or court ruling. In practice, a person who commits suicide is rarely deemed a halakhic suicide. Most authorities are of the opinion that nobody in his right mind would kill him- or herself. If the person were completely rational, suicide would not be a possibility. The very fact that the deceased committed suicide is enough evidence to deem him or her at least temporarily insane. For this reason the so-called suicide is usually accorded a respectful and dignified Jewish burial.

Endnotes

1   TB Nazir 43b.

2   Deuteronomy 21:23.

3   Sifrei on the verse, TB Sanhedrin 46a. R. Shimon bar Yohai stated that one who does not immediately bury his dead transgresses a negative command. TY Nazir 7:1; see Maimonides, *Yad*, Sanhedrin 15:8 and Avel, chap. 4.

4   The mystical tradition as well offers reasons for immediate burial. One has to do with the grief of the soul. As long as the body is not buried, the soul suffers from grief. Abraham Chill, *The Minhagim: The Customs and Ceremonies of Judaism* (New York: Sepher-Hermon Press, 1979), p. 326. Another reason mentioned by Chill has to do with the transmigration of the soul.

5   For a complete discussion of this issue, see Ovadia Yosef, *Yabia Omer*, vol. 4, p. 305 (YD 28:3).

6   Genesis 3:19.

7   Edward Koch with Daniel Paisner, *Citizen Koch: An Autobiography* (New York: St. Martin's Press, 1992), pp. 60–61.

8   See Ovadia Yosef, *Yabia Omer*, vol. 3, p. 190 (YD 24). *Yalkut Yosef* 7:1.

9   This custom is no longer widely practiced by Syrian Sephardic Jews.

10   Leviticus 21:2–3.

11   YD 372:1.

12   This exception does not apply to the *kohen gadol*; see Leviticus 10:19–20.

13   See TB Moed Katan 20b.

14   *Mekor Hayim*, vol. 5, chap. 284.

15   Ibid.

16   *Yalkut Yosef* 30:1.

17   *Shulhan Arukh*, YD 373:6.

18   Pirke Avot 4:29.

19   Bahya Ibn Pakuda, *Duties of the Heart*, chap. 4.

20   *Yalkut Yosef* 33:1; also see *Yabia Omer*, vol. 2, chap. 24 and vol. 6, chap. 36.

21   See *Yalkut Yosef* 33:2; also *Yabia Omer*, vol. 6, p. 262 (YD 36) on the subject of whether or not one who commits suicide has a portion in the world-to-come.

22   YD 345:2.

23   King Saul killed himself out of fear that if he were captured in battle the Philistines would torture him. His actions were not deemed to be immoral.

24   *Yalkut Yosef* 33:1.

25   Ibid. 33:3.

CHAPTER 6

The Funeral and the Burial

The Funeral Service

The traditional Sephardic Jewish funeral service is kept simple and to the point. Its purpose is not to comfort the mourners, for our sages, of blessed memory, tell us "there can be no comfort for one whose deceased lies before him."[1] Rather, the service is intended to offer further *kavod hamet*, honoring the deceased through the recitation of psalms, the gathering of family, friends, and the community, and articulating to those present the good deeds the deceased performed during his or her lifetime.

The basic structure of the funeral service is as follows:

- The service begins with the recitation of specific psalms.
- The *hesped* (eulogy) is delivered by the rabbi, a friend, or members of the family.
- *Tsiduk HaDin* (some communities do *Tsiduk HaDin* after burial).
- The Syrian community recites *Kaddish* after the eulogy and *Tsiduk HaDin*.
- *Levaya* (escorting the casket) to the cemetery or gravesite.
- Burial Service.

Recitation of Psalms

The psalms selected for this purpose give expression to the thoughts and emotions which emanate from the heart of one who seeks solace and comfort at a time of loss. The Book of Psalms stands out as different from the rest of the Bible in one important respect. In the Torah and the *Nevi'im*, the books of the prophets, God speaks to man. In the Book of Psalms man speaks to God. While the other books of the Bible are filled with God's message to us – God reaching out, as it were, through his prophets, to draw man near to Him – in the book of Psalms man's soul reaches out to God, yearning for knowledge and wisdom, nearness and comfort.

The Book of Psalms reminds us that all of life's experiences, the moments of joy and victory as well as the moments of affliction and bitterness, can be used as a means of striving toward better clarity of thought and purity of resolve before our Creator. All of life's experiences can inspire song and poetry. Even today the psalms serve to lift up to God the emotions of all those who seek Him to bring consolation and strength, and to inspire them to devotion. Unconditional trust in God is the dominant theme throughout the Book of Psalms. The words "Though I walk through the valley of the shadow of death, I will fear no evil, for You are with me, Your rod and Your staff, they comfort me" is the message mourners need to hear at the time of their loss.

While the choice of psalms selected for the service may vary from community to community, most begin with Psalms 49, 16, and 23. Other psalms that may also be recited include Psalms 1, 15, and 90.

The Hebrew and English texts of all of these psalms, together with commentaries, will be found in Appendix 1.

The Eulogy

The eulogy is often the focal point of the funeral service. It is important that the eulogy be prepared and delivered by an experienced and capable person, preferably a rabbi. The Talmud states, using very strong terms in order to emphasize the point, that one who is lax in the preparation and delivery of a eulogy deserves to be buried alive.[2]

Rabbi Joseph B. Soloveitchik, of blessed memory, writes that the *hesped* (eulogy) has a twofold objective. Its first objective is to make people weep, as is clearly stated in the Talmud: "It is obligatory for the eulogizer to raise his voice and speak in terms which will break the heart."[3] Rabbi Soloveitchik explains:

> The *Halakha* did not like to see the dead interred in silent indifference. It wanted to hear the shriek of despair and to see the hot tear washing away human cruelty and toughness.[4]

The second objective to be achieved by the eulogy, according to Rabbi Soloveitchik, is more "informative and instructional." Through the eulogy we tell the life story of the deceased. We ask the question: "Who was this person?" No matter how well we think we knew the deceased during his or her lifetime, ultimately we are each a "sealed book," even to those closest to us, until our last hour. Writes Rabbi Soloveitchik:

> Anonymity is an integral part of the human existential destiny. *Sof Davar Hakol Nishma* – "the end of the matter, all is heard" (Ecclesiastes 12:13). Only at the conclusion of the *Davar*, the human career, only at the end of the life story of man or woman, do people become inquisitive. Only then do they begin to inquire about him or her. Who was he or she? Only then *Hakol Nishma* – all kinds of questions are asked.

Jewish tradition insists that a person be mourned appropriately. The Talmud tells us:

> R. Simeon b. Pazzi said in the name of R. Joshua b. Levi in Bar Kappara's name: "When one sheds tears for a worthy person, the Holy One, blessed be He, counts them and lays them up in his treasure house, for it is said: 'Thou countest my grieving: Put thou my tears into thy bottle; are they not in thy book.'"[5]

The purpose of the eulogy is to show honor and respect for the deceased by expressing his or her good deeds and positive qualities, and to show how much he or she will be missed.[6]

It is very important to give the rabbi, or whoever will be delivering the eulogy, accurate information about the deceased. There is a tendency at times to exaggerate the qualities or glorify the traits of one who has just passed away. The *Shulhan Arukh* states that while we should not overstate the qualities of the deceased, we should try describe his or her best qualities.[7] An experienced rabbi knows how to gather the appropriate information needed to uncover the unique qualities and special virtues of the deceased.

TIMES WHEN THE EULOGY IS SCALED DOWN

Every person is deserving of an appropriate eulogy. There are times, however, when the deceased leaves special instructions regarding his or her eulogy. If the deceased clearly wished that no eulogy be delivered, that wish should be honored.

There are certain times of the year when it is appropriate to scale down the eulogy because excessive sadness and wailing is forbidden. The principle governing this law asserts that the joy of the community overrides the grief of the individual. Other opportunities for remembering and reflecting upon the life of the deceased can be created at the *Sheloshim* (thirty-day memorial service).

> **THE FOLLOWING ARE THE TIMES**
> **WHEN A EULOGY IS NOT PERMITTED:**
>
> If the funeral occurs on:
> - Pesah, Sukkoth, Shavuoth, Hanukkah, Purim, Rosh Hodesh (New Moon)
> - On the eve of the above holidays and on Friday
> - During the entire month of Nissan

TSIDUK HADIN

The *Tsiduk HaDin* prayer consists of various verses from the Bible. It is a prayer that affirms our faith in God and in His divine justice. It begins with the words: "You are righteous, O Lord, and upright are Your judgments.[8] The Lord is righteous in all His ways."[9] We acknowledge the fact that we do not and cannot ever understand God's ways and yet our faith does not waver. Life and death are in the hands of the Almighty, and its mystery we cannot fully fathom. At a time of loss, our lives are put into perspective; we accept our lot and reaffirm our belief that God provides and takes away. The earliest appearance of such a theme is found in *Ha'azinu,* the Song of Moses, and it is later used throughout the Bible: "The Rock – perfect is His work, for all His paths are justice; a God of faith without iniquity, righteous and fair is He."[10]

The first recorded association of this general theme with death and mourning dates back to the talmudic period. The Talmud records that at the end of the Jewish revolt against the Roman empire and the fall of the fortress of Bethar toward the end of the summer of 135 C.E., Rabbi Hanina ben Teradion was captured. Condemned to death for teaching Torah, he was wrapped up in a parchment Torah scroll and burned alive at the stake. Rabbi Hanina ben Teradion's entire family was also taken to be martyred, and the Talmud reports that they uttered the verses that form the basis of the *Tsiduk Hadin* prayer.[11]

Indeed, our tradition mandates that these words be stated on behalf of the mourner as a departure for healing and resolution. Human beings yearn for life, and yet we are reminded at a time of bereavement that it is only God who controls life and death, and that ultimately death will be our end.

Like *Keriah* and the blessing *Dayan Ha'emet, Tsiduk HaDin* should actually be recited at the time of death.[12] Today, in most Sephardic communities, the accepted custom is to recite the *Tsiduk HaDin* at the conclusion of the funeral service. It is also recited prior to the *Hashkavah* during the entire week of *Shivah.*

Below is an English translation of the *Tsiduk HaDin.* For the complete Hebrew text see the appendix.

You are righteous O Lord, and upright are Your judgments.
The Lord is righteous in all His ways,
and pious in all His deeds.
Your righteousness is an everlasting righteousness,
and your Torah is truth.

The judgments of the Lord are true, being righteous together.[13]

Since the word of the King reigns,
who could say to Him, what are You doing?
He is One, and who could possibly answer Him back?
Whatever His essence desires, He does.

There are those who are great and those who are small,
and the servant is free of his master.[14]

Behold, He has no faith in His servants,
and to His angels He attributes folly.
Certainly, the human, who is but worm,
the son of man, who is but maggot.

The Rock, perfect is His work, for all His ways are just,
trustworthy God, never unjust, righteous and upright is He,
the Judge of truth, who judges righteously and truthfully;
Blessed is the Judge of truth,
for all His judgments are righteous and true.

The words of the *Tsiduk HaDin* afford the mourner a sense of connection to a faith, to a past, and to a community. Like the *Kaddish*, the *Tsiduk HaDin* is recited with a quorum; a reminder that the mourner is not alone in his or her grief.

Levayath Hamet

A *hesed shel emet* is an act of kindness that is distinguished from other acts of kindness in that it is also an act of complete sincerity and *truth*. The term designates acts of kindness and love that are done without expecting or ever receiving anything back, not even a thank you. The *mizvah* of accompanying the deceased to burial, *levayath hamet*, is considered to be an act of *hesed shel emet*, a kindness of truth.[15] In fact, our sages liken the accompaniment of the deceased to accompanying the Lord.[16]

The importance of escorting the deceased to the cemetery is

underscored by the fact that one is permitted to cancel Torah study for this *mizvah*.[17] This is especially true if the deceased was a Torah scholar and teacher. The rule of canceling Torah study does not apply to a Torah teacher whose absence would mean canceling Torah study for students.[18] Therefore every effort should be made to accompany the family to the cemetery.

IF ONE CANNOT GO TO THE CEMETERY

If you can attend the funeral service but cannot go out to the cemetery, you should make a point of following the hearse a short distance as it drives away[19] and then stop and wait until the procession is out of sight. Psalm 91 is traditionally recited (text and translation will be found in Appendix 1), followed by the words:

לך לשלום ותנוח בשלום ותעמוד לגורלך לקץ הימים

Go in peace and rest in peace, and stand up for your destiny at the end of days.

> **IMPORTANT NOTE**
> From here on we have to make a distinction between that which falls into the category of law, which is observed by all who revere Jewish tradition, folklore specific to certain groups or families, and traditions observed uniquely by certain local communities. Many traditions and folkloric practices are cultural or superstitious. Readers are encouraged to learn more about their own *traditional* heritage.

GOING TO THE CEMETERY

In many Sephardic communities, the folkloric tradition prohibits women from attending funeral services and going to the cemetery. Similarly, in some communities men do not attend their father's burial service. The reason given for these customs is based on a passage in the *Zohar* which states that a sort of "spiritual danger" lurks at the cemetery, and while women are most at risk, men whose fathers have died are also at risk.[20] In earlier days, the statement in the *Zohar* combined with community superstition and the tendency not to question religious authorities ensured that people would observe this custom. Today, a rabbi would be hard-pressed to tell a woman who is in grief that she should not attend the funeral service or the cemetery for the death of a loved one. It is therefore an accepted fact that today women do attend the funeral service and the cemetery. It is not my purpose to suggest that communities that continue to observe this custom should change their ways.

The custom of men not attending their father's burial continues to be observed in many Sephardic communities, including the Sephardic community of Jerusalem. Rabbi Ovadia Yosef, former Sephardic chief rabbi of Israel, suggests that these customs should not be imposed on individuals and communities, yet if an individual or a family wants to observe this ancient tradition, they should not be discouraged.[21]

Rabbi Moshe Shamah[22] of Brooklyn, New York, responded as follows to a question on this matter:

> Although some discourage a son from attending his father's burial, this is a practice that is not mentioned in the Talmud or in a single classical Jewish source including *Shulhan Arukh*. Rabbi Solomon D. Sassoon *a"h* considered it contrary to the spirit of the Torah and countermanding the Mizvah of honoring one's father.
>
> An excerpt from the *Encyclopaedia Judaica* under the entry "Demonology" (vol. 5, col. 1530) may help place this matter into better perspective: "The sexual element in the relationship of man and demons holds a prominent place in the demonology of the Zohar …remarkably similar to the beliefs current in Christian and medieval demonology…. these demons …need the human semen in order to multiply. In the later Kabbalah it is pointed out that the demons born to man out of such unions are considered his illegitimate sons. At death and burial they come to accompany the dead man, to lament him, and to claim their share of the inheritance; they may also injure the legitimate sons. Hence the custom …in a number of communities (dating from the 17th century) of

not allowing the sons to accompany their father's corpse to the cemetery in order to prevent their being harmed by their illegitimate step-brothers."

STANDING WHILE THE BODY IS MOVED

Those who are present must stand when the dead body is moved from place to place. Standing is not only a sign of respect for the deceased but a show of respect for those performing the *mizvah* of *hesed* (kindness).[23]

PALLBEARERS

The handlers of the casket, or those carrying the bier, as well as those waiting to replace the pallbearers are performing an important *mizvah* and giving honor to the deceased. It is therefore important that the pallbearers selected for this task be Jewish.[24]

A good indicator of how esteemed this *mizvah* was in the eyes of our sages is related by the fact that the pallbearers are exempt from the *mizvah* of reciting the *Shema* as long as they are needed for the task.[25] The rest of the participants are required to recite the *Shema* but are exempt from reciting the *Amidah*.[26]

BLESSING BEFORE ENTERING THE CEMETERY

Before entering the cemetery, the appropriate blessing is recited by the rabbi or hazan.[27] This blessing should be recited by anyone who has not entered a Jewish cemetery within thirty days.

The blessing is as follows:

בָּרוּךְ אַתָּה יְהוָה אֱלֹהֵינוּ מֶלֶךְ הָעוֹלָם אֲשֶׁר יָצַר אֶתְכֶם בְּדִין, וְזָן אֶתְכֶם בְּדִין,
וְכִלְכֵּל אֶתְכֶם בְּדִין, וְהֶחֱיָה אֶתְכֶם בְּדִין, וְהֵמִית אֶתְכֶם בְּדִין, וְיוֹדֵעַ מִסְפַּר
כֻּלְּכֶם, וְהוּא עָתִיד לְהַחֲיוֹתְכֶם וּלְהַקִּימְכֶם בְּדִין לְחַיֵּי הָעוֹלָם הַבָּא: בָּרוּךְ אַתָּה
יְהוָה מְחַיֶּה הַמֵּתִים:

Blessed are You, Lord our God, King of the universe, who fashioned you with justice, nourished and sustained you with justice, took your lives with justice, knows the sum total of all of you with justice, and will restore and resuscitate you with justice. Blessed are You, who resurrect the dead.

Burial Service

Upon arriving at the cemetery, the pallbearers carry the casket to the gravesite, with the feet of the deceased always directed forward. At the gravesite the casket is turned around and buried with the head forward.

As the casket is escorted, those following it repeat the following verse three times:

והוא רחום יכפר עון ולא ישחית והרבה להשיב אפו ולא יעיר כל חמתו

And He, the merciful one, will forgive iniquity and not destroy man. He will frequently turn aside His anger and not arouse all His wrath.

Once at the grave, the casket is immediately lowered. The rabbi may use this opportunity to say a few closing remarks.

In some communities it is customary for the rabbi or the person officiating to symbolically ask the deceased, on behalf of those present, to forgive any pain caused during his or her lifetime or for any disrespect while preparing the burial.

In some communities, *Hakafot*, a procession encircling the grave seven times, may be enacted at the burial of a righteous and pious person.

SHOVELING EARTH INTO THE GRAVE

Hashkavah, the memorial prayer, cannot be recited until the entire casket is covered with earth. It is a *mizvah* for relatives and friends to assist in the burial of a loved one by helping to shovel earth back into the grave. For some this may seem difficult, but it is the last opportunity to do a physical act of love and kindness for the departed. This too is considered a *hesed shel emet*. By burying the deceased, we not only fulfill the *mizvah* of *kavod hamet* but we also provide an opportunity for the mourners to reconcile the death of their loved one. A healthy readjustment to society requires acceptance of the reality and finality of death.

I have officiated at many funerals where the family insists on doing more than simply the minimum of covering the casket with earth. They make a point of filling the entire grave with earth before leaving the cemetery.

I once officiated at the service of an elderly man in Seattle. This man had no children, but he had numerous loving nephews and nieces. After the burial service, as we were walking away from the grave, I noticed a young man, clearly not Jewish, whom I did not recognize, filling the grave with earth. I approached and asked him what he was doing. He answered that he owed this act of respect to the deceased. I must have looked baffled, because an explanation followed. The deceased had employed this man's father, and many years earlier, when the man's father had died, the deceased had attended the service. This being a non-Jewish service, the burial of the body was left to the custodian of the cemetery. The deceased, however, stayed behind after everyone left and personally buried his friend. When the young man asked the deceased what he was doing, he responded by saying: "I'm showing your father the utmost respect because I loved him, and when I die I want you to do the same for me." The man had promised he would, and he kept his promise.

PASSING THE SHOVEL

Another custom associated with the burial service is to take the shovel or digging utensil and not pass it from hand to hand. Rather the shovel is inserted back into the ground after it is used for the next person to take and use.[28] The reason for this custom is to symbolically avoid making the person who is handed the shovel the messenger of the previous person. Each person performs the *mizvah* individually, by personally picking up the shovel himself or herself.

While earth is being shoveled into the grave the following words are said:

כי עפר אתה ואל עפר תשוב. והוא רחום יכפר עון ולא ישחית והרבה להשיב אפו ולא יעיר כל חמתו.

From dust you are created, and to dust you shall return. And He, the merciful One, will forgive iniquity and not destroy man. He will frequently turn aside his anger and not arouse all His wrath.

The Memorial Prayer

Although the version of the *Hashkavah* may slightly vary between communities, the central themes are identical. The themes of the memorial prayer include an affirmation that God is compassionate and merciful, and that the deceased is no longer in the community of the living but among the community of the holy and righteous who have preceded him or her in death.

In some Sephardic communities,[29] the name of the deceased is not mentioned in the *Hashkavah* until after the *Shivah* period. Instead of using the name, reference is made to the deceased by saying *Haniftar lebet olamo*, "He who has gone to his eternal home."

In communities that have the custom of using the name of the deceased during *Shivah, Hashkavah* is said using the deceased's name followed by his or her mother's name.[30]

At the cemetery, some communities have the custom, following the *Hashkavah*, of having the children rise to ask *mehilah* (forgiveness) from the parent. The Syrian communities have the custom of blowing the shofar immediately following the *Hashkavah*.

Some have the custom of using this opportunity to recite *Hashkavah* for the parents of the deceased, if appropriate, or for any close relatives who may have preceded the deceased in death.

The complete text of the *Hashkavah* can be found in the appendix.

Proper Behavior at the Cemetery

It is important that people show appropriate respect at the cemetery. The cemetery is not a place for frivolous behavior and idle talk.[31] One should maintain a sense of solemnity and respect. It is forbidden to eat or drink in the cemetery proper. Those attending the cemetery should be encouraged to dress appropriately and modestly.

There is a principle that one should not indulge, in the presence of the dead, in religious activities that the deceased cannot perform. Therefore, one should not study Torah at the cemetery or carry a *talleth* or *tefillin*. Men who customarily wear the fringes of their *sisit* outside their garments should make a point of concealing them while in the cemetery.[32]

Leaving the Cemetery

After leaving the cemetery, those in attendance should ritually wash their hands. At the exit of the cemetery, there is usually running water for this purpose. Some have the custom of reciting the words of Isaiah:[33]

בלע המות לנצח ומחה יהוה אלהים דמעה מעל כל פנים וחרפת עמו יסיר מעל כל הארץ כי יהוה דבר

May He swallow up death forever, and may the Lord God wipe away tears from upon every face and remove the scorn of His people from the entire world, for the Lord has spoken. [34]

After washing, the hands should not be dried with a towel or kerchief, but should be left to dry naturally.[35]

Accompanying the Mourners Home

It is appropriate to accompany the mourners from the cemetery back to their home.[36] Once the funeral service is over, the mourners should not be left to grieve alone. Returning home with the mourner, affords them an anchor, a sense of belonging, and important comfort.

Disinterment

Disinterment, the opening of the casket after burial, may never be undertaken without first consulting an authority on Jewish law. Jewish law completely prohibits such an action with the exception of certain unusual cases.[37]

Even disinterment for the purpose of reinterment in another grave is strictly forbidden. Cases which may be considered by rabbinical authorities as exceptions to this rule include:

- When a deceased has been buried with the intent of being reinterred in another grave at a later time. The Spanish and Portuguese community inter all their dead with the condition that they may have to be reinterred at a later time.
- If the deceased will be reinterred in Israel.
- If the government appropriates the land for construction.
- If the gravesite will be destroyed by water or other natural disasters.

- If the deceased is being moved from a non-Jewish cemetery to a Jewish cemetery

These and other exceptions to the above rule are decided based on numerous factors, many of which are too complicated for the scope of the discussion here. Again, competent rabbinical counsel should be sought before making any decision on these matters.

Note that even when reinterment is permitted, a period of twelve months should elapse before disinterment is undertaken. Our sages regarded the transfer of bones as less of an assault on the dignity of the deceased than the transfer of a decomposing body.

If a body is disinterred, the grave and the monument cannot be sold or reused.[38] The principle that governs this law is that one cannot benefit from the deceased. This includes the grave, casket, shrouds, and monument of the disinterred. The only way to reuse any of these items would be for indigent cases in the community who could not otherwise afford a grave or monument.

Reinterment

An entire day of mourning must be observed at the time of reinterment of the remains of one's father, mother, or close relative. This includes the prohibitions against wearing shoes, sitting on chairs or couches, marital relations, bathing, and so on.[39] Similarly, *Keriah* and *Seudat Havra'ah* are performed immediately following the reinterment.[40] The day of mourning concludes with nightfall.

The utmost respect must be shown at all times to the remains of the body. If the remains will be traveling a distance, they must be accompanied by a *shomer*.[41]

Endnotes

1　Pirke Avot 4:23.
2　See TB Shabbat 105b and other such comments on eulogizing.
3　TB Berakhot 6a.
4　Joseph B. Soloveitchik, *Tradition* 17, no. 2 (Spring 1978): 73.
5　TB Berakhot 6a.

6 In TB Sanhedrin 46b our sages ask, "Is the eulogy for the dead or the living?" See *Torah Temimah* on Genesis 23:2 for the answer of the Gemara.

7 *Shulhan Arukh*, YD 344:1.

8 Psalms 119:137.

9 Psalms 145:17.

10 Deutcronomy 32:4.

11 TB Avodah Zarah 18a; Midrash Sifre on Deuteronomy 32:4; Midrash Rabbah Numbers 88:4. Also see *Encyclopaedia Judaica*. The full text of the story will be found in Appendix II.

12 *Shulhan Arukh*, YD 339:3.

13 They do not contradict one another.

14 The verse is making reference to the grave.

15 Mishnah 1:1 Peah; see Maimonides' Commentary on this Mishnah, also *Yad*, Avel 14:1. See Rashi on Genesis 47:29, *v'asita imadi hesed v'emet*; also TB Ketubot 72a.

16 Rashi on Rav Assi's statement about the *mizvah* of *levayath hamet*, TB Berakhot 18a.

17 *Shulhan Arukh*, YD 361:1. See Ketubot 17a and Tosafot.

18 See *Taz* on preceding note.

19 Rabbi Yehudah Shemuel Ashkenazi, *Siddur Bet Oved*, p. 442.

20 *Zohar*, Bereshit, p. 54.

21 Professor Meir Benayahu of Jerusalem wrote a book called *Ma'amadot U'Moshavot* on this subject. The work was inspired because after the death of his father, the Rishon LeZion, Hakham Izhak Nissim, and the rabbis of Jerusalem asked Benayahu and his brothers not to go to the cemetery. Professor Benayahu told them at the time that there is no room for such superstitions in Jewish law. He personally went to the cemetery and at the first annual memorial for his father delivered a lecture on the issue that subsequently was published as a book.

22 See Sephardic Institute web page under "Ask the Rabbi". Rabbi Moshe Shamah is the Rabbi of the Sephardic Institute of Brooklyn NY.

23 See *Shulhan Arukh*, YD 361:4; also *Tur* and *Taz*.

24 Mishnah Berakhot 3:1.

25 See Mishnah Berakhot 3:1; *Shulhan Arukh*, YD 358:1 and OH 72:1.

26 *Shulhan Arukh*, OH 106:1.

27 Ibid., OH 224:12. This blessing is recited any time one goes to the cemetery after thirty days.

28 *Hokhmat Adam* 158:30.

29 Specifically the Moroccan community.

30 See *Yalkut Yosef*, vol. 7, 23:22.

31 TB Megillah 29a.

32 *Shulhan Arukh*, OH 23:2. also YD 367:4

33 Ibid. 376:4.

34   Isaiah 25:8

35   *Kaf HaHayim* 4:8.

36   *Bet Yosef*, YD 378.

37   See note 1 in *Yalkut Yosef*, vol. 7, 32:1.

38   *Gesher HaHayim* 26, 3:2

39   *Shulhan Arukh*, YD 403:1.

40   Ibid., YD 403:2.

41   *Shulhan Arukh*, YD 403:10

CHAPTER 7

Kavod Habriot

Honoring the Living

Grief, like a wound, requires proper attention in order to heal. Mourning the loss of a loved one is the natural way to resolve grief. In order to work through and resolve grief appropriately, we must learn to face our feelings openly and honestly. This is a big order and requires not only courage to grieve but also support and a proper structure that allows grief to occur.

Unfortunately, we live in a society that values restraint and denial when confronted with loss. Judaism, on the other hand, requires the mourner to openly journey into the realm of pain and sorrow in order to heal and recover.

That we ultimately will recover from our grief may seem to be an amazing feat, yet we do recover. This is nature's way. Forests burn down and eventually grow anew. The Jewish response to death is not only about loss and mourning but also about recovery and restoration. Though at times this seems preposterous, we do conquer grief, we heal and even grow from the experience.

I have learned many lessons about grief from those who have trusted me as their rabbi. One of those lessons is that the only grief that does not end is the grief that was not grieved. We seek creative ways to avoid feeling the pain of the loss and act as if nothing has happened. I have seen it over and over again; no one succeeds in permanently denying the effects of loss. Fear is probably the number-one barrier to grieving. It may be the fear of rejection by others brought on by being honest and open about one's feelings. Some fear that if grief takes hold of them it will never let go. For this reason our sages, of blessed memory, transmitted to us laws, practices, and customs that govern our treatment of death. Our tradition mandates laws that govern not only the behavior of the mourner, but the behavior of the community. Until this point in the grief process, the entire focus has been on *kavod hamet*, maintaining the utmost respect and dignity of the deceased. From burial onward, the focus is now on *nihum aveilim*, comforting the mourners. The community must be a supportive anchor for the mourners and allow them the opportunity to express their grief in a safe, sensitive environment. Judaism, through *Shivah*, the seven-day period of mourning, offers the mourner a structure for open and uninhibited grief, allowing for an adequate response to the death of a loved one and a healthy way of coming to terms with grief.

Shivah means "seven" in Hebrew and refers to the seven days immediately following the burial of a relative that are set aside for the expression of grief. This period is the first stage of mourning in the process toward recovery. The tradition of *Shivah* dates back before the giving of Torah, as is evident from the story of Joseph, who mourned his father's death for seven days.[1]

Jewish tradition recognizes the need of those in mourning to confront their loss and not pursue regular daily living as if nothing unusual has taken place. During this period the mourner is placed in a safe and supportive atmosphere with family and friends to confront the difficult realities of life and death. The period of *Shivah* is designed to allow the mourner the opportunity to reflect upon moments and memories with the departed and gradually prepare the stage for a healthy transition to normal living.

This period is given unique significance by the presence of family, friends, and community volunteers who share in the mourner's grief and lend support and strength in order to adjust to life without the beloved who has just died. The family and friends are there to cater to the mourner's every need, be it physical or emotional.

Who Is a Mourner?

One is required to observe the laws of mourning for the following immediate relatives: father, mother, spouse, son, daughter, sister, brother, half-sister, and half-brother.[2] Children under the age of *mizvah* (boys thirteen, girls twelve) normally are not required to observe commandments; regarding the rituals of mourning, however, if they are capable of understanding the situation, they should be encouraged to observe the laws of mourning. Jewish law also has what is called empathetic mourning (see below for more details), which is appropriate to observe for one's father-in-law, mother-in-law, or stepmother if one's father is still living, as a sincere sign of respect for the deceased and for one's spouse.

Empathetic Mourning

Jewish law allows for a limited form of mourning for a select group of relatives. Empathetic mourners are those who mourn with the bereaved. The nature of this mourning is best described by Rabbi Yosef Karo in the *Shulhan Arukh*. He states as follows: "Whomever one mourns for, one mourns with."[3] In other words, the empathetic mourner is not considered a mourner according to *Halakhah* because he or she is not an immediate relative of the deceased. Instead, the empathetic mourner is mourning as a sign of respect and support for an immediate relative who is bereaved. Thus, if one of my nine immediate relatives suffers a certain type of loss (see below), I am obligated to participate in some of the mourning practices even though the deceased was not my blood relative. This halakhic rule was originally instituted as a sign of respect for the mourner. It affords the mourner comfort and support from the knowledge that those closest to him or her are also observing some form of mourning. It is traditionally accepted today that most mourners waive their right to this sign of respect.[4]

The empathetic mourner's obligation is limited until the conclusion of the Shabbat following the burial.

The laws of empathetic mourning particularly apply when one's spouse is in mourning for a parent.[5] It does not apply, however, when one's spouse is in mourning for a sibling or a child from another marriage. Another instance in which empathetic mourning would apply would be when one's parent is mourning a spouse from a second marriage.[6] Because parents would not want their children mourning, empathetic mourning does not apply when mourning the death of a grandparent. Similarly, it does not apply when a child is in mourning for a spouse.[7]

Since empathetic mourning is a sign of respect and support for the mourner, its rituals are only observed in the presence of the mourner but are not relevant if the mourner is in another place or city.

Voluntary Mourners

How does Jewish law respond to the loss of a beloved person when the deceased is not one of the nine immediate relatives (see above) whom one is required to mourn? The loss of a beloved rabbi or teacher, or of a grandparent or a dear friend can at times be as painful, if not more so, as the loss of a relative. Within the framework of the laws of *Avelut,* there is a category for voluntary mourning.[8] If the traditional response to death were not only symbolic, but also therapeutic, then it would make sense that *Halakhah* offers an opportunity to respond to any death religiously.

Jewish law allows us to engage in ritual mourning whenever we want to sincerely participate in the bereavement of a loved one even though the deceased is not a relative. The only restriction placed on voluntary mourners is that they may not violate any Torah commandments. Take, for example, the commandment to study Torah every day. This commandment is waived for mourners during the entire week of mourning because "Study of Torah brings joy."[9] However, it is not waived for the voluntary mourner.

Voluntary mourning is introduced as a means to respond to the loss of a loved one whom we are not obligated to mourn for and not as a license to mourn above and beyond that which the law prescribes. As was mentioned earlier, *Halakhah* has definite guidelines as to the extent to which we should mourn. In fact, the Talmud relates the story of a woman who excessively mourned the death of her sons and died as a result. The clear guidelines of mourning are designed to prevent the bereaved from wallowing in their mourning.

Counting the Seven Days

Shivah does not begin until the deceased is buried and the grave is filled with earth, and it lasts seven days.[10] A halakhic day is not necessarily always twenty-four hours. In Jewish law, part of a day is considered as a whole day; therefore, even if the period from the time of interment until that evening is less than twenty-four hours, it is considered day one. At sundown begins day two of the seven days. Similarly, the seventh day is only observed for a short period in the morning. Once again, the principle which states that part of a day is considered an entire day goes into effect. Therefore, shortly after morning services on the seventh day of *Shivah*, those present extend their last condolences and the mourner rises from his or her mourning.[11]

As is evident, the total number of days the mourner observes for *Shivah* are seven *halakhic* days but not necessarily seven twenty-four-hour days.

Times When *Shivah* Does Not Begin Immediately After Burial

HOLIDAY OR *HOL HAMOED*

If the burial took place on a holiday or during *Hol Hamoed*, the intermediate days of the holiday, the *Shivah* begins on *Motza'ey Yom Tov*, the night following the holiday.[12] In the Diaspora, *Shivah* also begins on *Motza'ey Yom Tov*; however, the last day of the holiday is counted as day one toward the seven-day count.

BURIAL OUT OF TOWN

If the burial is going to take place out of town (e.g., in Israel), the mourners who accompany the casket begin *Shivah* after the burial. The mourners who remain behind begin *Shivah* when the body leaves the city they are in.[13]

WHEN THE MOURNER IS NOT AT THE BURIAL

If you receive news that a relative has passed away in another city and are notified as to exactly when the burial will take place, *Shivah* begins after the burial of the deceased. If, however, it is unclear when the burial will take place, *Shivah* begins immediately upon hearing the news of the death.[14]

IF BURIAL IS DELAYED

If the deceased was going to be buried in another city and the mourners who stayed behind began their *Shivah* period, but a delay occurred and the deceased was not buried as scheduled, the mourners should not interrupt their mourning period. After burial, the mourners do not need to sit *Shivah* again.

NO CORPSE

If there is no corpse and the news of the death was reported within thirty days of the death, the mourners begin *Shivah* immediately upon hearing of the death.[15]

Times When *Shivah* Is Not Seven Days

National celebrations take precedence over the grief of the individual. Therefore, if one of the major holidays occurs during *Shivah*, the *Shivah* is considered complete with the onset of the holiday.[16] Even if mourning began only one hour before the holiday, that one hour is considered equivalent to the full seven days of mourning and counts toward the thirty-day memorial (this will be explained in further detail later on).

Hearing About the Death After Burial

One is obligated to sit *Shivah* even when the news of the death of a relative arrives after the burial, provided that it is within thirty days of the death according to the local time of the person who receives the news.[17] If the news arrives on the thirtieth day,[18] one must sit *Shivah*. If, however, the news of death arrives after the thirtieth day from the time of death, then one sits *Shivah* for only one hour.[19] This is true even for one's parents; however, while the *Shivah* restrictions do not apply when one is notified of a parents demise thirty days after the parent has died, the restrictions of the *Sheloshim* period (e.g., getting a haircut) do apply.[20]

A Double Grief

If two or more family members die on the same day, God forbid, the mourners observe only one *Shivah* period for all the deceased.[21]

If, however, a second family member dies while one is already sitting *Shivah* for a family member, the mourner begins counting *Shivah* from the time of burial of the second family member.[22] In other words, if a person has observed two days of mourning for a member of the family, and then a second member of the family dies and is buried on that day, the mourner now observes seven days of *Shivah* with the second day of the original *Shivah* counting as day one. At the conclusion of the *Shivah,* the mourner need not observe any further mourning. In total the mourner has observed eight days.

Rituals in the Home of a Mourner

THE ORDER OF RITUALS UPON ARRIVING

AT THE MOURNER'S HOME

- Removal of shoes
- *Keriah*
- Lighting a memorial candle
- Sitting on the floor or a low stool
- *Seudat Havra'ah,* the meal of consolation
- *Birkat Hamazon*
- Observance of *Shivah* restrictions

REMOVAL OF SHOES

Immediately upon arrival at the home the mourners remove their shoes. It is the custom of most Sepharadim that the mourners not wear shoes. even those made without leather.[23]

Keriah

As was mentioned above, with the burial of the deceased the emphasis now changes from *kavod hamet*, honoring the dead, to *nihum aveilim,* comforting the mourners. It is with this in mind that the *Shivah* begins with the *Keriah*,[24] the rending of one's clothing. *Keriah* allows mourners to vent out their anguish in a controlled, religiously sanctioned act in the presence of a rabbi and close family and friends. Though it is only symbolic, *Keriah* serves as a potent physical and emotional release of sorrow and anger at precisely the needed moment. *Keriah* also symbolizes the impermanent nature of our stay in this world and the ephemeral nature of material things.

The act of *Keriah* as a sign of grief dates back to biblical times. Jacob rent his garment when he saw Joseph's coat of many colors drenched in blood. So, too, King David tore his clothes after hearing of the death of King Saul.[25]

A rabbi or religious leader usually initiates *Keriah*. The garment is first cut with a knife or blade and then the mourner takes both ends of the cut and tears the garment. *Keriah* is done in a standing position.[26] Immediately prior to the tearing of the clothes the following blessing is recited:

Barukh Atah Adonai Eloheinu Melekh Ha'olam Dayan Ha'emet.
Blessed are You Lord our God whose Judgement is righteous.

The Blessing for *Keriah* is only recited within the first three days after death.

Our tradition uses ritual to give form and shape to its objectives. The act of rending a garment and reciting words that speak of divine justice allow mourners to express their inner selves in true human relatedness. In pagan cultures, the body of the mourner would be mutilated as a sign of mourning. In American Western culture, we choose to ignore the pain. Jewish tradition avoids these extremes. We rend our garments as a formal external expression of grief.

LAWS OF *KERIAH*

Both men and women must observe the *mizvah* of *Keriah*. Immediately following the *Keriah*, women should safety-pin their cut garment for modesty reasons.[27] Our sages of blessed memory sought to impress upon us the importance of the *Keriah* by stating that one who does not do *Keriah* at the time of the death of a relative is worthy of death.[28]

Keriah is observed for the relatives that one is commanded to mourn; namely, father, mother, spouse, son, daughter, brother, half-brother, sister, and half-sister.

A child who is old enough to understand that a family member has died and that *Keriah* is a sign of grief and mourning should be encouraged to perform *Keriah.*[29]

APPROPRIATE GARMENT FOR *KERIAH*

Keriah is done at the neck in the front of an outer garment that is worn indoors at normal room temperature.[30] Therefore one does not rend an undershirt or overcoat or other such garments for special temperatures. While the initial cut may be done with a knife, the rest of the cut must be done by hand. The appropriate garment to cut for men is a jacket, a vest, or a shirt if it is the outer garment, while for women a dress, blouse, or sweater. The custom of tearing a ribbon does not fulfill the *mizvah* of *Keriah* and should be strongly discouraged.

KERIAH FOR A PARENT

Some communities make a distinction between the rending when one is mourning for a parent versus the rending while mourning other relatives. For a parent, one tears one's clothing on the left side next to the heart.[31] Today, however, in most Sephardic communities, the *Keriah* is done on the left side for all relatives. The heart is on the left side and the tear is symbolic of a broken heart at this time of grief.

The tear must be visible at all times. It should be torn vertically, beginning near the neck and cut down approximately three and one-half inches.[32]

For a parent, the *Keriah* must be visible throughout the *Shivah* period. Therefore, for their parent(s), mourners must tear whatever garments they change into during the *Shivah.*[33] This is not the case for other relatives. Therefore, mourners who change their clothing during the *Shivah* do not need to tear the new clothing.[34]

Immediately following *Shivah* the rent garment can be removed.

IF *KERIAH* WAS NOT DONE ON TIME

If one did not do *Keriah* immediately following the burial service, it must be done sometime during the seven days of *Shivah.*[35] If it is done before the third day of *Shivah*, the appropriate blessing is recited. If it is done between the third and seventh days, the blessing is recited without the use of God's name.[36]

One does not perform *Keriah* after the *Shivah*. The reason for this is that *Keriah* is only performed at a time of intense grief. After *Shivah* it is assumed that the period of intense grief is over, and thus tearing a garment could not be justified because it would be considered wasteful.[37]

SLEEPWEAR

At night one may change into sleeping clothes and need not do *Keriah* on them.[38]

WHEN TWO DEATHS OCCUR SIMULTANEOUSLY

If two family members die at the same time, *Keriah* is only performed once for both deaths.[39]

If a second family member dies after *Keriah* has already been performed for a member of the family, the mourner can either extend the original tear another three and one-half-inches or cut the same garment in a different place. The same applies if the second death occurs after *Shivah* has concluded for the first family member.[40]

KERIAH ON HOL HAMOED

It is the accepted custom of the Sepharadim that *Keriah* is even performed on *Hol Hamoed*, the intermediate days of Pesah and Sukkoth, for all relatives as long as the burial takes place at this time.[41] When this is the case, the garment is removed immediately after the *Keriah* because there is no public mourning on the *Moed*.[42]

Lighting a Candle

Following the *Keriah* a candle is lit, and it is customary for it to remain burning during the entire *Shivah* in memory of the deceased. The most convenient kind of candle is a seven-day memorial candle. If a seven-day candle cannot be obtained, an ordinary candle should be kept burning at all times during the *Shivah*. The candle acts as a constant reminder of the deceased and represents the soul of the human being.

Lighting a candle in memory of the deceased during *Shivah* is an ancient custom that dates back to the time of the Talmud.[43]

A candle or lighted wick is a beautiful symbol for the soul of the human being. The Bible describes the soul of man as "God's candle." Just like the flame on a wick, the soul is attached to the human body, giving off light and realizing the physical body's potential. The candle we light at the time of death may also represent the internal flame we all possess within ourselves – a sacred refraction of the divine light that God has shared with every one of us. The internal light equips us not only with the ability to distinguish between good and evil, compassion and cruelty, truth and falsehood, but also confers supreme value upon us, making each and every one of us special and unique, each created in the image of God.

The following declaration is made immediately prior to the lighting of the candle:

הריני מדליק נר זה לעילוי נשמת אבי / אמי / אחי / אחותי / בני / בתי

Hareni madlik ner zeh le'lluy nishmat –avi (father) *–imi* (mother) *–ahi* (brother) *–ahoti* (sister) *–beni* (son) *–biti* (daughter) _________ ______
Name of Deceased

I light this candle in loving memory of my …

The Meal of Consolation

The mourners, seated on low chairs or on the floor, are served their first meal. The *Seudat Havra'ah*, or meal of consolation, our *hakhamim* state, must be supplied and prepared by friends, neighbors, and community. Rambam writes as follows: "On the first day of mourning it is prohibited for the bereaved …to eat from their own food"[44] (unless, of course, there is no one else to feed them). Our sages of blessed memory curse those who allow mourners to prepare their own *Seudat Havra'ah*: "A curse will come upon the neighbors if the mourner has to provide his own food."[45]

Preparing the mourners' food and serving them is subsumed under the *mizvah* of *nihum aveilim*, comforting the mourners. This *mizvah* not only provides for the mourners' physical well-being but also shows concern for their psychological needs. The *Shulhan Arukh* provides us with an interesting perspective regarding the meal of consolation. The bereaved, the *Shulhan Arukh* notes, "are anxious over their loss". The mourner psychologically identifies with the deceased to the point where death is the only comfort. Thus mourners may not find the inner strength to nourish themselves, let alone prepare their own food. Being required to eat a prepared meal, however, is an affirmation of life. It is therefore the duty of the community to feed the mourners. Immediately following *Keriah*, the mourners must sit. Although they are required to sit on the floor, they must eat and affirm one of the basic acts of life's regular patterns. This is not a mere gesture of kindness but a direct means of assisting the bereaved back into society.[46]

The concept of *nihum aveilim*, comforting the mourners, involves more than psychological and emotional comfort and support; it also involves taking an active role in the healing process of those in grief. While the mourners focus on their own emotional state, the community supplies their physical needs. The emphasis here is community and not individual. As individuals we have little or nothing to say to a person who has just buried a loved one. But as a community, by virtue of its very existence, we testify that death is not the end of life. Individuals live and die, whereas the community lives forever.

The meal of consolation must be the very first meal eaten by the mourners after the interment. While customs vary as to what is served, most include bread rolls for *Hamosi*, hard-boiled eggs, olives, raisins, and wine (some vegetables or fruit may be included).

Each of the foods, over time, has developed its own folkloric and symbolic meaning. Eggs, for example, represent birth, and their shape is symbolic of the cycle of life. At a time of grief we present the mourner with foods that remind us to affirm life. Other symbolic meanings of the egg may have to do with the fact that it is completely round, with no mouth or opening,[47] which is symbolic of the way we want to respond to the tragedy of death. We do not question God's will; we accept it in silence, just as Aaron, the High Priest, responded when his sons died during their service in the Temple. The Torah records: *Vayidom Aharon*, "Aaron remained silent."[48]

The hard-boiled egg is never served whole; it is cut in half as a symbolic act indicating that whatever decrees have been set upon us should be cut and severed.

The raisins also teach a beautiful lesson about life. A raisin is a dried, shriveled-up grape. From its appearance one could never believe that with this very same fruit the finest of wines are produced. So, too, humans being cannot be judged by their external appearance. Their real beauty and value, their soul, lies deep within themselves.

The wine too has important significance. Wine is served to mark this meal as a religiously significant act. The intent, of course, is not to get drunk or be lighthearted, but to add meaning to the ritual.[49]

EATING IN THE HOUSE OF MOURNING
Some Sepharadi communities have the custom that visitors do not eat in the house of mourning.[50] Those whose families observe this custom should not change it.

MISCELLANEOUS LAWS
- Jewish law is always concerned about seemingly improper acts that involve men and women. Therefore, it is proper practice at the meal of consolation that men serve men and women serve women.[51]
- If two mourners are sitting *Shivah* together and there is no one to serve them their meal of condolence, they can serve each other as long as it is not stipulated that they are exchanging meals.[52]
- A mourner who refuses to eat the meal of condolence can forgo it.[53]
- On the eve of Shabbat or Yom Tov, the meal of condolence must be served in the morning or early afternoon so that the mourner can have an appropriate appetite for Shabbat or the holiday.[54]
- If the burial took place more than thirty days before the mourner heard of the death, the meal of condolence is waived.[55]
- If two consecutive deaths occur, a meal of condolence must be served even while one is sitting *Shivah* for the first death.[56]

Birkat Hamazon

After the *Seudat Havra'ah*, a special *Birkat Hamazon* is recited. When three or more adult males eat bread together, *Birkat Hamazon,* the grace after meals, is introduced by a formal invitation called *Zimun*. When reciting the *Zimun* in the house of mourning, the invitation goes as follows:

> *Bila hamavet lanetzakh umakha Adonay Elokim dima me'al kol panim vekherpat amo yasir me'al kol ha'aretz ki Adonay Diber.*
> **He [God] will make death disappear forever, and the Lord will wipe away tears from upon every face, and He will remove the shame of His people from the entire world, for the Lord has spoken.**

> Let us bless Him who comforts those who mourn, from whose [food] we have eaten.

Response

> Blessed be He who comforts those who mourn, of whose bounty we have eaten, and through whose goodness we live.[57]

The regular *Birkat Hamazon* is recited until *Bimhera beyamenu*; then the following paragraphs conclude the prayer.
For the entire Hebrew text of Birkat Hamazon, see Appendix 1.

> Comfort, O Lord our God, those who mourn for Zion and Jerusalem and those who are mourning in this grief. Console them in their bereavement, and give them happiness after their sorrow. For it is written, "As one whom his mother comforts, so will I comfort you, and through Jerusalem shall you be comforted." Blessed are You, Lord who consoles those who mourn, and who will rebuild Jerusalem. May this be speedily and in our days, Amen. Yes, in our days may Zion's city be built up and Your worship re-established in Jerusalem.
> Blessed are you, Lord our God, ruler of the universe, God our Father and Ruler, our mighty redeemer. You, Holy one of Jacob, living King, You are good, and You do that which is good.

You are the God of truth, and Your decree is just. You take back our souls in Your universal rule, doing according to Your will; we are Your people and Your servants. Whatever may befall, we must acknowledge You and bless You.

May He who gives strength to the bereaved, in His compassion give solace in this bereavement to us and all His people Israel. May He who creates the harmony of the spheres, in His tender love create peace for us and for all Israel, Amen.

ON SHABBAT

On Shabbat, if the mourner is saying *Birkat Hamazon* with two or three men, he uses the special *Zimun*.[58] However, with more than three people the above *Zimun* is not used and the regular Shabbat *Birkat Hamazon* is recited. The reason for this is because there is no public mourning on Shabbat and a group of more than three people would be considered "public."

Endnotes

1   Genesis 50:10.
2   The seven immediate relatives are considered biblically ordained by most commentaries, while the maternal half-brother, married sister, and half-sister are rabbinically ordained. See TB Moed Katan 14b; Rambam, Avel 2:1; *Shulhan Arukh* 374:4.
3   *Shulhan Arukh,* YD 374:6; see also Rambam, Avel 2:4.
4   Rema 374:6. Rabbi Moses Isserlis, known as Rama (1525–1572), was the chief rabbi of Krakow. His glosses on the *Shulhan Arukh* are the authoritative *halakhic* rulings for Ashkenazic Jewry.
5   Regarding grandparents, the Rema claims this would not apply; see 374:6.
6   Regarding stepparents, see *Pithei Teshuvah*, loc. cit., no. 3.
7   Rambam, Avel 2:4; Shakh 374:6, those related only by marriage are not included.
8   See Rema on *Shulhan Arukh* 374:6, "If a person chooses to be stringent on himself and mourn for someone for whom he is not required to mourn, he should not be prevented from doing so."
9   See *Shulhan Arukh,* YD 384:1.
10   YD 375:1
11   Ibid. YD 395:1.

12   See YD 399:2 for private activities that are forbidden even during the holiday.

13   Ibid. YD 375:2; see also *Arukh HaShulhan* 375:8 and Moshe Feinstein, *Iggerot Moshe* for an elaborate discussion on this issue, YD 1:253 and 2:170.

14   See *Yalkut Yosef* 24:6 and n. 9; *Iggerot Moshe,* YD 1:253; *Gesher HaHayim* 19:4:10.

15   *Yalkut Yosef* 24:7.

16   *Shulhan Arukh,* YD 399.

17   *Yalkut Yosef,* vol. 7, 34:7.

18   *Yabia Omer,* vol. 5, p. 290 (EH 7:4).

19   TB Moed Katan 20a; Pesahim 4a, *miktzat hayom kekulo,* see Rashi there. *Tur, Shulhan Arukh* 402:1 states that a few moments is enough.

20   This is a dispute among the Rishonim. Maimonides and Meiri write that one can shave immediately. However, Ramban, in *Torat Ha'adam,* p. 61, writes that the restrictions of *Sheloshim* do apply and must be observed. My *pesak* is based on Rabbi Ovadia Yosef, *Yabia Omer,* vol. 1, YD 25:14, 26:5.

21   See *Bet Yosef,* YD 375.

22   *Shulhan Arukh,* YD 375:10.

23   See below, the discussion on wearing shoes.

24   With the exception of the Spanish and Portuguese, all other Sephardic communities follow the *minhag* to do *Keriah* after returning from the cemetery to the house of mourning. See Ovadia Yosef, *Yekhave Da'at,* vol. 4, p. 286.

25   1 Samuel 2:13–31.

26   *Shulhan Arukh* 340:1; TB Moed Katan 20a.

27   TB Moed Katan 22b; see commentaries on Gemara.

28   TB Moed Katan 24a.

29   *Shulhan Arukh* 340:27.

30   While the *Shulhan Arukh* states that one must also rend his *kamiza* (shirt), most communities do not follow this *pesak* and follow the *pesak* of Rabbi Hai Gaon and others that the outer garment is sufficient. See Ovadia Yosef, *Yabia Omer,* vol. 6, p. 252 (32:4).

31   While this distinction is not found among the early Sephardic *hakhamim,* it is mentioned by Rabbi Ovadia Yosef, who quotes the *Turey Zahav* 340:106.

32   YD 340:3; the required length is one tephah, or a handbreath, which is approximately 3.5 inches.

33   *Shulhan Arukh* 340:14.

34   Ibid.

35   Ibid. 340:18.

36   See *Yabia Omer,* vol. 2, p. 190 (YD 23:5); *Yalkut Yosef,* vol. 7, 4:4.

37   *Shulhan Arukh* 396:1 where the ruling is not applied to parents. If one did not rend clothing for the loss of a parent, one does so even after *shivah.*

38   This is the accepted *Minhag* in most communities

39   *Shulhan Arukh,* YD 340:23.

40   Ibid. 340:21, 23; TB Moed Katan 26b.

41 *Bet Yosef*, OH 547. YD 340:31 Some Syrian communities do not do *Keriah* on *Hol HaMoed*.

42 *Yalkut Yosef* 4:17.

43 See TB Ketubot 103a, also Mishnah Berakhot 52b and Gemara 53a, with Rashi's comment there.

44 Avel 4:9; see also TB Moed Katan 27b, *Shulhan Arukh*, YD 378:1.

45 TY Moed Katan 3:1.

46 Emanuel Feldman "Death as Estrangement: The Halakha of Mourning" in *Jewish Reflection on Death* Edited by Jack Riemer, pp. 80–85.

47 *Shulhan Arukh*, YD 378:8; see Shakh 8, TB Baba Batra 16b. Lentils are also mentioned as an appropriate food at this time: "As the lentil rolls, so does mourning roll from one person to the next."

48 Leviticus 10:3.

49 TB Ketuboth 8a.

50 Yosef, *Yabia Omer*, vol. 4, p. 327 (YD 35:4) mentions some of the sources of this custom.

51 *Shulhan Arukh* 378:2.

52 Ibid. 378:1; see Shakh.

53 Ibid 378:3. Shakh 5 notes that the mourner would be forbidden to eat his own fod until nightfall.

54 Ibid 378:5. The latest time is the "ninth hour of the day" (*sha't zemaniyot*). In order to calculate the ninth hour, one divides the time between sunrise and sunset into twelve equal parts. Each of these equal parts is one *halakhic* hour.

55 Ibid 393:6.

56 See *Arukh HaShulhan* 379.

57 Ibid.

58 *Siddur Bet Oved*, p. 452.

CHAPTER 8

Laws and Customs of *Shivah*

Where Is *Shivah* Observed?

Death, in the words of Rabbi Joseph B. Soloveitchik, represents man's "defeat." "Beaten by the fiend, his prayers rejected, forsaken and lonely, Man (woman) begins to question his singular worth."[1] With the beginning of the *Avelut*, or mourning process, Jewish law commands mourners to pick up the shattered pieces and begin reestablishing their personal dignity and uniqueness. Prior to the burial, the mourner grieved alone; with the start of *Shivah* the mourner is surrounded by family and friends, slowly reasserting his humanity and dignity.

In the most ideal situation there is one *Shivah* observance in the home of the deceased with the entire family. If for some reason the *Shivah* cannot take place in the home of the deceased, the next-best situation is to observe *Shivah* in the home of a close relative. The family should be together in one place for the entire seven days. The mourners should not leave the house of mourning during the *Shivah* period unless there are extenuating circumstances,[2] such as:

- Being needed in one's own home to care for children and or spouse

97

- Not having enough room for everyone to sleep together in the house of mourning
- A mourner losing, God forbid, another relative and needed to make the funeral arrangements
- Not having a *minyan* that is able to convene in the house of mourning, the mourner must attend services in order to say *Kaddish*
- Being the only *mohel* in a city, the mourner is needed to perform a circumcision

A mourner who must leave the house of *Shivah* must do so inconspicuously and never be alone.[3]

Sitting on the Ground During *Shivah*

The *Halakhah* states that mourners do not sit on chairs; they either sit on the floor or on low stools. This tradition is first recorded in the Book of Job. The Bible tells us that Job and his friends sat on the floor. Rabbi Emanuel Feldman suggests that intimate contact with death has diminished the mourner's identity as a human being and therefore the mourner does not sit in the accepted mode on a chair or couch.[4] The mourner sits on the ground as a sign of lowliness and diminution. Elderly people and those who are not fit physically to sit on the floor or lower stools may sit in regular chairs.

Personal Grooming

During the period of *Shivah* the mourner must show a disregard for personal vanity and physical comfort. There is a temporary withdrawal from society in order to deal with the personal loss. The mourner experiences the timeless words of King Solomon: *Hevel havalim*, "Vanity of vanities, saith Koheleth; Vanity of vanities, all is vanity."[5] One grooms oneself in order to take part in society with others, to build relationships and engage in social activities. In contrast, the mourner is dealing with relationships ended. One forms relationships in order to plan for the future. The mourner, in contrast, is obsessed with reviewing the past. Therefore, Jewish law states that during *Shivah* mourners do not bathe their entire body at one time. Washing different body parts in cold or lukewarm water is permitted.[6] If a mourner is excessively dirty or uncomfortable it would be permitted to be lenient in this law. The *Halakhah* intends to prohibit bathing for pleasure, not for necessity.[7] Similarly, a sick person whose doctor recommends bathing may do so even in hot water during *Shivah*.[8]

Laws Related to Personal Grooming

- The mourner is not permitted to bathe for pleasure or for comfort. Bathing for pleasure or comfort means washing or soaking the entire body at one time with hot water. A mourner is permitted, for purposes of cleanliness, to wash different parts of the body with cool water. The exception to this rule is, of course, one who is ill and under the advice of a physician is required to bathe.
- Similarly, mourners may not soak or anoint their bodies with oils and cosmetics.[9]
- Haircutting and shaving are not permitted during *Shivah*.[10] (This will be discussed further in the section dealing with *Sheloshim*.) This prohibition does not include combing one's hair.[11] In fact, cleanliness and neatness should not be compromised during *Shivah*.
- Mourners are prohibited from cutting their fingernails or toenails with an instrument.[12]

GREETINGS AND INQUIRING ABOUT ANOTHER'S WELFARE
- Mourners do not greet guests during the *Shivah* period nor they inquire about another's welfare. If others ask about their welfare, they should just respond by saying they are mourners.[13]
- A mourner is not expected to rise in respect for any visitor, even if the guest is a renowned *hakham*. A mourner who would like to show respect for a Torah scholar, however, may do so.[14]
- Greetings may be extended on Shabbat because not doing so would be considered a public form of mourning.[15]

LEATHER SHOES
- Mourners are not permitted to wear leather shoes.[16] Rabbi Yaakov Hayim Sofer (1870–1935), one of the leading Sephardic *halakhic* authorities and author of *Kaf HaHayim*, insists that one should not even wear shoes that do not have any leather in them; one should

only wear socks during *Shivah*.[17] This is the accepted custom among the Sepharadim.

- A woman within thirty days of giving birth is permitted to wear shoes during *Shivah*. Similarly, a sick person, upon the recommendation of a doctor, can wear shoes.[18]
- If a mourner must walk a long distance and not wearing shoes would be painful or dangerous, then he or she may wear shoes.[19]

LAUNDRY DURING *SHIVAH*

- Mourners are not permitted to wash or iron clothes during *Shivah*.[20] This prohibition includes soaking the clothes in water.[21] Mourners are also not permitted to wear freshly laundered clothing or clothing that may have been washed by someone else during *Shivah*.[22]
- Mourners are forbidden to wear new clothing even if it was bought before they became a mourner.[23]
- Under extenuating circumstances, such as two consecutive *Shivah* periods, or if for some reason there are absolutely no clean clothes, a mourner can have some clothes washed without any laundering chemicals or agents.[24]
- Children's clothing, especially soiled clothes, may be washed by people other than the mourners.[25]

MARITAL RELATIONS

- A mourner is not permitted to have marital relations with his/her spouse during *Shivah*. This law applies even on Shabbat, because, while all public practices of mourning are suspended, all private and personal demonstration of mourning are in effect.[26]
- A woman is not permitted to go to the *mikveh* while sitting *Shivah*.[27]

WORK AND BUSINESS DURING *SHIVAH*

Jewish law states that during *Shivah*, mourners are not permitted to work, manage a business, or invest any moneys by themselves or through the assistance of an agent. This prohibition includes non-Jewish hired employees of the mourner. These laws, however, vary so much in circumstance and case, and have so many exceptions, that one should consult a rabbi to address one's personal situation.

Expressions of Joy and Celebration

- The *Shulhan Arukh* states that mourners should not hold a child on their her lap during *Shivah* because this is joyful and may lead to laughter.[28]
- Similarly mourners should not engage in frivolous conversation or laughter with adults. This is deduced by Maimonides as follows: The mourner is prohibited from asking about the welfare of others; all the more so, then, the mourner should be prohibited from indulging in conversation and laughter.[29]

Torah Study

As was just mentioned, mourners should not engage in things that bring them joy and delight. Therefore the usual study of Torah is prohibited during *Shivah* because it is considered to be a source of great joy and delight.[30] This prohibition is limited to study that brings joy; for example, the process of analysis of Talmud and Halakhah that challenges the mind, or the study of Torah and its exegesis that inspires the spirit. The mourner is still obligated to fulfill the *mizvah* of *Talmud Torah,* the study of Torah.[31] The mourner, therefore, must fulfill the *mizvah* with the study of texts that do not inspire joy and delight. These texts include the Book of Job, Lamentations, certain parts of Jeremiah, and the laws that relate to mourning. The mourner is also permitted to study Pirke Avot (Ethics of our Fathers) and other such texts that focus on the development of character.

- A teacher of Torah who is in mourning and has no one to replace him is permitted to teach Torah and to study in preparation for his classes.[32]

Brit Milah

Many Sephardic communities have the custom of inviting family and friends to their home the night before the *Brit Milah* for a festive evening of prayer, study, and food. This custom can be observed during *Shivah*. However, the focus of the evening should be the recitation of the appropriate study and prayers, and not the festive meal.[33]

- The father of a child to be circumcised is permitted during *Shivah* to wear Shabbat clothing and leather shoes. Similarly, he is permitted to wear freshly laundered clothing.[34]
- The father recites the *Sheheheyanu* blessing at the *Brit Milah* of his son.[35]
- The father may attend the festive meal as long as there is no music and dancing, but he should not sit at a head table and participate publicly.[36]
- During *Shivah*, a mourner may be a *sandak*, which means that he may hold the baby during the circumcision, but he does not change his mourning clothing.[37] This leniency does not apply to the honor of carrying the baby and handing him over to the *sandak*.

Pidyon Haben

Parents who are in mourning are permitted to participate in the redemption of the firstborn ceremony for their son. They may wear Shabbat clothes and leather shoes for the occasion. Similarly, they can partake of the festive meal as long as they do not sit down at a table.[38]

- The father recites the *Sheheheyanu* blessing at the *Pidyon* of his son.[39]

Weddings

- A mourner does not attend a wedding ceremony for twelve months if he or she is mourning the death of a parent, and thirty days for all other relatives.[40]
- A parent of a bride or bridegroom who is in mourning may attend the wedding because his or her presence will bring unique joy to the bride and groom.[41] The mourning parent can even partake of the festive meal but may not sit at a table of honor.[42]
- The mourners should not enjoy the music and certainly not participate in the dancing at a wedding.[43]
- A mourner is not permitted to marry within thirty days of his or her

bereavement, even without a reception, unless the wedding had been planned already.[44]

- If the death occurred within seven days of the planned wedding, then the wedding must be postponed.[45]
- A mourner who is scheduled to marry may get a haircut, shower, and shave in preparation for the wedding even during *Shivah*.[46]
- In such a situation, nothing is held back from the wedding festivities of the bride and bridegroom.[47]

Leaving the House of Mourning

- Mourners are prohibited from leaving their home during the entire *Shivah* period.[48] If *Shivah* is being observed in another's home and it would be difficult for the mourner to sleep there, the mourner is permitted to go to his or her own home at night.[49]
- Mourners are permitted to leave their home in order to fulfill certain *mizvot*.[50] Such *mizvot* include making burial arrangements for a deceased who had no relatives to make the preparations, or a *mizvah* that the mourner is obligated to personally fulfill and can only be done outside the home (e.g., *Brit Milah*). In such cases the mourner is not only permitted but obligated to leave the home and fulfill his religious duty.
- On Shabbat a mourner is permitted to go to the synagogue for services.[51]
- During the week of *Shivah* every effort must be made to provide a *minyan* in the mourner's home. If services at home are impossible, the mourner is permitted to attend services and pray with a *minyan*.[52]
- When a mourner must leave the home of *Shivah*, many Sephardic communities observe the custom that the mourner should not leave the house alone, but should be accompanied by one or two people. A larger group of people should not accompany the mourner.[53]

Services in the House of Mourning

It is important to secure a *minyan* for services in the house of mourning during *Shivah*. This practice, the Talmud tells us, is a great *zekhut* (merit) and source of comfort for the mourners.[54] Ideally, services should be held in the home where the deceased lived.[55] The order of services when held in the house of mourning is given below.

SHAHARIT:

The order of the prayers for *Shaharit* is the same as that of a regular morning service. Note that *Birkat Kohanim* (the priestly blessing) is recited during the repetition of the *Amidah.*[56] (If the mourner is a *kohen*, he does not perform the blessing and must leave the room during the repetition.) The *Tahanunim*[57] and Psalm 20 before *Uva L'tzion* are omitted. On Rosh Hodesh and Hanukkah, *Hallel* is recited. The mourner, however, does not participate in this part of the service.[58] Some communities have the custom of reciting *Kaddish Yehe Shelamah Raba* instead of *Kaddish Titkabal.*[59] Psalm 49 is recited instead of the psalm of the day (see below), after which the mourners recite *Kaddish.* At the conclusion of the service, *Tzidduk Hadin* is recited, followed by the *Hashkavah* and *Bila Hamavet.*

MINHAH

In some communities, *Pitum Haketoret* is not recited in a house of mourning. Other communities begin with the *Pitum Haketoret* even in a house of mourning. *Tahanunim* are omitted. As was mentioned above, some communities have the custom of not reciting *Kaddish Titkabal,* and instead reciting *Kaddish Yehe Shelama Raba.* If *Arvith* does not immediately follow *Minhah,* then *Tzidduk Hadin, Hashkavah,* and *Bila Hamavet* are recited at the conclusion of the *Tefilah.*

ARVITH

On a weeknight the service begins with Psalm 49, followed by *Kaddish* and *Arvith.* In some communities *Kaddish Titkabal* is not recited, and instead *Yehe Shelama Raba* is said. At the conclusion of the service, *Tzidduk Hadin, Hashkavah,* and *Bila Hamavet* are recited.

Services in the Synagogue

When the services are not being held in the house of mourning, the mourners should be encouraged to go to a synagogue and say *Kaddish* with a *minyan.* The regular synagogue service is not changed when a mourner is present.

The following are the *halakhic* rules that affect the mourner in synagogue:

- Mourners do not sit in their regular seats. Many synagogues have designated seats for mourners. This *halakhah* applies for two weeks following burial.[60]
- Mourners do not recite *Tahanunim*. They sit down while the *minyan* is saying *Tahanunim*.[61]
- At the conclusion of the service, *Tzidduk Hadin, Hashkavah*, and *Bila Hamavet* are recited.

The *Kaddish*

Today most people associate the recitation of the *Kaddish* with death and mourning. In reality the *Kaddish* has little to do with death. It praises God, and affirms life without making mention of the dead. There are actually five forms of the *Kaddish*. Two are recited during the prayer service, one after the study of Torah, and four are associated with mourning.

1. *Hazi-Kaddish*, the first paragraph of the *Kaddish*, is the earliest form of this prayer. It is recited in the middle of the service or before the *Amidah*. In the Syrian community, it is customary for the mourner to recite this *Kaddish* along with the *shaliah tzibbur*.
2. *Kaddish Shalem*, which includes *Titkabal, Yehe Shelama Raba*, and *Oseh Shalom Bimromav*, is always recited after the *Amidah*.
3. *Kaddish al Israel* (also known as *Kaddish deRabbanan* and as the *Rabbis' Kaddish*) is recited after the study of *Halakhah*, Midrash, or Aggadah.[62] The mourner recites this *Kaddish* at every opportunity that arises.
4. *Kaddish Yatom* is identical to the *Kaddish Shalem* except that *Titkabal* is omitted. The mourner recites this *Kaddish* throughout the year for a parent.
5. *Kaddish Lehadeta* is recited immediately following the burial service at the gravesite. The text of this *Kaddish*, unlike the ones above, varies slightly from community to community.

The original *Hazi-Kaddish* first appeared in the liturgy in *Seder Rav Amram Gaon* (ca. 860), the first prayer book, compiled by Rabbi Amram ben Sheshna Gaon, head of the Sura academy in Babylonia (856–874).[63] *Titkabal, Yehe Shelama Raba, Oseh Shalom Bimromav,* and the *Rabbis' Kaddish* are all later additions.[64]

The format of the *Kaddish* recited by the Sepharadim comes from the *siddur* (prayer book) of Rabbi Saadia ben Yosef Gaon (882–942), who followed Rabbi Amram Gaon as head of the academy in Sura.[65] This *Kaddish* went through various versions before it took on the final form that is recited today by Sephardic communities throughout the world.[66] The earliest version that is close to the one recited by the Sepharadim today is found in a classic work on liturgy by Rabbi David Abudarham (ca. 1340), a Spanish scholar from the city of Seville. *Kaddish* was a flexible liturgy that was often customized to different communities by their leaders. The early versions of the *Kaddish* often include the name of the rabbi of the community and other matters specific to the community.[67]

The earliest reference to the *Kaddish,* or more specifically a Hebrew version of a line in the *Kaddish,* is found in Tractate Berakhot of the Talmud. It goes as follows:

> Rabbi Yose related that once, when he entered one of the ruins of Jerusalem to pray, Elijah the prophet appeared to him and berated him for endangering his life in such a way. Elijah then asked R. Yose: "What sound did you hear there?" His answer was that he heard a sound like that of a dove cooing: "Alas … that I destroyed My house, burned My Temple, and exiled My children among the nations of the world!" The prophet Elijah then assured him that whenever Jews enter their synagogues or houses of Torah study and respond: *Yehe shemo hagadol mevorakh,* the Holy One, blessed be He, as it were laments: "Happy is the king who is so praised in His own house, and woe to the Father who drove His own children into exile!"[68]

Rabbi Hayim David HaLevy, in his book *Mekor Hayim,* points out that this allegorical talmudic passage makes a connection between the *Kaddish* and mourning for the destruction of Jerusalem and the dispersion of the Jews.[69] He further notes that this passage proves that the *Kaddish* became part of the liturgy only after the destruction of the Temple, and that part of its message is messianic in nature.

The first words of the *Kaddish,* "Exalted and sanctified be His great name" (*Yitgadal veyitkadash sheme raba*), echo the words of Ezekiel the prophet: "Thus will I be exalted and sanctified, and I will make Myself known in the eyes of many nations, and they shall know that I am the Lord" (*Vehitgadalti vehitkadashti*).[70] Ezekiel is speaking to a humiliated and disconsolate people in exile. His words boost their morale and kindle a spark of hope for national and individual redemption. The *Kaddish,* then, is meant to be a declaration of hope and faith in our people's national purpose and personal relationship with God. It is a prayer of longing for a time when all people will accept the heavenly mission that gives meaning to life and transcends death.

The reason for its popularity may be precisely because *Kaddish* is such a powerful response to death.[71] It involves not only the reader but also those present at the time of its recitation. "Through the *Kaddish,*" writes Rabbi Joseph B. Soloveitchik, "we hurl defiance at death and its fiendish conspiracy against man." The Rav continues:

> When the mourner recites "glorified and sanctified be the Great name…" he declares more or less the following: No matter how powerful death is, notwithstanding the ugly end of man, however terrifying the grave is, however nonsensical and absurd everything appears, no matter how black one's despair is and how nauseating an affair life itself is, we declare and profess publicly and solemnly that we are not giving up, that we are not surrendering, that we will carry on the work of our ancestors as if nothing had happened, that we will not be satisfied with less than the full realization of the ultimate goal of the establishment of God's kingdom.[72]

The reader not only makes this declaration himself but he calls out to the congregation to join him. The reader begins with the words "Exalted and sanctified be His great name throughout the world that He created." The congregation then answers the reader's declaration with the following words: "Amen. May His great name be blessed forever and ever."[73] Our sages of blessed memory regarded this response as the main theme of the entire *Kaddish*. They comment that the response *Amen. Yehe sheme raba mevorakh*, and so on, is so powerful that it has the ability to inspire *teshuvah*, or transformation, on those who recite it in a meaningful way.[74]

AMEN

Kaddish is recited at every service on a daily basis, beginning immediately after burial throughout the twelve-month mourning period for a parent. It is one of those prayers that is considered *davar shebekedusha*, a prayer of special significance, and requires a *minyan*, a quorum of ten men to be recited. The mourner, therefore, never stands alone when reciting the *Kaddish*. He is in the presence of others who respond Amen, not only as part of the prayer but also as an acknowledgment of the mourner's loss.

The response *Amen* is used throughout the Bible as a means of endorsing a blessing or in some cases a curse.[75] Its literal meaning is "so be it" or "truly." Our sages of blessed memory viewed the response of *Amen* as an affirmation and acceptance of faith.[76] A Jew is therefore obligated, according to Rambam,[77] to respond *Amen* when hearing a benediction, because his response is a testimony to the truth of the blessing and an expression of his own faith. *Amen* is indeed so powerful a response that it is considered tantamount to having said the blessing itself. According to one opinion in the Talmud, the response *Amen* outweighs the recitation of the blessing itself.[78] The reason for this extraordinary statement may have to do with the root of the word *Amen,* which according to the Talmud is made up of three letters: *alef, mem*, and *nun,* which stand for *El melekh ne'eman* "God is a faithful King."[79] While a blessing is restricted in its scope, the response *Amen* is all-encompassing and all-inclusive in meaning.[80]

In light of all this, we can now better understand the comment found in the Talmud, which states: "One who responds *Amen* with the fullest devotional concentration, the gates of paradise are open [for him]."[81] In other words, by saying *Amen* in a sincere and devout fashion, one expresses total faith in God, and this indeed leads to a sense of peace and serenity that is likened to Paradise.

Amen should therefore not be said in haste or mispronounced.

It should not said in ignorance of the benediction to which it is a response.[82]

RECITING *KADDISH*

In the process of dealing with grief, many emotional ups and downs are experienced. At times the sense of loss is especially intense, while at other times it feels more resolved. The Talmud tells the story of the death of Rav,[83] one of the great scholars and the founder of the Babylonian academy of Sura. Rav's disciples met on a riverbank shortly after his burial. Upon completing their meal, they discussed a matter of Jewish law which they were unable to resolve. One of the disciples, Rav Ada bar Ahava, got up and made a second tear in his garment, which he had previously rent in grief. He said: "Our teacher is dead and we haven't even learned from him some basic laws!" Tragically, at that moment they felt the intense loss of their revered teacher differently than they had felt it before. Their teacher was gone and his loss was especially poignant when they needed to resolve a matter of Jewish law. All mourners experience these kinds of moments. The *Kaddish* serves as a daily response to grief's surprises throughout the first year of mourning.

LAWS RELATED TO *KADDISH*

- In Israel it is the custom among Sephardim that the mourner recites his first *Kaddish* immediately prior to burial. This is not the generally accepted custom outside Israel.[84]
- *Kaddish* is recited for twelve months, beginning on the day of burial.[85] Some have the custom of reciting *Kaddish* for eleven months and resuming for one more month after the first *Hazkarah*.[86] From then on *Kaddish* is recited annually during the week preceding the year anniversary of death.
- Some have the custom of reciting *Kaddish* until one week before the year anniversary of death.[87]
- If one dies without children or has children who will not recite *Kaddish,* another family member or friend may recite the *Kaddish* instead.[88]
- A stepson or adopted son may choose to recite *Kaddish* for a deceased step-parent or adopted parent.

- Grandchildren can recite *Kaddish* if the deceased has no living children or none of the children of the deceased will be reciting *Kaddish*.[89]
- If a rabbi dies without leaving sons, *Kaddish* may be recited by one of his students.[90]
- If a parent asked one or more of his children not to recite *Kaddish* after his or her death, some authorities suggest that the child not honor the parent's request. Other authorities disagree.[91]
- If one only heard of the death long after the burial, *Kaddish* is recited from the moment one hears the news until the eleventh month from the time of burial (or whatever is the local custom).[92]
- If one heard of the death after the twelve-month period, *Kaddish* is not recited. Some authorities disagree with this ruling.[93]
- Women are permitted to recite *Kaddish*.[94] Because some authorities strongly disagree with the practice of women reciting *Kaddish,* I personally suggest that readers consult their own rabbis on this question.
- A child, even if younger than age thirteen for a boy or twelve for a girl, should recite *Kaddish* for a parent.[95]

Converts

"A *ger* [convert] is like a newborn babe."[96] The implication of this statement is that converts do not align themselves genetically with their mother or father. This principle has significant *halakhic* ramifications in a wide variety of areas. Two examples include the law of inheritance and the *mizvah* of procreation. According to biblical law, a convert does not inherit from his or her father's estate[97] and does not fulfill the biblical mandate to be fruitful and multiply through the children born while still a gentile.[98] In other words, there is a complete genealogical break between converts and their parents.

This genealogical break is limited, however, to matters that do not affect the honor and respect that must be shown one's natural parents. Maimonides, in his *Yad HaHazakah,* states that although *halakhically* and formally the convert is considered to be a newborn child, the natural parents must continue to have and deserve a unique place in the child's life.[99] This, in fact, is the law, because the *Halakhah* mandates the convert to show love, honor, and respect to his or her natural parents in life and in death. Therefore, there is no doubt that converts can mourn the death of their gentile parents if they choose to do so.

Of course, the mourning practices must be Jewish rituals and not those of the convert's former religion. Rabbi Yosef Karo, in his *Bet Yosef* code, discusses this issue and suggests that converts exemplify self-respect by mourning appropriately in a way that fits their own (Jewish) religious outlook and philosophy.[100] Converts may observe all of the mourning practices for their parents that Jews observe. They may serve as pallbearers, bury the dead at the cemetery, and fill the grave. Regarding the complete observance of *Shivah, Sheloshim,* and the twelve months, there are various opinions and one's personal rabbi should be consulted.

Rabbi Ovadia Yosef encourages converts to recite *Kaddish* for their parents.[101] Similarly, he encourages the recitation of *Hashkavah*, the memorial prayer, at the appropriate times. "Since his parents struggled to bring him [her] into this world," writes Rabbi Yosef, "should he [she] not help them cross the threshold into the world-to-come?"

Based on the principle of "a convert is like a newborn babe," Halakhah could not mandate that converts respect and show honor to their parents by formally practicing the laws of mourning. It is the parent/child relationship that determines the obligation.

Shivah on Shabbat

All mourning observances are divided into two categories: (1) those that reflect a public mourning, and (2) those that are of a personal and private nature. On Shabbat one's mourning is diminished. All mourning observances that are of a public nature are suspended, but all private and personal practices are observed.[102]

The following laws are relevant during Shabbat:

- Mourners cease to observe all public mourning on Friday afternoon approximately two and a half hours before sunset in order to prepare themselves and their households for Shabbat.[103]
- Mourners can wear leather shoes and leave the house in order to go to synagogue.[104]

- Mourners do not wear the torn garment usually worn during *Shivah*; instead, freshly washed clothes may be worn in honor of Shabbat.[105]
- The private mourning practices that must be observed even on Shabbat include abstinence from marital relations and bathing.[106]
- The study of Torah is forbidden even on Shabbat, except for study of the weekly Torah portion.[107]
- In most Sephardic communities the mourners sit in their regular seats on Shabbat.[108] In some *kehilot*, however, the mourner sits in a designated area for mourners.[109] Today the ancient custom continues in many Sephardic communities that the congregants take turns sitting behind or opposite the mourners during the service as a sign of comfort and support.[110]
- A mourner does not get an *aliyah* to the Torah, nor is he honored with any of the *mizvot* on Shabbat.[111]
- A mourner who is a *kohen* can go up to the *Sefer Torah* for his *aliyah* if there are no other *kohanim* in the synagogue.[112]
- A *kohen* who is a mourner performs the Priestly Blessing during *Shivah*.[113]
- A mourner who eats alone or with three or fewer people recites the mourner's *Birkat Hamazon* after each of the Shabbat meals. If the mourner eats with more than three people, the regular *Birkat Hamazon* is recited.[114]

MOTZA'EY SHABBAT

When Shabbat ends, the mourner removes his leather shoes without touching them immediately following the *Barekhu et Adonay Hamevorakh* of the *Arvith* service. If services are being held in the home of the mourner. some communities omit the verse *Vihi noam* and begin with *Yoshev beseter elyon*. If services are held in the synagogue, they proceed as usual.

HAVDALAH

A mourner who recites *Havdalah* does not recite the introductory verses and begins immediately with the blessing over the wine. Immediately following *Havdalah,* the mourner must change out of his Shabbat clothing and put on his mourner's garments.

Concluding *Shivah*

As was mentioned above, in Jewish law, part of a day is considered an entire day; therefore, on the seventh day of *Shivah,* shortly following the morning services, *Shivah* officially terminates. After services the *Hashkavah* is recited. Before the mourners rise from their mourning period, all those present gather around them and recite the following verses:

לֹא יָבֹא עוֹד שִׁמְשֵׁךְ וִירֵחֵךְ לֹא יֵאָסֵף כִּי יְהֹוָה יִהְיֶה לָךְ לְאוֹר עוֹלָם וְשָׁלְמוּ יְמֵי אֶבְלֵךְ: וּכְתִיב כְּאִישׁ אֲשֶׁר אִמּוֹ תְּנַחֲמֶנּוּ כֵּן אָנֹכִי אֲנַחֶמְכֶם וּבִירוּשָׁלַם תְּנֻחָמוּ:

Thy sun shall no more go down, nor thy moon wane. For the Lord shall be thy everlasting light and the days of thy mourning ended. As one whom his mother comforts, so will I comfort you, and through Jerusalem shall you be comforted.

Rabbi Yehudah Ashkenazi, author of the *Bet Oved Siddur,* describes how those present physically lift the mourner. In other words, the comforters help to clearly distinguish the period of grief from the period of healing (post-*Shivah*) by actually raising the mourner from the ground.[115]

Some have the custom of taking the mourner outside the house to walk a short distance as a sign that he or she is ready to enter back into society.

It is the custom of the Sepharadim to permit bathing of the entire body even in hot water immediately after *Shivah.*[116]

If the conclusion of *Shivah* falls on Rosh Hodesh, the above verses should be said to the mourner immediately following the *Amidah* so that the mourners can participate in the recitation of *Hallel.*[117]

Customs Pertaining to the Concluding Service of *Shivah*

LADINO SEPHARADIM

On the night of the seventh day after burial, the Ladino-speaking Sepharadim hold a *meldatho* at the home where *Shivah* was observed. This service is called *El Corte de Siete,* meaning "the end of the seven days." Before the evening services, those present study Mishnah in memory of the deceased. At the conclusion of the study, the Mourner's *Kaddish* is recited, followed by the *Arvith* service; after *Arvith, Hashkavah* is recited. Those present partake of some food that is prepared by the hosts. A charity plate or container from the synagogue is passed around. Because many synagogues had, and some still have, an oil lamp with wicks, which are lit during a *meldatho*, any money collected by passing around this charity container was designated as being for *shemen lamaor* (oil for the lamp).

MOROCCAN SEPHARADIM

Among the Moroccan Jews the concluding service, which is called *Mishmarah*, takes place the night before the end of *Shivah*; in other words, on the night of the sixth day of mourning. The study consists of reading the *Zohar*, portions of Torah, and Prophets. At the *Mishmarah* for a man, *Shuva Israel* (Hosea 14:2–10) is recited. At the *Mishmarah* for a woman, *Vatitpalel Hanah* (Samuel 2:1) is recited. The name of the deceased is spelled by reciting the appropriate paragraphs from Psalm 119, the *Alfa Beta*. At the conclusion of the study, *Hashkavah* and *Kaddish* are recited, and again those present are invited to partake of some food.

SYRIAN COMMUNITY

Among the Syrians, this service is *Arayat* and is held on the afternoon of the final day of *Shivah*. The *Arayat* is held after *Minhah*. The study for this service includes *Zohar* and portions of the Torah. Again food is served for those present. After the meal *Arvith* is recited, followed by *Hashkavah* and *Kaddish*.

GOING TO THE CEMETERY AFTER *SHIVAH*

It is the custom in some communities to go to the cemetery after the services on the seventh day.[118] If the seventh day falls on Shabbat, however, one may not go to the cemetery before Sunday.

After leaving the graveside one should place his hand on the grave and say the following words:

וְנָחֲךָ יְהוָֹה תָּמִיד וְהִשְׂבִּיעַ בְּצַחְצָחוֹת נַפְשֶׁךָ וְעַצְמֹתֶיךָ יַחֲלִיץ וְהָיִיתָ כְּגַן רָוֶה
וּכְמוֹצָא מַיִם אֲשֶׁר לֹא־יְכַזְּבוּ מֵימָיו (ישעיהו נח, יא): אָז יִבָּקַע כַּשַּׁחַר אוֹרֶךָ
וַאֲרֻכָתְךָ מְהֵרָה תִצְמָח וְהָלַךְ לְפָנֶיךָ צִדְקֶךָ כְּבוֹד יְהוָה יַאַסְפֶךָ (ישעיהו נח, ח):
The Lord shall guide you continually, satisfy your soul in

drought, and strengthen your frame. And you shall be like a watered garden, yes, like a spring of water whose waters fail not. Then shall you find delight in the Lord, and I will make you to ride on the heights of the earth and nourish you with the heritage of Jacob your father; for the mouth of the Lord has spoken it.,

IF *SHIVAH* WAS NOT OBSERVED

If for some reason *Shivah* was not observed immediately after burial, it should be observed within thirty days of the death.[119] After the thirtieth day, *Shivah* is not observed even if it began within the thirty days after death. In other words, there is no *Shivah* observance at all after the thirtieth day of death. Therefore, if one began *Shivah* on the twenty-fifth day after death, it terminates on the thirtieth day.

Unusual Situations

HEARING ABOUT A DEATH AFTER *SHIVAH*

Jewish law states that if one hears about the death of a relative within thirty days of the relative's demise, the news is deemed recent and the mourner must observe *Shivah*.[120] On the day the news is reported to the mourner, he or she must immediately tear *Keriah*, be served a *Seudat Havra'ah*, a meal of condolence, and must observe all the laws of mourning.

If, however, one is notified of the death of a relative after the thirtieth day from the burial, Jewish law regards it as news that is not recent. In this case, the mourner only observes a short mourning period on the very same day the news is reported.[121] The moment the mourner is informed that a relative has died, he or she must remove shoes, recite the blessing *Dayan Ha'emet*,[122] and sit on the floor for approximately one hour.

If the deceased is a parent, *Keriah* is performed after the blessing of *Dayan Ha'emet*.[123] Furthermore, if the deceased is a parent, the mourner does not get a haircut for at least thirty days – until he is so unkempt that he is socially awkward.[124]

INFORMING ANOTHER ABOUT A DEATH

If a person does not know that a family member has died, the *Shulhan Arukh* states that there is no obligation to inform him immediately.[125] If, for example, the person is going to attend a wedding ceremony, there is nothing wrong with holding the news from him or her until after the wedding. Similarly if, God forbid, there is fear that the news of the death will harm the person, it can be withheld until a more opportune time. Of course, it is forbidden to lie. If the person asks about the relative, the truth must be stated.

Endnotes

1   Ibid

2   *Yalkut Yosef,* vol. 7, 12:25.

3   See *Magen Avraham,* OH 239:7; he quotes Gemara Berakhot 54b.

4   See his essay, "Death as Estrangement: The Halakhah of Mourning," in *Jewish Reflections on Death,* ed. Jack Riemer (New York: Schocken, 1979), p. 84.

5   Ecclesiastes 1:2.

6   *Shulhan Arukh* 381:1; *Bet Yosef* 381.

7   *Shulhan Arukh* 381:3; *Arukh HaShulhan* 381.

8   *Shulhan Arukh* 381:3; *Arukh HaShulhan* 381:5; *Gesher HaHayim* 21:3:1.

9   *Shulhan Arukh* 381:2.

10   Moed Katan 14b.

11   *Shulhan Arukh* 390:6.

12   Ibid. 390:7, however, cutting with ones teeth or hands is permitted.

13   TB Moed Katan 15b; *Shulhan Arukh* 385:2. During the first three days the mourner's response should be to declare that he/ she is a mourner. From the fourth day onward the mourner may return a greeting. The mourner is forbidden to inquire about the welfare of others during *Shivah* but may do so immediately after.

14   Yosef, *Yabia Omer,* vol. 3, p. 200 (YD 27).

15   *Shulhan Arukh* 381:3.

16   Ibid. 375:1, 376:4, 382:1; *Bet Yosef.*

17   Kaf Hachaim 554:70.

18   *Shulhan Arukh* 382:2.

19   Ibid. 382:4.

20   Ibid. 389:1.

21   Ibid. 389:4.

22   Ibid.

23   Ibid.

24   Ibid. 389:1; see also OH 551:15 regarding *Shivah* following Tisha Be'Av.

25   Ibid. 389:2.

26   Ibid. 383:1; see *Bet Yosef,* also Moed Katan 15b.

27   *Shulhan Arukh* 381:5.

28 Ibid. 391:1.

29 Rambam, *Avel* 5:20.

30 It is important to note that the mourner is not exempt from the *mizvah* of *Talmud Torah*; see *Yalkut Yosef* 13:2 and n. 2.

31 See *Yabia Omer*, vol. 2, YD 27:2; *Yalkut* 7, 13:2, and fn.

32 *Shulhan Arukh* 384:1.

33 See *Kol Bo*, p. 293; *Mekor Hayim*, vol. 5, chap. 287:15.

34 *Mekor Hayim*, vol. 5, chap. 287:16.

35 Yosef, *Yabia Omer*, vol. 7, 18:2.

36 Ibid :15; see also *Sedeh Hemed*, Avelut 50.

37 *Mekor Hayim*, loc. cit.

38 Rema 391:2.

39 Yosef, *Yabia Omer*, vol. 7, 18:2.

40 *Mekor Hayim* 287:17.

41 Ibid. 287:18.

42 See ibid.; *Yalkut Yosef* 18:8; *Iggerot Moshe*, YD 11:169. See also *Arukh HaShulhan* 391:10.

43 *Mekor Hayim* 287:18.

44 See *Shulhan Arukh*, YD 392:1; *Mekor Hayim* 287:21. See also *Bet Yosef* 392.

45 *Yalkut Yosef* 18:7 and footnote. There are exceptions to this rule and a Halakhic authority should be consulted.

46 See *Mekor Hayim* 287:22; *She'elot U'Teshubot Hayim Sha'al*, vol. 1, chap. 21.

47 Ibid.

48 *Shulhan Arukh*, YD 393:2.

49 Nachmanides, *Hokhmat Adam* 165:11.

50 *Gesher HaHayim* 21:13:4.

51 Ibid.

52 *Shulhan Arukh* 393:3.

53 See *Magen Avraham*, OH 239:7; he quotes Gemara Berakhot 54b.

54 See TB Shabbat 152b.

55 Rama YD 384:3.

56 See *Bet Yosef*, OH end of chap. 128; *Yalkut Yosef*, vol. 7, 10:7.

57 *Bet Yosef*, loc. cit.; see also TB Moed Katan 16b, 27b. The Hida states, in *Pirke Yosef* 131:3, that even if there are no mourners, *Tahanunim* are not said in a house of mourning.

58 Again there are varying customs; see Rabbi Ovadia Yosef, *Yabia Omer*, vol. 4, YD 33, who writes that it is a *minhag ta'ut* those who do not recite *Hallel* in a house of mourning on Rosh Hodesh and Hanukkah.

59 For a discussion on the varying customs on the issue, see Yosef, *Yabia Omer*, vol. 4, p. 320 (YD 32:6). Rabbi Ovadia Yosef is *posek* that the *Kaddish* is not changed.

60 *Shulhan Arukh* 393:2. See also Moed Katan 23a.

61 For a complete discussion on this issue, see *Yalkut Yosef*, vol. 7, 10:9 and n. 9.

62   See Rambam, *Mishneh Torah,* Kafih ed., Seder Tefilot.

63   For the text, see David Telsner, *The Kaddish: Its History and Significance* (Jerusalem: Tal Orot Institute, 1995), p. 43.

64   See *Arukh HaShulhan,* OH 56:1.

65   See *Siddur Rab Saadia Gaon.*

66   For the text of the Rambam's *Kaddish,* see *Mishneh Torah,* Ahavah, Seder Tefilot Kol Hashanah.

67   For a discussion on this, see David de Sola Pool, *The Old Jewish Aramaic Prayer: The Kaddish* (Leipzig, 1909); also see Telsner, *The Kaddish.*

68   TB Berakhot 3a.

69   *Mekor Hayim,* vol. 1, 40:1.

70   Ezekiel 38:23.

71   *Ottiyot deRabbi Akiva,* a geonic text, describes Rabbi Akiva meeting a spirit in the guise of a man carrying wood. The wood, the man tells Rabbi Akiva, is for the fire in which he burns daily. He would be released from the fire if his son would recite *Kaddish* in a minyan and the congregation responded Amen. Rabbi Akiva finds the son and educates him so as to release the father from the punishment of Gehinom.

72   Soloveichik, Rabbi Joseph B. Sitting Shivah is Doing Teshuva, Man of Faith in the Modern World. Reflection of the Rav Volume II by Rabbi Abraham Besdin.

73   This phrase is taken almost verbatim from Daniel 2:20. The word *raba* is substituted for *elaha* in Daniel. The Talmud, in t Pesahim 56a, claims that this phrase was coined by Jacob our patriarch on his deathbed. Indeed the Jerusalem Targum translates *Barukh shem kevod* as *Yehe sheme rabbah,* etc. See Jerusalem Targum, end of Genesis.

74   TB Shabbat 119a.

75   See Numbers 5:22, Deuteronomy 27:15, and Jeremiah 28:6.

76   TB Shevuoth 36a.

77   Mishnah Berakhot 1:13; *Shulhan Arukh,* OH 215.

78   TB Berakhot 53b.

79   TB Shabbat 119b.

80   See Maharal MiPrague, *Netivot Olam.*

81   TB Shabbat 119.

82   See Mishnah Berakhot 8:8; *Encyclopedia Talmudit,* s.v. Amen.

83   Rav passed away in the year 4007 (247 CE).

84   *Mekor Hayim,* vol. 5, 291:3.

85   *Shulhan Arukh,* OH 132:2; *Mekor Hayim* 291:4.

86   *Mekor Hayim* 291:15–16 for a variety of customs on this issue.

87   Ibid. 291:15.

88   *Bet Yosef,* end of chap. 403.

89   *Kaf HaHayim* 55:28; *Mekor Hayim* 291:10.

90 Rema, end of 376.

91 *Pithei Teshuvah* 344:1.

92 *Gesher HaHayim* 30:9:5.

93 *Kol Bo al Aveilut,* p. 378.

94 Rabbi Hayim David Halevi, *Aseh Lekha Rav,* vol. 5, no. 33, p. 230–236. See also Rabbi Yosef Eliyahu Henkin, *Sefer Teshuvot Ibra,* vol. 2, no. 4 (2), p. 6, entitled Amirat Kadish al Yedei Habat. For a complete discussion on this issue, see Joel Wolowelsky, "Women and Kaddish," *Judaism* 44, 3 (1995) 282–290. Also by the same author "Comunal and Individual Mourning Dynamics within Traditional Jewish Law", *Death Studies* 20 (1996) 469–480.

95 See *Mekor Hayim* 291:8; *Kol Bo al Avelut,* p. 373, n. 29.

96 TB Yevamot 22a.

97 TB Kiddushin 17b.

98 TB Yevamot 62a.

99 *Yad,* Mamrim 5:11.

100 *Bet Yosef,* YD 274.

101 Yosef, *Yabia Omer,* vol. 6, YD 36; *Yehave Da'at,* vol. 6, chap. 60.

102 TB Moed Katan 23a–24a; *Shulhan Arukh,* YD 400.

103 See *Shulhan Arukh,* YD 396; *Mekor Hayim* 286:40; *Arukh HaShulhan* 400:5.

104 *Shulhan Arukh* 400:1.

105 ibid.

106 *Shulhan Arukh* 400:1 also Mekor Hayim 286:41.

107 ibid.

108 *Shulhan Arukh* YD 393:4.

109 See *Mekor Hayim* 286:45 and footnote.

110 See ibid.

111 *Shulhan Arukh* 400:1. If the mourner was mistakenly called up to the Torah, he should accept the Aliyah because if he were to decline the honor it would be a public display of mourning.

112 *Mekor Hayim* 286:48.

113 See ibid. 286:54 and footnote.

114 *Shulhan Arukh* 379:4.

115 *Bet Oved Siddur,* p. 238.

116 See Rambam, Avel 6:12; *Shulhan Arukh* 390:6; *Bet Yosef,* end of chap. 400; *Yabia Omer,* vol. 4, YD 34.

117 *Hazon Ovadia,* vol. 2, p. 186.

118 This custom is mentioned in the *Shulhan Arukh,* YD 340:15.

119 Ibid. 396:1.

120 Ibid. 402:1.

121 Ibid.

122 Ibid. OH 222.

123 Ibid. 402:4.

124 Ibid. 402:1. One is considered to have reached such a state when friends encourage
the mourner to get a haircut.

125 Ibid. 402:12.

CHAPTER 9

Yom Tov and *Hol Hamoed*

Holidays Cancel Mourning

Judaism has afforded us the wisdom of a healthy response to grief and loss in which we can work out our bereavement and journey toward resolution. In this book, I have argued the need to mourn the loss of a loved one. I also believe that our tradition has afforded us rituals and structure that enable mourners to develop the inner resolve necessary to reenter society stronger both emotionally and spiritually. The *Shivah* period enables the bereaved to acknowledge the tragedy of death in a safe and secure environment and at the same time to reaffirm their relationship with God, who is the source of both life and death. This time of adjustment has a unique dimension insofar as it mandates the members of the community to be present for the mourner, to cater to the needs of the bereaved and share in their loss. It is no wonder that contemporary health care professionals have written, and continue to write, so much about the healthy structure Judaism offers the bereaved as a way to work out loss and grief. It then becomes evident that the laws and rituals of *Avelut* are important aids in the expression of loss and overcoming of grief.

Yet there comes a time when *Shivah* and the mourning rituals are not observed despite the benefit they afford the bereaved. This happens

121

when *Shivah* is interrupted by *Yom Tov*, that is to say, a holiday. The guiding principle is as follows: "national celebration takes precedence over the bereavement of the individual."[1] Rabbi Joseph B. Soloveitchik *z"l*, in an article entitled "Catharsis," deals precisely with this issue and describes the halakhic tension the individual experiences under these circumstances:

> [*Avelut*] is an inner experience of black despair, of complete existential failure, of the absurdity of being. It is a grisly experience which overwhelms man, which shatters his faith and exposes his I-awareness as a delusion. Similarly the precept of Simhat Yom Tov (to rejoice on a holiday) includes, not only ceremonial actions, but a genuine experience of joy, as well. When the Torah decreed *Vesamahta behageha*, "And thou shall rejoice in thy feast," it referred, not to merrymaking and entertaining, to artificial gaiety or some sort of shallow hilarity, but to an all penetrating depth-experience of spiritual joy, serenity and peace of mind deriving from faith and the awareness of God's presence. Now let us visualize the following concrete situation. The mourner, who has buried a beloved wife or mother, returns home from the graveyard where he has left part of himself, where he has witnessed the mockery of human existence. He is in a mood to question the validity of our entire axiological universe. The house is empty, dreary, every piece of furniture reminds the mourner of the beloved person he has buried. Every corner is full of memories. Yet the Halakha addresses itself to the lonely mourner, whispering to him: "Rise from your mourning; cast the ashes from your head; change your clothes; light the festive candles; recite over a cup of wine the Kiddush extolling the Lord for giving us festivals of gladness and sacred seasons of joy; pronounce the blessing *Sheheheyanu*: 'Blessed art thou …who has kept us in life and has preserved us and has enabled us to reach this season'; join the jubilating community and celebrate the holiday."[2]

Rabbi Soloveitchik describes what is indeed a most difficult experience, a time when Jewish law intervenes in the most intimate and personal aspects of our lives. It is an example of when the Jew is called upon to subject himself or herself in a total fashion to the divine call.

Jewish law mandates that when a festival interrupts a mourning period, it completely consumes the individual grief and cancels it. Therefore, if mourning began even one hour before dark on the eve of a Jewish holiday, the onset of the festival cancels the remainder of the *Shivah*. The one hour of mourning that was observed becomes equivalent to seven full days of mourning. This point takes on great significance when we calculate the remainder of the thirty days of mourning, as we will see later on.

The following holidays interrupt and cancel the mourning of *Shivah* and *Sheloshim*: Pesah, Sukkoth, Shavuoth, Rosh Hashanah, and Yom Kippur.[3] This applies when mourning is observed before the holiday even for a short time. If, however, the mourner did not observe any form of mourning before the holiday, the *Shivah* period is not cancelled. In such a situation the mourning is observed immediately after the festival.

When the festival holiday is going to interrupt and cancel the mourning period, the mourner is permitted to prepare after midday on the eve of the holiday. At that time, mourners can launder their clothes, but may only wear them after the holiday begins.[4] Bathing is permitted after midday even in hot water in order to prepare for the holiday. The prohibitions against getting a haircut and shaving, however, are not affected by the holiday. The mourner can get a haircut or shave only after he is reprimanded by his social peers for his unwieldy appearance.[5]

If Death Occurs on *Yom Tov*

If death occurs on *Yom Tov*, during the holiday, or so close to the holiday that there is no time to make arrangements for a funeral, the body must be left untouched until after the holiday. Only under extenuating circumstances may the body be moved during a holiday. If death occurs in a hospital or nursing home on a holiday, and the hospital or nursing home does not allow the body to remain on its premises until the end of the holiday, a non-Jew should be asked to contact a funeral home that has non-Jewish employees. The body is then picked up and held until the conclusion of the holiday. The funeral service should be scheduled immediately after the holiday, even on *Hol Hamoed,* the intermediate days of the holiday.

EULOGY, KERIAH, AND SEUDAT HAVRA'AH
On *Hol Hamoed,* no eulogy is delivered even for a scholar whose body is present and not yet buried. *Keriah* is never performed on the holiday, not even in the Diaspora on the second day.[6] On *Hol Hamoed,* the mourners return home after the funeral and *Keriah* is performed. Shortly after the *Keriah* the rent garment is removed and the mourner wears regular clothing until after the holiday.[7] A meal of consolation is served the mourner but is not eaten on the floor. Rather, it is eaten at the table in the company of others[8] and should not consist of eggs but of cakes and the like.[9] At the conclusion of the holiday, the mourner puts on the rent garment and observes all the restrictions of *Shivah.*

Counting Shivah and Sheloshim
When burial takes place on *Hol Hamoed, Shivah* begins immediately at the conclusion of the festival. In the Diaspora the last day of the holiday is counted as day one of *Shivah* even though the restrictions of *Shivah* are not observed until after the holiday.[10]

Sheloshim, however, is counted from the day of burial.[11] Therefore it is not necessarily twenty-three days after the *Shivah.*

Comforting the Mourner
Even though *Shivah* does not begin until after the holiday, mourners can be comforted on the holiday.[12] Care should be taken to make sure visits take place not only during the holiday but also throughout the seven days of *Shivah.*

Laws Relating to the Calendar Cycle
TISHRI
- On the eve of Yom Kippur, the mourner is permitted to sit on a chair at the table and eat the *Seudah Ha'mafseket,* the last meal before the fast, joined by others.[13]
- The period between Yom Kippur and the end of Sukkoth is considered an especially festive time because it is the period in which

King Solomon finished building the Temple in Jerusalem. Therefore many have the custom not to fast during this period. Sepharadim, however, make an exception on the anniversary date of the death of a parent. A person who has the custom of fasting on that date should continue to do so even between Yom Kippur and Sukkoth.[14]

- The mourner is obligated to perform the *mizvah* of dwelling in the *sukkah*.[15] If, however, sitting in the *sukkah* is not enjoyable or is painful, the mourner is exempt.
- During Simhat Torah the mourner is permitted to carry a Torah scroll and encircle the *tevah* (readers' podium) but cannot participate in the dancing with the Torah.[16]

KISLEV

- Hanukkah does not interrupt or cancel any mourning practices and prohibitions.[17]
- On Hanukkah the deceased is not eulogized.[18]
- *Meldathos, Mishmarah,* and *Ariyat* services can be held during Hanukkah. Going to the cemetery, however, is not permitted.
- The mourner can light a *menorah* at home with the appropriate blessings, including *Sheheheyanu* on the first night. The mourner is not permitted, however, to light the *menorah* in the synagogue on the first night during the twelve-month period following the death of a parent and the thirty-day period following the death of a relative.[19]
- *Hallel* is not recited in the home of the mourner. Therefore those who pray in a house of mourning must recite *Hallel* on their own after the service.[20]

ADAR

- Purim is similar to Shabbat in that any form of public mourning is prohibited, whereas personal mourning is required.
- Mourners are permitted to wear shoes, change their rent clothes, and go to synagogue and listen to the reading of the *Megillah* even when mourning the death of a parent.
- Mourners are not permitted to bathe or shave on Purim.
- Purim day is counted toward the completion of *Shivah*.

- If the burial takes place on Purim day, no eulogy is delivered. *Keriah* is performed but the garment is immediately removed, and the meal of consolation is served the mourner.[21]
- The question of whether a mourner within twelve months of the death of a parent can read the *Megillah* in synagogue is disputed by the *halakhic* authorities, and each community must follow its own custom.
- Mourners are obligated to fulfill all the *mizvot* of Purim, including *Mishloah Manot* (sending food gifts), giving charity, and partaking in a festive meal. The community, however, should not send the mourner *Mishloach Manot* during the year of death of a parent or within thirty days of the death of a relative.[22]
- A mourner who is within twelve months of the death of a parent may play music in honor of Purim and in order to make the Purim meal festive.[23]

NISSAN

- It is permitted to fast during the month of Nissan on the anniversary date of the death of a parent.
- A mourner during *Shivah* who is a firstborn is not permitted to attend a *Siyum* (the festive meal celebrating the completion of a tractate of Talmud) in order to eat. A *Siyum* is traditionally observed on the eve of Pesah. After *Shivah*, the mourner may attend the *Siyum* if mourning the loss of a relative other than a parent. For a parent the mourner may attend the *Siyum* only after the first thirty days of mourning.[24]

SIVAN

- Mourners are permitted to attend a *Tikun Le'l* on Shavuoth even during *Shivah* as long as this is something they customarily do every year.[25]

AV

- On Tisha Be'Av the mourner attends services in synagogue in order to participate in the *Kinot* and *Eikha* service.[26]
- Even during Shivah, a mourner may be called up to the Torah and

Maftir at the morning service on Tisha Be'Av.[27] This does not apply at Minhah.

Endnotes

1   TB Moed Katan 14b.
2   Soloveichik, "Catharsis," *Tradition* 17, no. 2 (Spring 1978).
3   *Shulhan Arukh*, YD 399:1, 6.
4   *Shulhan Arukh* 399:5, also OH 548:10.
5   Ibid 399:4.
6   Ibid. 340:31.
7   Ibid. 340:31, also OH 547:6.
8   Ibid. 401:4.
9   *Yalkut Yosef* 26:14.
10 *Shulhan Arukh*, OH 548:1.
11 Ibid.
12 Ibid., YD 399:1.
13 *Yalkut Yosef* 25:2.
14 Ibid., vol. 7, chap. 25:1.
15 OH 640:5.
16 *Kaf HaHayim* 669:33.
17 *Kaf HaHayim*, OH 670:20.
18 *Shulhan Arukh* 670:1.
19 *Rav Pe'alim*, vol. 4, OH 32; *Yalkut Yosef* 25:5.
20 See *Magen Avraham* 131:10, *Mishnah Berurah* 131:20.
21 See *Yabia Omer*, vol. 4, YD 26; *Yalkut Yosef* 25:6. There is an apparent contradiction in the *Shulhan Arukh* regarding the observance of mourning practices on Purim. In OH 696:4 it seemingly states that all the laws of mourning apply on both Purim and Hanukkah. In YD 401:7, however, it states that mourning practices are not observed on the fourteenth and fifteenth of Adar. Shakh reconciles this apparent contradiction by making a distinction between deaths occurring on Purim and before Purim; thus the passage in OH which states that the laws of mourning apply refers to a case where death occurs on Purim, and the passage in Yoreh De'ah refers to a case where death occurs before Purim.
22 *Shulhan Arukh*, OH 696:6. See also Rama YD 385:3.
23 *Yalkut Yosef* 25:11.
     Yalkut Yosef 25:13.
24 *Sha'arey Teshuvah* 664:1.
25 OH 559:6.
26 See *Kaf HaHayim* 554:56. On the ninth of Av all Jews are considered mourners. In the morning prayers this is evident from the special Torah reading. Thus there is

no difference between the person sitting *Shivah* and the rest of the congregation regarding *Aliyoth*. At *Minhah* the Torah portion is the same as other fasts on which the congregation does not have the status of mourner. Therefore at *Minhah* the mourner cannot be called up to the Torah during *Shivah*.

CHAPTER 10

Getting Married When in Mourning

When Death Occurs Prior to a Scheduled Wedding
If the death of an immediate relative of a bride or bridegroom occurs within seven days of their planned wedding, the wedding must be postponed. It can take place, however, if the scheduled date is after the conclusion of the *Shivah*, even if this is before the conclusion of the *Sheloshim*.[1] A wedding date can be scheduled anytime after the *Sheloshim* period even if it is to take place before the end of the twelve-month mourning period for a parent.[2]

When Death Occurs Immediately After a Wedding
A newly wed couple within seven days of their *Hupah* (marriage ceremony) falls into a unique category when it comes to mourning. If the death of an immediate relative of either the bride or groom takes place during the seven festive days immediately following their *Hupah*, all mourning practices are postponed until after the seven days.[3] In such a case the following *halakhic* laws must be observed:
- There is no *Aninut* period.[4]
- *Keriah* is not observed even if the deceased was a parent.[5]

- The mourner recites the blessing *Dayan Ha'emet*.[6]
- The bride and groom do not attend the funeral service.[7]

Throughout the week of festive celebration following the wedding, the bride or groom who is bereaved is exempt from all the prohibitions on mourners. In other words, they may eat with people, be festive, launder their clothing, and even get a haircut and shave. A bereaved groom can study Torah during the entire week of festivity. The mourner is, however, prohibited from having marital relations with his or her new spouse.[8]

A bride or groom who is the only mourner observes an entire *Shivah* period after the week of festivity. If, however, the mourner will join parents or siblings in mourning after the seven days of festive celebrations, or *Sheva Berakhot,* the newlywed concludes the *Shivah* with the other mourners[9] even if this means that he or she does not observe a full seven days of mourning. Jewish law recognizes that mourning is not a strictly private experience but also a familial experience. Therefore the *Shivah* period is dependent on the larger family or the elder of the family.

Second Marriage

The laws outlined above apply only when it is appropriate to have the *Sheva Berakhot.* The seven days of rejoicing are observed only for a first marriage for both the bride and groom. If, however, this is a second marriage for either of them, only three days of rejoicing are appropriate. In such a situation, the laws of mourning are suspended for only three days.

The seven or three days of suspended mourning do not count toward the *Sheloshim.* The count of the thirty days of *Sheloshim* begins with *Shivah*, the mourning period.[10]

Endnotes

1   *Yalkut Yosef* 18:7 and fn. 7.
2   *Mekor Hayim* 287:21.
3   *Bet Oved*; see also *Yabia Omer,* vol. 6, p. 256, YD 34; *Yalkut Yosef,* vol. 7 chap. 24:5.
4   *Kol Bo,* p. 133; *Gesher HaHayim,* pt. II, 15:3.
5   See *Yalkut Yosef,* vol. 7, chap. 24:5, fn. 7.

6   *Gesher HaHayim* 19:7; *Yalkut Yosef,* loc. cit.

7   *Bet Oved.*

8   *Shulhan Arukh* 383:2.

9   *Yalkut Yosef,* vol. 7 chap. 27:4.

10   *Shulhan Arukh* 383:2.

CHAPTER 11

Zakhor: Remember

One should not grieve too much for the dead, and whoever grieves excessively is really grieving for someone else. [The Torah sets limits for every stage of grief]: three days for weeping, seven for lamenting, and thirty for abstaining from laundered garments and from cutting hair.

Whoever does not mourn as the law has prescribed is considered callous.

– Shulhan Arukh, YD 394:1–4

Post-*Shivah*

With the conclusion of *Shivah,* the second mourning period begins. This period is called *Sheloshim,* the thirty-day period that begins with the burial of the deceased[1] and concludes on the morning of the thirtieth day. Maimonides, in his code of Jewish law, the *Yad HaHazakah,* writes as follows regarding the thirty-day mourning period:

It is a rabbinical enactment that the mourner must observe certain practices of mourning for the entire thirty days. On what did the sages base the thirty-day mourning period? On

133

the verse "She shall weep for her mother and father for a month" (Deuteronomy 21:13). This implies that the mourner grieves for thirty days.[2]

Throughout this period of time it is appropriate to extend condolences if they were not extended during *Shivah*.[3] The twenty-three days immediately following *Shivah* are marked by the continued observance of certain restrictions. These restrictions include:

- The mourner is prohibited from getting a haircut or shaving during the *Sheloshim* period.[4] Certain communities permit a mourner to shave after *Shivah* if he can prove that the deceased parent requested that he not observe this requirement.[5]
- It is forbidden to cut one's fingernails and toenails with an instrument like a clipper or scissors.[6]
- Mourners do not wear new clothing or freshly laundered clothing during this period.[7]
- Mourners should not attend festive meals, parties or celebrations.[8]
- Mourners should not attend live music performances, operas, and similar performances.
- Mourners should not listen to recorded music unless it is incidental music, such as the background music of a commercial.
- On Purim, the mourner is not given *Mishloah Manot* but must observe the *mizvah* by sending *Mishloah Manot* to at least two people.[9]

Permitted Social Gatherings
- Mourners may attend a *Kiddush* in their own synagogue.
- Mourners may partake of Shabbat meals with friends and guests.
- A mourner who is a musician, photographer, or caterer and must attend a large social function for income purposes may do so.

Counting the Thirty days of *Sheloshim*
While the word *Sheloshim* means "thirty," the *Sheloshim* period does not always last thirty days. As in the case of *Shivah,* the beginning of a day counts as an entire day. Therefore *Sheloshim* concludes in the morning of

the thirtieth day. Furthermore, the *Sheloshim* period can be dramatically shortened when a major festival occurs during this period. The actual duration of the *Sheloshim* is subject to a number of variables.

- While *Sheloshim* begins immediately following interment, its restrictions manifest themselves only after the *Shivah* period.
- A major festival (Rosh Hashanah, Yom Kippur, Sukkoth, Pesah, or Shavuoth) cancels the *Sheloshim* period provided that the *Shivah* period has been completed or was terminated by one of the major festivals. For example: (1) If *Shivah* is completed even one day before Pesah, Pesah cancels *Sheloshim*. (2) If Rosh Hashanah occurs during *Shivah*, *Shivah* is canceled, because Yom Kippur, which occurs ten days later, will cancel the *Sheloshim*.[10] Similarly if Yom Kippur cancels the *Shivah*, Sukkoth cancels the *Sheloshim*.[11]
- If Pesah cancels one's *Shivah*, that *Shivah* observance, even for one hour is considered seven days. Those seven days are added to the eight days that the festival is observed, making fifteen days completed toward the thirty days of *Sheloshim*. In other words, there are now only fifteen days left of *Sheloshim* restrictions.
- All the major festivals (Pesah, Shavuoth, Sukkoth, Shemini Atzeret) are considered to equal seven days. Therefore, if *Shivah* is terminated by Shavuoth: *Shivah* = seven days and Shavuoth = seven days (even though it is only a two-day holiday), which means that the mourner has completed fourteen days toward the *Sheloshim* observance.[12]
- When *Shivah* is terminated by Sukkoth, at the end of the holiday there are only eight days toward the completion of *Sheloshim*: seven days of *Shivah* plus seven days of Sukkoth plus seven days for *Shemini Atzeret* means that twenty-one days have been counted toward the thirty days of *Sheloshim*.[13]

Conclusion of *Sheloshim*

There are numerous customs as to how the conclusion of *Sheloshim* is observed. Some communities hold the memorial service at the home of the mourner. Immediately following the service, food is served and portions of the Torah, Mishnah, and *Zohar* are studied. This memorial observance is concluded with the *Hashkavah*, the memorial prayer for the deceased and a visit to the cemetery on the next day. Unlike our brethren, the Ashkenazim, the Sepharadim have so many different customs and variations of this memorial observance that it would be a futile attempt on my part to begin listing them. I encourage you, the reader, to find out how this memorial service is observed in your community and to follow that custom.

Excessive Grief

Jewish law affords the mourner a complete structure and spiritual response for grief. Indeed, our sages, of blessed memory, understood the need to confront loss directly and accept the reality of death consciously. Through the laws and rituals of mourning, the bereaved, in a time of confusion, are assisted in focusing their attention and emotions on the loss and on their need to resume the familiar patterns of normal living.

Most people do not intuitively know how to respond to grief. How much sadness is appropriate? Am I crying enough? Why am I not feeling more? Why can't I stop feeling depressed and sad? Why can't I stop crying? These are some of the questions asked by many who grieve without a structure.

By following a prescribed structure of laws and rituals, mourners are comforted by knowing that their response to the loss of a loved one is adequate. Their demonstration of love and honor is framed in a noble and dignified tradition that walks the mourner through this most difficult time in life. There is a great deal of comfort in knowing that our response to death is religiously ordained, and that no matter how observant we may be, we are fulfilling God's will by honoring the life of the deceased in the appropriate fashion.

Jewish tradition not only mandates a minimum amount of grief – "One who does not mourn the death of a loved one in the manner commanded by our sages is cruel"[14] – but also states that we are not permitted to excessively mourn the loss of a loved one. As was quoted earlier in this book, the Talmud relates the frightening story of a woman who grieved excessively and as a result died:

A certain woman lived in the neighborhood of Rabbi Huna. She had seven sons. One of them died. She wept over his death excessively. Rabbi Huna said to her: "Do not weep this way." She did not pay attention to his advice. He said to her: "If you do not listen to my advice, you may have to prepare shrouds for the rest of your children!" They all died. She again wept excessively. He said to her: "Do not weep excessively or you will have to prepare shrouds for yourself." She did not listen to his advice and died.[15]

Rabbi Yosef Karo, author of the *Shulhan Arukh*, states that it is forbidden to excessively mourn the death of a loved one. Halakhah prescribes appropriate mourning: "the first three days for weeping, seven days for eulogizing, thirty days for refraining from haircutting and laundering. One should not grieve more than this."[16]

Indeed, left to our own intuitive devices, we might run the risk of not knowing how to limit our mourning. Because the emotional wounds incurred from the loss of a child, or the loss of a life-long companion, or the loss of a parent or sibling never fully heal, a mourner risks getting caught in a web of endless grief. Jewish law clearly marks the beginning and end of the mourning practices. In its infinite wisdom, our tradition prevents the bereaved from getting pulled into an interminable grief. There can be limits to the grief felt no matter how tragic and how painful it may be. The framework our tradition affords us prevents us from mourning too little and from mourning too long.

Twelve-Month Restrictions for Loss of a Parent

The *Sheloshim* restrictions described above apply to all mourners who have lost a close relative. When one loses a parent, the restrictions listed above should be observed for twelve months.[17]

Regarding personal grooming, however, the law provides for the principle of "social reproach."[18] This means that after thirty days of mourning for a parent, if someone makes a comment to the mourner that his hair is too long or his beard unwieldy, he is permitted to shave and get a haircut. If no one makes a comment but the mourner's hair is so long that it is quite out of character, then he can use his own judgment and get a haircut.

Throughout the twelve-month period following the death of a parent, mourners should abstain from attending festive celebrations, parties, social gatherings, even public religious celebrations. The exceptions to this rule are:

- Attending the *Brit Milah* (circumcision) or *Pidyon Haben* (redemption of the firstborn) of one's own child is permitted even during *Shivah*. The father of the child may dress in new clothing and partake of the *Seudat Mizvah* (festive meal).[19]
- Mourners may attend a *Brit Milah* even when the child being circumcised is not their own. They can also partake of a full formal meal.
- Attending the *Bar* or *Bat Mizvah* of one's own child is permitted as long as there is no music or dancing.[20]
- Attending the *Hupah* (wedding ceremony) of one's own child or grandchild is permitted. One may even attend the festive meal.[21]
- After the *Sheloshim* of a parent and within the *Sheloshim* for a relative who is mourned, a mourner may attend the *Hupah* of a friend or relative as long as there is no musical accompaniment.
- Attending community business meetings is permitted.

Because of the complex nature of these issues and the many different situations, one should consult a rabbi before making final decisions on these matters.

Memorial Services

Memorial services for a loved one commemorate the enormous tragedy of death and are a tribute of love and honor to the deceased. It is a time set aside to reflect and remember the impact the deceased may have had in one's life. These services are referred to by different names. In the Judeo-Spanish community they are called *Meldathos*, in the Syrian community they are called *Ariyat*, and the Moroccan community calls it a *Mishmarah*. These services are observed primarily for parents, spouses, children, and siblings but can be observed for other relatives and friends.

There are various times during the first year of mourning that a memorial service is traditionally held. The various communities have different customs as to how many such services are observed.

Hazkarah

The last memorial service of the first twelve months of mourning is commonly known by its Hebrew name, *Hazkarah*. The custom in many communities is to hold the first-year *Hazkarah* of the deceased on the date of burial; in subsequent years it is held on the date of death.[22] In a leap year the first-year *Hazkarah* is observed twelve months from the date of burial. There is an alternative custom that commemorates the first-year *Hazkarah* and subsequent *Hazkarot* on the date of death.[23]

The Hebrew anniversary does not coincide with the anniversary on the Gregorian calendar in secular use. Therefore one should consult a rabbi or synagogue for the date of the *Hazkarah*. The rule is that the *Hazkarah* is always observed in the same month and on the same day.

LEAP YEARS

- When death occurs in Adar I of a leap year, the *Hazkarah* is always observed on the day of death.
- When death occurs in Adar II of a leap year, the *Hazkarah* is observed in Adar during a regular year and Adar II in a leap year.
- When death occurs in Adar of a regular year, the *Hazkarah* is observed in Adar II of a leap year.[24]

DIFFERENT TIME ZONES

If a death occurs on a certain date and the mourners are in another country where it is the next day, the rule is the *Hazkarah* is observed according to the date of the place where the death occurred.[25]

WHEN ONE DOES NOT KNOW THE DATE OF *HAZKARAH*

If one does not know the date of either parent's *Hazkarah,* a date should be selected, and that date should be commemorated annually as the *Hazkarah.*

HAZKARAH OBSERVANCES

The saintly mystics taught that we must observe the anniversary of the death of a parent even for one hundred years because of its auspicious nature and benefit to the soul of the deceased.[26]

The custom is to recite *Kaddish* with a *minyan* beginning on the

Shabbat before the *Hazkarah*.[27] On the day of *Hazkarah* for a parent, some have the custom to fast the entire day.[28] If the *Hazkarah* falls on a holiday or Shabbat, one should not fast, as it would conflict with the joyous spirit of the day; the fast can be postponed to the next day.[29]

It is appropriate to light a candle on the day of *Hazkarah* either at home or in the synagogue. On the day of *Hazkarah*, one studies psalms, *mishnayot*, and *Zohar* and recites the *Hashkavah*.

One should observe this day by abstaining from participating in parties or festive gatherings. It is customary to visit the cemetery and recite Psalm 119.[30]

On Shabbat of the week of *Hazkarah* it is customary to either be called up for *Mashlim* (the last of the seven *aliyoth*) and recite *Kaddish* or be called up for the *Haftarah*. Many congregations will give priority to those observing *Hazkarah* for a parent, over the *Hazkarah* for a spouse, child, or sibling. On Shabbat of the week of *Hazkarah*, after the *Haftarah* is recited or after one's *aliyah* to the Torah, one recites *Hashkavah*, the memorial prayer.

Visiting the Grave

Visiting the graves of parents, loved ones, and ancestors is an ancient custom, a show of respect and honor to the deceased and to the cherished memories shared with the loved one. The *Zohar* tells the story of Rabbi Yitzhak, who requested three things of Rabbi Yehudah before he died.[31] One of these three things was that Rabbi Yehudah visit his grave and pray for his soul. This reference and other such references suggest that we honor the deceased through prayer and the recitation of psalms at the gravesite.

Other rabbinical references suggest that visiting the gravesite of parents, ancestors, or righteous people affords us an opportunity to pray for ourselves or for others. This does not mean that the souls of the deceased function as intermediaries between God and us.[32] Each of us has direct access to God through prayer. Our sages nevertheless saw the gravesite as a place that may inspire heartfelt prayer and thereby result in personal transformation of the individual.

The Torah records that Jacob our forefather told his son Joseph that he had buried Rachel (Joseph's mother) "on the road to Ephrat."[33] Rashi comments that Jacob did this by divine command, so that when their descendants were exiled from the land of Israel by Nebuzaradan, they would pass by the gravesite of Rachel, the matriarch, and she would beseech God to have mercy on her children. The verses in Jeremiah tell the story of the exile: "A voice is heard in Ramah…. Rachel weeps for her children." God responds: "There is reward for your deed … and your children will return to their borders."[34] Another powerful talmudic reference to the visitation of graves comments on the verse "He [Caleb] came to Hebron."[35] Caleb, one of the twelve spies Moses sent into the land of Israel, apparently left the group and went on his own. Our sages tell us:

> This teaches us that Caleb withdrew from the scheme of the spies and went to pray at the tomb of the patriarchs [the Cave of Machpelah]. He said to them: "My fathers, beseech the Lord to have mercy on me that I may be saved from the scheme of the spies."[36]

It is therefore customary to pray at the gravesite of the deceased for health and healing, protection, fertility, or any situation of trouble that, God forbid, may befall us.

The appropriate times to visit the cemetery are:

- Fast days[37]
- On the seventh day of *Shivah*
- On the thirtieth-day memorial
- On the day of *Hazkarah* each year
- Some communities have the custom of visiting the cemetery before Rosh Hashanah and before the month of Nissan.

If one of the days that is appropriate to visit the cemetery falls on a Shabbat or holiday, the visit should be done the next day. The custom is to not visit the cemetery during the entire month of Nissan except for the visit on the *Hazkarah*.

ENTERING THE CEMETERY

If one has not seen Jewish graves for thirty days, one recites the blessing before entering the cemetery (see appendix)

Upon arriving at the grave, it is customary to place one's left hand on the grave or headstone and recite the following verse:

וְנָחֲךָ יְהֹוָה תָּמִיד וְהִשְׂבִּיעַ בְּצַחְצָחוֹת נַפְשֶׁךָ וְעַצְמֹתֶיךָ יַחֲלִיץ וְהָיִיתָ כְּגַן רָוֶה וּכְמוֹצָא מַיִם אֲשֶׁר לֹא־יְכַזְּבוּ מֵימָיו (ישעיהו נח, יא): אָז יִבָּקַע כַּשַּׁחַר אוֹרֶךָ וַאֲרֻכָתְךָ מְהֵרָה תִצְמָח וְהָלַךְ לְפָנֶיךָ צִדְקֶךָ כְּבוֹד יְהֹוָה יַאַסְפֶךָ (ישעיהו נח, ח):

After reciting the above verse, one takes a small pebble or stone and places it on the headstone or grave. This is a sign of honor to the deceased and a marker that someone has visited this place. When placing the stone the following words are said:

תשכב בשלום עד בו מנחם משמיע שלום.[38]

Lie in peace until the coming of the Consoler who will announce peace.

RECITING PSALMS AT THE GRAVESITE

It is most appropriate to recite psalms at the gravesite. Psalms 16, 17, 33, 72, 91, 104, and 130 are all suitable. One can recite the verses of Psalm 119 beginning with the letters that spell the name of the deceased and the word *neshamah* (soul). *Hashkavah* is said after the recitation of psalms, and if there is a *minyan, Kaddish Yehe Sheme Raba* is said.

LEAVING THE CEMETERY

When leaving the cemetery, it is customary to ritually wash one's hands. No blessing is said on the washing of the hands, and it is the custom not to dry them with a towel or kerchief.

Erecting a Monument

Erecting a monument as a marker over the grave of a loved one is an ancient tradition in Judaism. The earliest record of such a tradition dates back to biblical times, when Jacob placed a monument on his wife Rachel's grave.[39] Our sages in Mishnah Shekalim 2:5 state: "With the remainder of the money collected for the needs of the deceased, they built a monument for his grave." Jewish law is clear about the fact that the immediate family of the deceased is responsible for providing a monument on the grave. It is part of the *mizvah* of showing honor to the deceased.[40]

The monument has several purposes. It is there to indicate that someone is buried in the ground and proper respect must be shown to that place. It also serves as an indicator that *kohanim* should avoid that place in order not to defile themselves. Finally, it is a sign of honor for the deceased, so that friends and family can identify the place of burial and visit the gravesite when appropriate.

The monument is made of stone. In Hebrew the word for "stone" is *tzur*. The same word is also one of God's names describing his ever-present nature. Just as a stone lasts forever, so too God is ever-present in our lives. Erecting a monument of stone is a way of saying that the memory of the deceased will linger forever.

Arranging for a proper monument is considered an integral part of the burial arrangements. Immediately following *Shivah*, the family must begin the process of preparing the monument. Cemeteries usually have guidelines as to the maximum size for acceptable monuments. One should be cautious not to be overly ostentatious. The monument should be dignified and in good taste.

The inscription on the monument should include the full Hebrew name of the deceased and his or her mother's name as well as the full English name, the date of death, and the deceased's Jewish status (i.e., *kohen* or *levi*).

Along with the above information, the inscription will include, above the inscription, the Hebrew letters *peh nun* which stand for *poh nitman* "here rests," or *mem kof, matzevet kevarah*, "monument of the grave of." Underneath the inscription the monument will also include the following Hebrew letters: *taf nun tzadik bet heh*, which stand for *Tehe nishmato/nishmatah tzerurah bisror hahayim* "May his/her soul be bound up in the bond of eternal life."

UNVEILING SERVICE

The unveiling service is the formal dedication of the monument erected at the grave of the deceased. The ideal time to dedicate the monument is between the *Shivah* and the beginning of the eleventh month. The unveiling should not be scheduled on *Hol Hamoed* (the intermediate days of Pesah and Sukkoth), Rosh Hodesh, Hanukkah, Purim, Lag La'Omer, or during the month of Nissan. The general rule is that the unveiling should not take place on any day when the penitential *Tahanunim* prayers are not recited.

The unveiling service is centered around the recitation of Psalm 119, known as the *Alfa Beta*. The name of the deceased is spelled out with the appropriate verses of Psalm 119 (see appendix). If one has not been to the cemetery for thirty days, the blessing before entering the cemetery should be recited.

The recitation of the appropriate paragraphs of Psalm 119 is followed by *Barukh Eloheinu, Kaddish,* and *Hashkavah.*

Endnotes

1   Rabbi Yosef Hayim, *Responsa Rav Pe'alim,* vol. 1, YD 51.
2   Maimonides, Avel 6:1.
3   *Shulhan Arukh* 380:2.
4   Ibid. 390:1.
5   Shaul Matlub Abadi, *Magen Ba'adi,* pp. 133–144.
6   *Shulhan Arukh* 390:6.
7   Ibid. 389:7.
8   Ibid. 391.
9   *Siddur Bet Oved,* p. 177.
10 *Shulhan Arukh,* YD 399:9, OH 548:14.
11 Ibid., YD 399:10, OH 548:15.
12 The first day of *Shavuoth* is considered to be seven days. In the diaspora, where a second day is observed, that day will count as the 15th day towards the *Sheloshim*.
13 The second day of *Shemini Aseret,* known as *Simhat Torah,* counts as the 22nd day of Sheloshim.
14 Ibid.
15 TB Moed Katan 27b.
16 *Shulhan Arukh* 394:1. This applies to ordinary people; for a sage and scholar one can weep for thirty days and eulogize for twelve months. See also Rambam, Avel 13:11; Moed Katan 27b.
17 *Shulhan Arukh,* YD 391:1.
18 TB, Moed Katan 22b; *Shulhan Arukh* 390:1. The expression "social reproach" is taken from Rabbi Maurice Lamm's book *The Jewish Way in Death and Mourning.*

19 *Yalkut Yosef* Ibid. 18:12–13.

20 Ibid. 18:14.

21 Ibid. 18:8.

22 Rabbeinu Hayim Phalagi, *Responsa Hayim Beyad,* chap. 118. See also Taz YD 402.9.

23 *Yalkut Yosef* 22:3.

24 *Shulhan Arukh* 391:2, OH 568:7.

25 *Gesher HaHayim* 32:14.

26 See *Rav Pe'alim,* Teshuvot Sod Yesharim, end.

27 *Mekor Hayim,* vol. 5, 291:17.

28 *Shulhan Arukh,* OH 568:7; also Rama YD 402:12; *Responsa Rav Pe'alim,* pt. 4, OH 11.

29 *Shulhan Arukh,* OH 568:9.

30 *Shulhan Arukh* 344:20.

31 *Zohar* Vayekhi; see also *Gesher HaHayim.*

32 Such an idea is precluded by Deuteronomy 18:11.

33 Genesis 48:7.

34 Jeremiah 31:15–16.

35 Numbers 13:22.

36 Sotah 34a.

37 See *Shulhan Arukh* 579:10, Ta'anit 17b.

38 *Kaf HaHayim* 224:42.

39 Genesis 35:20.

40 See *Bet Yosef* 348; also Rambam, Avel 4:4; *Kol Bo* 378–379.

CHAPTER 12

When a Baby Dies

King David said …"But now he is dead, can I bring him back
again? I shall go to him, but he will not come back to me."

– II Samuel 12:23

Grieving for a Baby

Parents do not mourn for children according to how long they lived.
Grieving the death of a baby is a natural response to the loss, and yet it
is very different from grieving for a spouse, parent, sibling, older child, or
any other loved one. There are numerous factors that affect the course of a
person's grief, but the death of a baby is especially difficult to endure.

The entire experience of death and mourning in Judaism is a process that enables the bereaved to strengthen themselves, their families,
and their community ties. Every stage of the grief process, from the
moment one is confronted with an ailing relative and must assist the
dying with the recitation of the *Viduy*, the personal confession, all the
way through the first-year anniversary of the death, integrates the loss
and the memory of the deceased into the life of the bereaved. All these
rituals afford mourners a structure that leads to resolution and places it
within a theological perspective.

When a child dies in infancy, that is, after the age of thirty days, the bereaved are afforded the same complete framework of religious observances, necessary rituals, and support in order to accept the death, grieve, and go on living.

What happens, however, when a pregnancy ends in a miscarriage or a stillbirth, or a baby dies less than thirty days after birth? From the standpoint of Jewish law, an infant who has not completed the nine-month gestation period is referred to as "nonviable," and one does not observe any kind of mourning ritual or grief period for this baby. The *halakhic* principle is as follows: A baby that dies before reaching the age of thirty days is presumed nonviable unless it can be absolutely ascertained that the infant completed a full nine months of gestation. The only way to be absolutely certain, from a *halakhic* viewpoint, that the baby has completed the nine-month gestation period would be if the couple did not have intercourse from conception until the birth of the baby.[1] The nine-month clock stops running after the couple resumes intimacy, and Jewish law makes the basic assumption that married couples will engage in intimacy on an ongoing basis. Thus there is always a doubt as to when a baby has been conceived.

The reason for this ruling may have to do with the fact that such losses were so commonplace years ago. Had our sages instituted mourning rituals for nonviable babies, families would have found themselves grieving three and sometimes four times out of every five pregnancies.

This ruling is consistent with the attitudes espoused by medical and psychological professionals that were so prevalent only ten and twenty years ago. Bereaved parents were encouraged to forget their loss, to pretend that it had never happened. Such a practice deprived the parents of the opportunity to show an expression of love for their baby. No matter how short the baby's life, the bond between parent and child cannot be denied. Research is finally being done on the effects of miscarriage, stillbirth, and infant death. As a result, health professionals and pastoral professionals are learning what parents have known all along: the sorrow and pain of losing a baby are as profound as any other loss and in some ways even more complicated.

As a result of the *halakhic* view of this problem, traditional Jewish couples who have suffered such a loss experience bereavement and consider themselves bereaved but do not have a formal structure of mourning to follow as an outlet for their grief. The painful silence of Judaism at this time creates a climate of isolation. The basic needs for comfort and support of the bereaved, *nihum aveilim,* is overlooked by many pastoral caregivers. The unstated assumption is that if the law does not offer a religious framework for such grief or the religious structure to offer comfort to those who have experienced such a loss, this must mean either that the bereaved really do not need to grieve and be comforted, or that it is best that they not grieve and be comforted.

Of course, neither of these two assumptions is valid. They are born out of ignorance and denial of the true and most profound feelings of pain that the bereaved experience.

The need for formal religious mourning after the loss of a baby became especially clear to me after my wife and I experienced such a loss myself and did not have a religious structure available for grief, guidance, and support. Through our grief, I learned of the amazing power a modest ritual can have. We felt an intense need to respond spiritually and there was nothing available. We felt somewhat abandoned.

I discussed this in total candor with my rabbinical colleagues and found them to be understanding and supportive. Those who had experienced a similar loss shared my sense of abandonment and expressed a need for a change in attitude. Ever since my personal experience with the loss of a baby, I have counseled numerous couples who also expressed how they would have found comfort in a religious spiritual response to their loss. Indeed, the loss is painful, the silence unbearable. During the nine-month period that I was writing my book *Confronting the Loss of a Baby: A Personal and Jewish Perspective,* I received many letters from men and women who had lost a baby and were courageous enough to share their experience. Here is one of the many letters I received from a Jewish woman describing her need for a religious response to her loss.

Dear Rabbi Levy,

I am very interested in the work you are doing on grief and mourning for a newborn child. As I told you over the phone our daughter was born on the way to the hospital and she was not breathing. The hospital staff could not resuscitate her. It wasn't until we left the hospital without our baby that her death became a reality. We called our rabbi who has known our family for years. He was very supportive and comforting but that was all he offered. I inquired about saying *Kaddish,* about sitting on the floor and tearing *Keriah* and he said that is not done under these circumstances. "What circumstances?" I asked. He went on to explain how this kind of death is different. I was truly at a loss. I needed a religious anchor and there was none. We grieved silently and alone.

It is a huge misconception to view the laws and rituals of mourning as a burden on the bereaved. If anything, they are an incredible source of support and validation that ultimately pave the way to a complete healing. Bereaved parents, those who lose a child to miscarriage, stillbirth, or shortly after birth, need to heal and need some kind of spiritual and religious response to their grief. The alternative is either repressing the grief, which makes the pain more complicated, or going elsewhere for support and validation.

> Halakhah offers a means of working through and completing the grief process. It is a process that encourages us to face our feelings openly and honestly, to express and release them in a safe and supportive environment. It takes courage to feel pain and to face the unfamiliar.

Rabbi Jack Riemer, one of the important pioneers in bringing the Jewish perspective on death to the English-reading public, recently edited a book called *Wrestling With the Angel: Jewish Insights on Death and Mourning.* As opposed to his first book, which was published in the mid-seventies, this one has a section dealing with miscarriage, stillbirth, and early infant death. Rabbi Riemer introduces the chapter "How Shall We Mourn The Stillborn?" with the following comments:

> And I am now aware, as I never was before, of the pain of those who lose a child by miscarriage or at birth. We used to know what was appropriate at such a time. The social worker would say: "Don't see the baby, don't take a lock of its hair, don't get

attached, for it will only add to your pain if you do." And the rabbi would say: "Don't give the baby a name, don't sit *Shivah*, don't say *Kaddish*, for it will only add to your pain." Now we know better. Now we know that although they meant well, this advice was faulty. Now we realize that listening to this kind of advice only repressed the pain; it did not heal it.

And so now a new generation of social workers and rabbis grope for ways in which people can acknowledge and cope with this kind of loss. It is not enough to tell the parents that the mourning rites are not necessary, as if the rites were an onerous burden from which we are trying to spare them. The mourning rites are a therapy, not a burden, and if we excuse those who are suffering from that form of therapy we do them no favor.

Today we recognize that holding one's baby before and after death is an opportunity to love and gather positive memories of the child. Feeling sad, angry, or lonely is a healthy reaction associated with grief. Talking about the baby with someone who can listen is correctly viewed as therapeutic and healing. Even taking pictures and gathering mementos can become very important at a later time. The need to arrange a religious funeral service, attend the burial, recite *Kaddish*, and recognize a mourning period with rituals that offer support and comfort to the bereaved should not be overlooked.

The bereaved who allow themselves the necessary time and afford themselves appropriate responses to grieve are more likely to be on the road to resolving their grief. Those who do not, eventually recognize that their lives are burdened by a grief they have never resolved.[2]

That we can grieve and recover from a loss of this nature seems to be an amazing feat, yet human resilience is amazing.

I strongly suggest that those who have lost a baby read my *Confronting the Loss of a Baby: A Jewish Perspective* for a religious and spiritual response, in the context of Halakhah.

Counting Thirty Days of Life

There is a dispute among the halakhic authorities as to whether we count thirty *halakhic* days or thirty twenty-four-hour days. A *halakhic* day can actually, under certain circumstances, be a fraction of a twenty-four-hour day. For example, if one begins the mourning period at midday or even late afternoon on any given day, then at sundown of that day the mourners have completed one halakhic day of the seven-day mourning period. In other words, a portion of the day is considered an entire day for purposes of counting *Shivah*, the seven days of mourning. This is also true at the end of the counting of seven days. Mourners conclude the seven-day period of *Shivah* on the morning of the seventh day because a portion of the day is counted as an entire day.

How is the thirty days of life counted in order to determine whether or not a baby is viable and whether or not a family is required to mourn the death of their infant?

The general rule with regard to the laws of *Avelut* is that when in doubt you follow the more lenient opinion.[3] Our sages of blessed memory always sought out a way to absolve us from required mourning. It was assumed that if you did not have to mourn, it would be best not to. Regarding the counting of the thirty days, since it would be a determining factor as to whether or not the family should mourn the death of the baby, Jewish law rules in a way that would minimize the chances of a family mourning. We therefore count thirty twenty-four-hour days.[4]

Endnotes

1   See *Shulhan Arukh*, EH 156, on the subject of *yibum*.
2   I.G. Leon, *When a Baby Dies: Psychotherapy for Pregnancy and Newborn Loss* pp. 97–131, records numerous cases of unresolved grief of prenatal loss which becomes especially complicated later on in life.
3   TB Moed Katan 18a.
4   *Rav Pe'alim*, pt. 1, YD 51; see *Sefer Asya*, vol. 8.

Services Associated with Death and Mourning

- Viduy
- Funeral Service
- Service at the cemetery
- Kaddish De'Achadeta
- Kaddish DeRabbanan
- Kaddish Yehe Shelama
- Hashkavot for men and women
- Birkat Hamazon
- Tziduk Hadin
- Psalm 119

Viduy Service

רבון העולמים בעל הסליחות והרחמים. יהי רצון מלפניך יי אלקי ואלקי
אבותי שיעלה זכרוני לפני כסא כבודך לטובה. וראה בעניי כי אין מתום
בבשרי מפני זעמך אין שלום בעצמי מפני חטאתי. ועתה אלוק סליחות הטה
אלי חסדיך. ואל תבא במשפט את עבדך. ואם קרבה עת פקודתי למות.
אחדותך לעד מפי לא תמוש ככתוב בתורתך שמע ישראל יי אלקינו יי אחד:
ברוך שם כבוד מלכותו לעולם ועד:

153

מודה אני לפניך יי אלקי ואלקי אבותי. קל אלקי הרוחות לכל בשר.
שרפואתי בידיך. ומיתתי בידיך. יהי רצון מלפניך שתרפאני רפואה שלמה.
ויעלה זכרוני ותפלתי לפניך כתפלת חזקיהו בחלותו. ואם קרבה עת פקודתי
למות. תהא מיתתי כפרה לכל חטאתי ולכל עונותי ולכל פשעי שחטאתי
ושעויתי ושפשתי לפניך מיום היותי על האדמה עד השעה הזאת ותן חלקי
בגן עדן. וזכני לעולם הבא הצפון לצדיקים. ותודיעני ארח חיים שבע
שמחות את פניך נעימות בימינך נצח: ברוך אתה יי שומע תפלה:

אנא בכח גדולת ימינך, תתיר צרורה:
קבל רנת עמך, שגבנו, טהרנו נורא:
נא גבור, דורשי יחודך כבבת שמרם:
ברכם, טהרם, רחמי צדקתך, תמיד גמלם:
חסין קדוש, ברוב טובך, נהל עדתך:
שועתנו קבל, ושמע צעקתנו, יודע תעלומות:
(בלחש) ברוך שם כבוד מלכותו לעולם ועד:
ואומר ויהי נועם יושב בסתר עליון ואחר כך:

ויהי בשלשים שנה ברביעי בחמשה לחדש ואני בתוך הגולה על נהר כבר
נפתחו השמים ואראה מראות אלקים: בשנת מות המלך עזיהו ואראה את
אדני ישב על כסא רם ונשא. ושוליו מלאים את ההיכל: שרפים עמדים
ממעל לו. שש כנפים שש כנפים לאחד. בשתים יכסה פניו. ובשתים יכסה
רגליו. ובשתים יעופף: וקרא זה אל זה ואמר קדוש קדוש קדוש יי צבקות
מלא כל הארץ כבודו: שמע ישראל יי אלקינו יי אחד: יי הוא האלקים. יי
הוא האלקים: יי מלך. יי מלך. יי ימלך לעלם ועד: משה אמת ותורתו אמת:
לישועתך קויתי יי: שמח נפש עבדך. כי אליך יי נפשי אשא: בידך אפקיד
רוחי. פדיתה אותי יי קל אמת: יהיו לרצון אמרי פי. והגיון לבי לפניך יי צורי
וגואלי:

Funeral Service
INTRODUCTORY PSALMS AT THE FUNERAL SERVICE:

Psalm 49

פרק מט

א לַמְנַצֵּחַ | לִבְנֵי־קֹרַח מִזְמוֹר: ב שִׁמְעוּ־זֹאת כָּל־הָעַמִּים הַאֲזִינוּ כָּל־יֹשְׁבֵי חָלֶד: ג גַּם־בְּנֵי אָדָם גַּם־בְּנֵי־אִישׁ יַחַד עָשִׁיר וְאֶבְיוֹן: ד פִּי יְדַבֵּר חָכְמוֹת וְהָגוּת לִבִּי תְבוּנוֹת: ה אַטֶּה לְמָשָׁל אָזְנִי אֶפְתַּח בְּכִנּוֹר חִידָתִי: ו לָמָּה אִירָא בִּימֵי רָע עֲוֹן עֲקֵבַי יְסוּבֵּנִי: ז הַבֹּטְחִים עַל־חֵילָם וּבְרֹב עָשְׁרָם יִתְהַלָּלוּ: ח אָח לֹא־פָדֹה יִפְדֶּה אִישׁ לֹא־יִתֵּן לֵאלֹהִים כָּפְרוֹ: ט וְיֵקַר פִּדְיוֹן נַפְשָׁם וְחָדַל לְעוֹלָם: י וִיחִי־עוֹד לָנֶצַח לֹא יִרְאֶה הַשָּׁחַת: יא כִּי יִרְאֶה | חֲכָמִים יָמוּתוּ יַחַד כְּסִיל וָבַעַר יֹאבֵדוּ וְעָזְבוּ לַאֲחֵרִים חֵילָם: יב קִרְבָּם בָּתֵּימוֹ | לְעוֹלָם מִשְׁכְּנֹתָם לְדֹר וָדֹר קָרְאוּ בִשְׁמוֹתָם עֲלֵי אֲדָמוֹת: יג וְאָדָם בִּיקָר בַּל־יָלִין נִמְשַׁל כַּבְּהֵמוֹת נִדְמוּ: יד זֶה דַרְכָּם כֵּסֶל לָמוֹ וְאַחֲרֵיהֶם | בְּפִיהֶם יִרְצוּ סֶלָה: טו כַּצֹּאן | לִשְׁאוֹל שַׁתּוּ מָוֶת יִרְעֵם וַיִּרְדּוּ בָם יְשָׁרִים | לַבֹּקֶר וְצִירָם [וְצוּרָם] לְבַלּוֹת שְׁאוֹל מִזְּבֻל לוֹ: טז אַךְ־אֱלֹהִים יִפְדֶּה נַפְשִׁי מִיַּד־שְׁאוֹל כִּי יִקָּחֵנִי סֶלָה: יז אַל־תִּירָא כִּי־יַעֲשִׁר אִישׁ כִּי־יִרְבֶּה כְּבוֹד בֵּיתוֹ: יח כִּי לֹא בְמוֹתוֹ יִקַּח הַכֹּל לֹא־יֵרֵד אַחֲרָיו כְּבוֹדוֹ: יט כִּי־נַפְשׁוֹ בְּחַיָּיו יְבָרֵךְ וְיוֹדֻךָ כִּי־תֵיטִיב לָךְ: כ תָּבוֹא עַד־דּוֹר אֲבוֹתָיו עַד־נֵצַח לֹא יִרְאוּ־אוֹר: כא אָדָם בִּיקָר וְלֹא יָבִין נִמְשַׁל כַּבְּהֵמוֹת נִדְמוּ:

1. To the chief musician, a psalm by the sons of Korach.
2. Hear this, all peoples, listen, all inhabitants of the decaying world!
3. Sons of Adam and sons of men, rich and poor together.
4. My mouth shall speak wisdom, and the meditation of my heart shall be of understanding.
5. I will incline my ear to a parable, I will begin to solve, to the accompaniment of a harp, my riddle.
6. Why should I fear in the days of evil? The iniquity I trod upon surrounds me.
7. Those who trust in their wealth and take pride in their great riches.
8. A man will not redeem his brother, neither can he give to God his ransom.
9. The redemption of their soul is too costly, and it shall cease to be forever.
10. Shall he then live forever, shall he never see the grave?
11. For he sees that wise men die, the fools and senseless perish equally and leave their wealth to others.
12. Their inner thoughts are that their house [will last] forever, their homes for generation after generation; [for] they have proclaimed their names throughout the lands.
13. But man does not endure in his splendor, he is likened to the silenced animals.
14. This is their way – their folly remains with them, and [yet] their descendants take pleasure in their speech, Selah.
15. Like sheep, they are destined for the grave; death shall be their shepherd, and the upright shall dominate them at morning, their form will be consumed in the grave; [it will not remain] their dwelling-place.
16. But God will redeem my soul from the [grasp of] the grave, for He will take me [to Himself], Selah.
17. Fear not when a man grows rich, when the glory of his house is increased.
18. For when he dies, he shall carry nothing away, his glory will not descend after him.

19. Because while he lived, he blessed his soul [saying]: they will praise you because you have done well for yourself.
20. He will join the generation of his fathers, they shall not see light for all eternity.
21. Man with [all his] splendor, [but] without understanding, is likened to the silenced animals.

COMMENTARY

The primary theme of Psalm 49 deals with the relationship between our material possessions and our moral and spiritual purpose in life. It is through the fulfillment of our spiritual and moral purpose in life and an understanding that all of our material possessions are but a means to this end that we can rescue our spiritual existence in this world. Our goal in this world is to transcend our fleeting existence on earth and enter into the immortal when our body dies. If, however, we fail to recognize our true purpose in life, and regard the acquisition of material wealth as an end in itself, then we will forfeit our immortality not only here on earth but also in heaven above, and our existence will not continue beyond the grave. This psalm calls upon all the communities of men, as well as upon every one of us irrespective of class and social position, to take this truth to heart. This is a basic truth, writes the psalmist, which no one can afford to dismiss lightly.

Psalm 16

פרק טז

א מִכְתָּם לְדָוִד שָׁמְרֵנִי אֵל כִּי־חָסִיתִי בָךְ: ב אָמַרְתְּ לַיהֹוָה אֲדֹנָי אָתָּה טוֹבָתִי בַּל־עָלֶיךָ: ג לִקְדוֹשִׁים אֲשֶׁר־בָּאָרֶץ הֵמָּה וְאַדִּירֵי כָּל־חֶפְצִי־בָם: ד יִרְבּוּ עַצְּבוֹתָם אַחֵר מָהָרוּ בַּל־אַסִּיךְ נִסְכֵּיהֶם מִדָּם וּבַל־אֶשָּׂא אֶת־שְׁמוֹתָם עַל־שְׂפָתָי: ה יְהֹוָה מְנָת־חֶלְקִי וְכוֹסִי אַתָּה תּוֹמִיךְ גּוֹרָלִי: ו חֲבָלִים נָפְלוּ־לִי בַּנְּעִמִים אַף־נַחֲלָת שָׁפְרָה עָלָי:

זְ אֲבָרֵךְ אֶת־יְהֹוָה אֲשֶׁר יְעָצָנִי אַף־לֵילוֹת יִסְּרוּנִי כִלְיוֹתָי:
ח שִׁוִּיתִי יְהֹוָה לְנֶגְדִּי תָמִיד כִּי מִימִינִי בַּל־אֶמּוֹט: ט לָכֵן
שָׂמַח לִבִּי וַיָּגֶל כְּבוֹדִי אַף־בְּשָׂרִי יִשְׁכֹּן לָבֶטַח: י כִּי
לֹא־תַעֲזֹב נַפְשִׁי לִשְׁאוֹל לֹא־תִתֵּן חֲסִידְךָ לִרְאוֹת שָׁחַת:
יא תּוֹדִיעֵנִי אֹרַח חַיִּים שֹׂבַע שְׂמָחוֹת אֶת־פָּנֶיךָ נְעִמוֹת
בִּימִינְךָ נֶצַח:

1. A Michtam of David. Preserve me, Almighty, for I have taken refuge in You.

2. You said to Adonay, "You are my Master, I have no well-being without You."

3. Due to the holy that are in the earth, and the mighty, are all my desires [fulfilled].

4. Let their sufferings multiply, those who follow another [sovereignty]; I will not pour their libations of blood, nor carry their names upon my lips.

5. Adonay is the portion of my inheritance and of my cup; You guide my fate.

6. The portions that have fallen to me are in pleasant places; a beautiful inheritance is mine.

7. I will bless Adonay, who has given me counsel; even for the nights in which my mind admonished me.

8. I have set Adonay before me always; for surely He is at my right hand, I will not be moved.

9. Therefore my heart rejoices and my soul exults; also my flesh will dwell in safety.

10. For You will not abandon my soul to the grave, nor will You allow Your devoted one to see the pit.

11. You will make known to me the path of life; fullness of joy is in Your presence; pleasantness is at Your right hand, evermore.

COMMENTARY

The superscription "Michtam" seems to denote a psalm which King David has recorded for himself as an everlasting memorial, a tenet to which he would adhere forever.[1] Psalms 56–60 all have the same superscription and seem to record David's emotions and thoughts at crucial moments in his life.

In this psalm, David records for everlasting remembrance a moment at which he escaped unscathed from direst peril.

King David, the most powerful man in his period, recognized his mistake and devised for himself the motto *Shomreini El,* "Protect me, O God," thus placing himself completely and trustingly under the sole and direct care of God.

Psalm 90

פרק צ

א תְּפִלָּה לְמֹשֶׁה אִישׁ־הָאֱלֹהִים אֲדֹנָי מָעוֹן אַתָּה הָיִיתָ לָּנוּ בְּדֹר וָדֹר: ב בְּטֶרֶם | הָרִים יֻלָּדוּ וַתְּחוֹלֵל אֶרֶץ וְתֵבֵל וּמֵעוֹלָם עַד־עוֹלָם אַתָּה אֵל: ג תָּשֵׁב אֱנוֹשׁ עַד־דַּכָּא וַתֹּאמֶר שׁוּבוּ בְנֵי־אָדָם: ד כִּי אֶלֶף שָׁנִים בְּעֵינֶיךָ כְּיוֹם אֶתְמוֹל כִּי יַעֲבֹר וְאַשְׁמוּרָה בַלָּיְלָה: ה זְרַמְתָּם שֵׁנָה יִהְיוּ בַּבֹּקֶר כֶּחָצִיר יַחֲלֹף: ו בַּבֹּקֶר יָצִיץ וְחָלָף לָעֶרֶב יְמוֹלֵל וְיָבֵשׁ: ז כִּי־כָלִינוּ בְאַפֶּךָ וּבַחֲמָתְךָ נִבְהָלְנוּ: ח שַׁתָּ [שַׁתָּה] עֲוֹנֹתֵינוּ לְנֶגְדֶּךָ עֲלֻמֵנוּ לִמְאוֹר פָּנֶיךָ: ט כִּי כָל־יָמֵינוּ פָּנוּ בְעֶבְרָתֶךָ כִּלִּינוּ שָׁנֵינוּ כְמוֹ־הֶגֶה: י יְמֵי שְׁנוֹתֵינוּ | בָּהֶם שִׁבְעִים שָׁנָה וְאִם בִּגְבוּרֹת | שְׁמוֹנִים שָׁנָה וְרָהְבָּם עָמָל וָאָוֶן כִּי־גָז חִישׁ וַנָּעֻפָה: יא מִי־יוֹדֵעַ עֹז אַפֶּךָ וּכְיִרְאָתְךָ עֶבְרָתֶךָ: יב לִמְנוֹת יָמֵינוּ כֵּן הוֹדַע וְנָבִא לְבַב חָכְמָה: יג שׁוּבָה יְהוָה עַד־מָתָי וְהִנָּחֵם עַל־עֲבָדֶיךָ: יד שַׂבְּעֵנוּ בַבֹּקֶר חַסְדֶּךָ וּנְרַנְּנָה וְנִשְׂמְחָה בְּכָל־יָמֵינוּ: טו שַׂמְּחֵנוּ כִּימוֹת עִנִּיתָנוּ שְׁנוֹת רָאִינוּ רָעָה:

טז יֵרָאֶה אֶל־עֲבָדֶיךָ פָעֳלֶךָ וַהֲדָרְךָ עַל־בְּנֵיהֶם: יז וִיהִי |
נֹעַם אֲדֹנָי אֱלֹהֵינוּ עָלֵינוּ וּמַעֲשֵׂה יָדֵינוּ כּוֹנְנָה עָלֵינוּ
וּמַעֲשֵׂה יָדֵינוּ כּוֹנְנֵהוּ:

1. A prayer of Moses, the man of God: My Master, a dwelling [-place] have You been for us in every generation.

2. Before the mountains were born, and You brought forth the earth and the inhabited world, from world to world You are Almighty.

3. You push man down until the crushing point, and You say, "Return, children of man!"

4. For a thousand years are in Your eyes like the yesterday that has just passed, and like a night watch.

5. The stream of their life is [but] slumber, in the morning, they are as grass, freshly grown.

6. [If] in the morning it blossoms and grows afresh, by evening it is cut off and shriveled.

7. So are we consumed by Your anger, and by Your rage are we terrified.

8. You have set our iniquities before You, the sins of our youth before the light of Your countenance.

9. For all our days vanish in Your wrath; we terminate our years like an unspoken word.

10. The days of our years in them [total] seventy years, and with strength, eighty years, and their pride is frustration and falsehood; for, cut off quickly, we fly away.

11. Who can [get to] know the force of Your anger? And like the fear of You, so is Your wrath.

12. To count our days, teach us and we will acquire a heart of wisdom.

13. Turn Adonay – how long? And change Your mind about Your servants.

14. Satisfy us in the morning with your kindness, and we will sing and rejoice throughout our days.

15. Make us rejoice like the days You afflicted us, the year [when] we saw evil.

16. Let be revealed to Your servants, Your deeds and Your splendor be upon their children.

17. May the pleasantness of my Master our God be upon us, and the work of our hands established for us, and the work of our hands – establish it.

COMMENTARY

Psalm 90 is a *tefilah* in which Moses, the man chosen by God as the instrument of His sovereignty, reminds himself of the significance of his historic mission among mankind. He does so by reviewing the significance of the centuries of human development that had passed before he was entrusted with his great calling. The central theme of this psalm is that man would descend to utter nonentity if it were not for his rebirth, which can be expected to come to pass if Israel fulfills its mission.

OPTIONAL PSALMS

Psalm 1

פרק א

א אַשְׁרֵי־הָאִישׁ אֲשֶׁר לֹא הָלַךְ בַּעֲצַת רְשָׁעִים וּבְדֶרֶךְ חַטָּאִים לֹא עָמָד וּבְמוֹשַׁב לֵצִים לֹא יָשָׁב: ב כִּי אִם־בְּתוֹרַת יְהֹוָה חֶפְצוֹ וּבְתוֹרָתוֹ יֶהְגֶּה יוֹמָם וָלָיְלָה: ג וְהָיָה כְּעֵץ שָׁתוּל עַל־פַּלְגֵי מָיִם אֲשֶׁר פִּרְיוֹ | יִתֵּן בְּעִתּוֹ וְעָלֵהוּ לֹא יִבּוֹל וְכֹל אֲשֶׁר־יַעֲשֶׂה יַצְלִיחַ: ד לֹא־כֵן הָרְשָׁעִים כִּי אִם־כַּמֹּץ אֲשֶׁר־תִּדְּפֶנּוּ רוּחַ: ה עַל־כֵּן | לֹא־יָקֻמוּ רְשָׁעִים בַּמִּשְׁפָּט וְחַטָּאִים בַּעֲדַת צַדִּיקִים: ו כִּי־יוֹדֵעַ יְהֹוָה דֶּרֶךְ צַדִּיקִים וְדֶרֶךְ רְשָׁעִים תֹּאבֵד:

1. Fortunate is the man who has not walked in the counsel of the wicked, and in the way of the sinful he has not stood, and in the seat of the scornful he has not sat.

2.	But only in the Torah of Adonay is his desire, and in His Torah he meditates day and night.

3.	He will be like a tree set into the ground near streams of water, which yields its fruit in its season, and whose leaf does not wither; and in whatever he does he will succeed.

4.	Not so the wicked, who are like the chaff which the wind drives away.

5.	Therefore, the wicked will not stand up in judgment, nor the sinful in the assembly of the righteous.

6.	For Adonay regards the way of the righteous, and the way of the wicked will be lost.

COMMENTARY

Psalm 1, *Ashrei Ha'Ish*, is a lesson concerning the questions "To whom shall the future belong?" and "Who shall truly stride forward toward all the goals of mankind?" The answer is the righteous person who has never taken counsel from the wicked and whose life knows of no deliberate transgression of the law. This is the person who will attain the spiritual goals of humanity. The righteous individual is likened to a tree that has deliberately planted itself in the place where it can receive the best nourishment. The term *palgei mayim* (verse 3) denotes many separate branches of water all springing from the same source. Torah as well emanates from the One Source of the Divine Truth and saturates life within and without in all its aspects, making it bear fruit. The wicked person is influenced by passion and levity, whereas the righteous person is influenced and nourished by the Torah, which will give "its fruit in its due season."

Psalm 15

פרק טו

א מִזְמוֹר לְדָוִד יְהֹוָה מִי־יָגוּר בְּאָהֳלֶךָ מִי־יִשְׁכֹּן בְּהַר
קָדְשֶׁךָ: ב הוֹלֵךְ תָּמִים וּפֹעֵל צֶדֶק וְדֹבֵר אֱמֶת בִּלְבָבוֹ:
ג לֹא־רָגַל | עַל־לְשֹׁנוֹ לֹא־עָשָׂה לְרֵעֵהוּ רָעָה וְחֶרְפָּה
לֹא־נָשָׂא עַל־קְרֹבוֹ: ד נִבְזֶה | בְּעֵינָיו נִמְאָס וְאֶת־יִרְאֵי

יְהֹוָה יְכַבֵּד נִשְׁבַּע לְהָרַע וְלֹא יָמִר: ה כַּסְפּוֹ | לֹא־נָתַן בְּנֶשֶׁךְ וְשֹׁחַד עַל־נָקִי לֹא־לָקָח עֹשֵׂה אֵלֶּה לֹא יִמּוֹט לְעוֹלָם:

1. A Psalm of David. Adonay, who will sojourn in your Tabernacle? Who will dwell upon Your holy mountain?
2. He who walks with wholehearted integrity and deals righteously and speaks truth in his heart.
3. He who has no slander on his tongue, who has done his friend no evil, nor cast disgrace upon his fellow man.
4. In whose eyes a vile person is despised, and those who fear Adonay he honors; though he makes a vow to his own hurt, he does not change [his oath].
5. His money he has not lent out at usury, and a bribe against the innocent he has not taken; whoever does these things will not be moved forever.

COMMENTARY

Psalm 15 speaks of the traits of the individual who is worthy of living in the sanctuary of the Lord. This individual is one who puts all his trust in his dutiful striving to fulfill the will of the Lord. The central features that the psalmist selected relate to interpersonal relationships. The psalmist reminds us that we should not be misled to believe that only the fulfill-ment of our duties to God is of importance in the House of the Lord. Rather, human relationships of everyday life and the way we treat other human beings are fundamental to being worthy of entering the House of the Lord.

Psalm 23

פרק כג

א מִזְמוֹר לְדָוִד יְהֹוָה רֹעִי לֹא אֶחְסָר: ב בִּנְאוֹת דֶּשֶׁא יַרְבִּיצֵנִי עַל־מֵי מְנֻחוֹת יְנַהֲלֵנִי: ג נַפְשִׁי יְשׁוֹבֵב יַנְחֵנִי בְמַעְגְּלֵי־צֶדֶק לְמַעַן שְׁמוֹ: ד גַּם כִּי־אֵלֵךְ בְּגֵיא צַלְמָוֶת

לֹא־אִירָא רָע כִּי־אַתָּה עִמָּדִי שִׁבְטְךָ וּמִשְׁעַנְתֶּךָ הֵמָּה
יְנַחֲמֻנִי: ה תַּעֲרֹךְ לְפָנַי | שֻׁלְחָן נֶגֶד צֹרְרָי דִּשַּׁנְתָּ בַשֶּׁמֶן
רֹאשִׁי כּוֹסִי רְוָיָה: ו אַךְ טוֹב וָחֶסֶד יִרְדְּפוּנִי כָּל־יְמֵי חַיָּי
וְשַׁבְתִּי בְּבֵית־יְהֹוָה לְאֹרֶךְ יָמִים:

1. A Psalm to David, Adonay is my shepherd, I shall lack nothing.

2. In lush pastures He makes me lie, beside tranquil waters, He leads me.

3. My soul, He restores, He directs me in paths of righteousness for the sake of His name.

4. Though I walk in the valley of the shadow of death, I will fear no evil, for You are with me; Your rod and Your staff, they comfort me.

5. You prepare a table for me in the full presence of my enemies, You anoint my head with oil; my cup overflows.

6. [May] only good and kindness pursue me all the days of my life, and I shall dwell in the House

7. of Adonay for long days.

COMMENTARY

Psalm 23 expresses the most intimate relationship of the individual human being with God and gives us a strikingly clear insight into King David's soul. The Lord is my shepherd, therefore I suffer no want. I do not miss what I do not have. I do not feel its lack, since it is God, my shepherd, who has seen fit to deny me of it. He shows me His love and compassion by providing me with that which is good for me and denying me that which will harm me. "I will fear no evil" because the ever-presence of the Lord is my guiding light even in the darkest of moments.

The following verses are recited immediately after the eulogies:

גדל העצה ורב העלילייה אשר עיניך פקחות על כל דרכי בני אדם לתת
לאיש כדרכיו וכפרי מעלליו (ירמיהו לב, יט): להגיד כי ישר ידוד צורי ולא
עולתה בו (תהלים צב, טז): ידוד נתן וידוד לקח יהי שם ידוד מברך (איוב א,
כא): והוא רחום יכפר עון ולא ישחית והרבה להשיב אפו ולא יעיר כל חמתו
(תהלים כ, י):

NULLIFICATION OF VOWS

Some communities have the custom to nullify the vows of the deceased

For a male the following is recited:

אחינו אתה: מותרים לך, מותרים לך, מותרים לך.
מחולים לך, מחולים לך, מחולים לך:
שרוים לך, שרוים לך, שרוים לך:

אין כאן נדרים, אין כאן שבועות, אין כאן קבלות, אין כאן הסכמות, אין
כאן מנהגים, אין כאן חרמים, אין כאן אסורים, אין כאן קונמות, אבל יש
כאן מחילה וסליחה וכפרה בין בעולם הזה בין בעולם הבא: כשם שהסכימו
והתירו לך בית דין של מטה כך יסכימו ויתירו לך בית דין של מעלה וסר
עונך וחטאתך תכופר (וחוזרים ג'פ):

אנא בכח גדולת ימינך, תתיר צרורה:
קבל רנת עמך, שגבנו, טהרנו נורא:
נא גבור, דורשי יחודך כבבת שמרם:
ברכם, טהרם, רחמי צדקתך, תמיד גמלם:
חסין קדוש, ברוב טובך, נהל עדתך:
שועתנו קבל, ושמע צעקתנו, יודע תעלומות:
(בלחש) ברוך שם כבוד מלכותו לעולם ועד:

בשנת מות המלך עזיהו ואראה את אדני ישב על כסא רם ונשא ושוליו
מלאים את ההיכל: שרפים עמדים ממעל לו שש כנפים שש כנפים לאחד
בשתים יכסה פניו ובשתים יכסה רגליו ובשתים יעופף: וקרא זה אל זה ואמר
קדוש קדוש קדוש ידוד צבקות מלא כל הארץ כבודו: וינעו אמות הספים
מקול הקורא והבית ימלא עשן:

For a female the following is recited:

אחותנו את: מותרים ליך, מותרים ליך, מותרים ליך.
מחולים ליך, מחולים ליך, מחולים ליך:
שרוים ליך, שרוים ליך, שרוים ליך:

אין כאן נדרים, אין כאן שבועות, אין כאן קבלות, אין כאן הסכמות, אין
כאן מנהגים, אין כאן חרמים, אין כאן אסורים, אין כאן קונמות, אבל יש

כאן מחילה וסליחה וכפרה בין בעולם הזה בין בעולם הבא: כשם שהסכימו
והתירו לך בית דין של מטה כך יסכימו ויתירו לך בית דין של מעלה וסר
עונך וחטאתך תכופר (וחוזרים ג"פ):

The mourners recite Half Kaddish   האבלים אומרים חצי קדיש:

קדיש יהא שלמא

Yitgadal veyitkadash shmeh raba. Be'alma di bera chiruteh ve'yamlich Malchuteh Ve'yatzmach purkaneh, vikarev meshichah (amen) Be'cha-ye-chon uv-yo-me-chon uv-chayeh dechol bet Yisrael ba'agalah uvizman kariv ve-imru Amen.

יתגדל ויתקדש שמה רבא: אמן בעלמא די ברא כרעותה, וימליך מלכותה, ויצמח פרקנה, ויקרב משיחה: אמן בחייכון וביומיכון, ובחיי דכל בית ישראל, בעגלא ובזמן קריב, ואמרו אמן: אמן

Ye'he she-meh rabah mevarach le-alam U'l-almeh almaya yitbarach, ve-yish-ta-bach, ve-yit-pa-ar, ve-yitromam ve-yitnaseh ve-yit-hadar ve-yit-aleh, ve-yit-halal shemeh de-kud-shah berich hu. (amen) Le-ela min kol birchata shirata tush-be-cha-ta ve-ne-cha-ma-ta, da'amiran be'alma ve'imru Amen.

יהא שמה רבא מברך, לעלם ולעלמי עלמיא יתברך, וישתבח, ויתפאר, ויתרומם, ויתנשא, ויתהדר, ויתעלה, ויתהל, שמה דקדשא בריך הוא: אמן לעלא מן כל ברכתא, שירתא, תשבחתא ונחמתא, דאמירן בעלמא, ואמרו אמן: אמן

Yehe shelamah rabah min shemaya, chayyim ve-sava vishuah ve-nechamah ve-shezava ur-fuah ug-ulah us-lichah ve'chaparah, ve-revah ve'hatsalah lanu ul-chol amo Yisrael ve-imru Amen.

יהא שלמא רבא מן שמיא, חיים, ושבע, וישועה, ונחמה, ושיזבא, ורפואה, וגאלה, וסליחה, וכפרה, ורוח, והצלה, לנו ולכל עמו ישראל, ואמרו אמן: אמן

Oseh shalom bim-ro-mav, hu be-rachamav ya-aseh shalom alenu ve-al kol amo Yisrael ve-imru Amen.

עושה שלום במרומיו, הוא ברחמיו, יעשה שלום עלינו, ועל כל עמו ישראל, ואמרו אמן: אמן

Some communities recite Tzidduk Hadin prior to going to the cemetery

צידוק הדין

צַדִּיק אַתָּה יְהֹוָה וְיָשָׁר מִשְׁפָּטֶיךָ: צַדִּיק יְהֹוָה בְּכָל דְּרָכָיו וְחָסִיד בְּכָל מַעֲשָׂיו:
צִדְקָתְךָ צֶדֶק לְעוֹלָם וְתוֹרָתְךָ אֱמֶת: מִשְׁפְּטֵי יְהֹוָה אֱמֶת צָדְקוּ יַחְדָּו: בַּאֲשֶׁר
דְּבַר מֶלֶךְ שִׁלְטוֹן וּמִי יֹאמַר לוֹ מַה תַּעֲשֶׂה: וְהוּא בְאֶחָד וּמִי יְשִׁיבֶנּוּ וְנַפְשׁוֹ
אִוְּתָה וַיָּעַשׂ: קָטֹן וְגָדוֹל שָׁם הוּא וְעֶבֶד חָפְשִׁי מֵאֲדֹנָיו: הֵן בַּעֲבָדָיו לֹא יַאֲמִין
וּבְמַלְאָכָיו יָשִׂים תָּהֳלָה: אַף כִּי אֱנוֹשׁ רִמָּה וּבֶן אָדָם תּוֹלֵעָה: הַצּוּר תָּמִים פָּעֳלוֹ
כִּי כָל דְּרָכָיו מִשְׁפָּט אֵל אֱמוּנָה וְאֵין עָוֶל צַדִּיק וְיָשָׁר הוּא: דַּיַּן הָאֱמֶת. שֹׁפֵט
צֶדֶק וֶאֱמֶת. בָּרוּךְ דַּיַּן הָאֱמֶת. כִּי כָל מִשְׁפָּטָיו צֶדֶק וֶאֱמֶת:

While the coffin is being escorted the following Psalm is recited
Introduction to Psalm:

ויהי נעם אדני אלקינו עלינו ומעשה ידינו כוננה עלינו ומעשה ידינו כוננהו:

Psalm 91

פרק צא

א יֹשֵׁב בְּסֵתֶר עֶלְיוֹן בְּצֵל שַׁדַּי יִתְלוֹנָן: ב אֹמַר לַיהֹוָה
מַחְסִי וּמְצוּדָתִי אֱלֹהַי אֶבְטַח־בּוֹ: ג כִּי הוּא יַצִּילְךָ מִפַּח
יָקוּשׁ מִדֶּבֶר הַוּוֹת: ד בְּאֶבְרָתוֹ | יָסֶךְ לָךְ וְתַחַת כְּנָפָיו
תֶּחְסֶה צִנָּה וְסֹחֵרָה אֲמִתּוֹ: ה לֹא־תִירָא מִפַּחַד לָיְלָה מֵחֵץ
יָעוּף יוֹמָם: ו מִדֶּבֶר בָּאֹפֶל יַהֲלֹךְ מִקֶּטֶב יָשׁוּד צָהֳרָיִם:
ז יִפֹּל מִצִּדְּךָ | אֶלֶף וּרְבָבָה מִימִינֶךָ אֵלֶיךָ לֹא יִגָּשׁ: ח רַק
בְּעֵינֶיךָ תַבִּיט וְשִׁלֻּמַת רְשָׁעִים תִּרְאֶה: ט כִּי־אַתָּה יְהֹוָה
מַחְסִי עֶלְיוֹן שַׂמְתָּ מְעוֹנֶךָ: י לֹא־תְאֻנֶּה אֵלֶיךָ רָעָה וְנֶגַע
לֹא־יִקְרַב בְּאָהֳלֶךָ: יא כִּי מַלְאָכָיו יְצַוֶּה־לָּךְ לִשְׁמָרְךָ
בְּכָל־דְּרָכֶיךָ: יב עַל־כַּפַּיִם יִשָּׂאוּנְךָ פֶּן־תִּגֹּף בָּאֶבֶן רַגְלֶךָ:

יג עַל־שַׁחַל וָפֶתֶן תִּדְרֹךְ תִּרְמֹס כְּפִיר וְתַנִּין: יד כִּי בִי
חָשַׁק וַאֲפַלְּטֵהוּ אֲשַׂגְּבֵהוּ כִּי־יָדַע שְׁמִי: טו יִקְרָאֵנִי
וְאֶעֱנֵהוּ עִמּוֹ אָנֹכִי בְצָרָה אֲחַלְּצֵהוּ וַאֲכַבְּדֵהוּ: טז אֹרֶךְ
יָמִים אַשְׂבִּיעֵהוּ וְאַרְאֵהוּ בִּישׁוּעָתִי:

1. He who dwells in the shelter of the Supreme One, under the protection of Shaddai, He will abide.

2. I say of Adonay, "[He is] my refuge and my stronghold, my God in whom I trust."

3. For He will save you from the snare-trap, from destructive pestilence.

4. With His wings He will cover you and beneath His wings, you will find refuge; His truth is a shield, a full shield.

5. You will not fear the terror of night, nor the arrow that flies by day.

6. The pestilence that prowls in darkness, nor the deadly plague that ravages at noon.

7. A thousand will fall at your [left] side, and ten thousand at your [right] side, but it shall not come near you.

8. Only with your eyes will you behold and see the punishment of the wicked.

9. For you [have proclaimed]: "Adonay is my refuge," the Supreme One you have made your dwelling

10. No evil shall befall you, and no plague shall come near your tent.

11. For His angels He will command on your behalf – to guard you in all your ways.

12. They will carry you upon their hands, lest you hurt your foot on a rock.

13. You will tread upon lion and snake, you will trample young lion and serpent.

14. Because he clings to Me with desire, I will save him; will strengthen him, for he knows My name.

15. When he calls upon Me, I will answer him; I am with him in distress, I will free him and honor him.

16. I will satiate him with longevity, and will let him see My deliverance.

COMMENTARY

This psalm continues the thought expressed in Psalm 90, in which Moses spoke of the turning point that his mission marked in the history of mankind. Moses declares that the nation which he had been called to lead was to receive both freedom and law from the hands of God and thus was assured of attaining a state of supreme bliss on earth. In this psalm Moses sings of the protection and the historic immortality that the nation will find under the direct guidance of God.

The Funeral Service – at the Cemetery סדר הלוייה בבית העלמין

מי שלא הי' תוך שלשים יום בבית העלמין, כשרואה אל הקברים, מברך:
One who has not been to a cemetery for thirty days recites the following blessing upon seeing the graves:

בָּרוּךְ אַתָּה יְהֹוָה אֱלֹהֵינוּ מֶלֶךְ הָעוֹלָם אֲשֶׁר יָצַר אֶתְכֶם בְּדִין, וְזָן אֶתְכֶם בְּדִין, וְכִלְכֵּל אֶתְכֶם בְּדִין, וְהֶחֱיָה אֶתְכֶם בְּדִין, וְהֵמִית אֶתְכֶם בְּדִין, וְיוֹדֵעַ מִסְפַּר כֻּלְּכֶם, וְהוּא עָתִיד לְהַחֲיוֹתְכֶם וּלְהָקִימְכֶם בְּדִין לְחַיֵּי הָעוֹלָם הַבָּא: בָּרוּךְ אַתָּה יְהֹוָה מְחַיֵּה הַמֵּתִים:

יִחְיוּ מֵתֶיךָ, נְבֵלָתִי יְקוּמוּן, הָקִיצוּ וְרַנְּנוּ שֹׁכְנֵי עָפָר, כִּי טַל אוֹרֹת טַלֶּיךָ, וָאָרֶץ רְפָאִים תַּפִּיל: וְהוּא רַחוּם יְכַפֵּר עָוֹן וְלֹא־יַשְׁחִית וְהִרְבָּה לְהָשִׁיב אַפּוֹ וְלֹא־יָעִיר כָּל־חֲמָתוֹ:

BURIAL קבורה

בשעת כסוי הקבר בעפר אומרים:
As the coffin is covered with earth, the following is recited:

וְהוּא רַחוּם יְכַפֵּר עָוֹן וְלֹא־יַשְׁחִית וְהִרְבָּה לְהָשִׁיב אַפּוֹ וְלֹא־יָעִיר כָּל־חֲמָתוֹ:
אַתָּה גִיבּוֹר לְעוֹלָם אֲדֹנָי מְחַיֶּה מֵתִים אַתָּה רַב לְהוֹשִׁיעַ. מְכַלְכֵּל חַיִּים בְּחֶסֶד
מְחַיֶּה מֵתִים בְּרַחֲמִים רַבִּים סוֹמֵךְ נוֹפְלִים וְרוֹפֵא חוֹלִים וּמַתִּיר אֲסוּרִים וּמְקַיֵּם
אֱמוּנָתוֹ לִישֵׁנֵי עָפָר, מִי כָמוֹךָ בַּעַל גְּבוּרוֹת וּמִי דוֹמֶה לָךְ מֶלֶךְ מֵמִית וּמְחַיֶּה
וּמַצְמִיחַ יְשׁוּעָה. וְנֶאֱמָן אַתָּה לְהַחֲיוֹת מֵתִים:

וְנָחֲךָ יְהֹוָה תָּמִיד וְהִשְׂבִּיעַ בְּצַחְצָחוֹת נַפְשֶׁךָ וְעַצְמֹתֶיךָ יַחֲלִיץ וְהָיִיתָ כְּגַן רָוֶה
וּכְמוֹצָא מַיִם אֲשֶׁר לֹא־יְכַזְּבוּ מֵימָיו (ישעיהו נח, יא): אָז יִבָּקַע כַּשַּׁחַר אוֹרֶךָ
וַאֲרֻכָתְךָ מְהֵרָה תִצְמָח וְהָלַךְ לְפָנֶיךָ צִדְקֶךָ כְּבוֹד יְהֹוָה יַאַסְפֶךָ (ישעיהו נח, ח):

After the grave is *completely* filled with earth, Hashkavah is recited.
After the Hashkava, Kaddish is recited.

Some communities recite Kaddish Le'Achadeta (facing page) while other
communities just recite Kaddish DeRabbanan (page following)

Introduction to Kaddish

רבי חנניה בן עקשיה אומר, רצה הקדוש ברוך הוא לזכות את ישראל, לפיכך
הרבה להם תורה ומצותו, שנאמר, יי חפץ למען צדקו יגדיל תורה ויאדיר:

Yitgadal veyitkadash shmeh raba. De-hu atid lehadata alma, ul-aha-a mitaya, Ul-shach-lala e-he-la, ulmifrak ha-ya-ya, ul-mivneh karta dirushlem, ul-me-ekar pulchanah de-elilayah me-ar-ah, ul-atavah pulchanah yakira dishmaya le-adreh ve-ziveh vikareh.

יתגדל ויתקדש שמה רבה. דהוא עתיד לחדתה עלמא, ולאחאה מיתיא, ולשכללא היכלא, ולמפרק חייא, ולמבני קרתא דרושלם, ולמעקר פלחנא דאליליא מארעא, ולאתבא פלחנא יקירא דשמיא להדרה וזיוה ויקרה.

Be'cha-ye-chon uv'yo-me-chon uv'chayeh dechol bet Yisrael ba-agalah uvizman kariv ve-imru Amen.

בחייכון וביומיכון ובחיי דכל בית ישראל בעגלא ובזמן קריב ואמרו אמן:

Ye-eh she-meh rabah mevarach le-alam le-almeh almaya yitbarach, ve-yish-ta-bach, ve-yit-pa-ar, ve-yit-aleh, ve-yit-alal shemeh de-kud-shah berich hu.

יהא שמה רבא מברך לעלם לעלמי עלמיא יתברך, וישתבח, ויתבאר, ויתרומם, ויתנשא, ויתהדר, ויתעלה, ויתהלל שמה דקדשא בריך הוא:

Le-ela min kol birchata shirata tush-be-cha-ta ve-ne-cha-ma-ta, da-amiran be-alma ve-imru Amen.

לעלא מן כל ברכתא שירתא תשבחתא ונחמתא, דאמירן בעלמא, ואמרו אמן:

Tit-keleh charbah, ve-haf-nah, umotanah, umar-inbeesheen, yaddeh minanah uminechon, ume-al amech Yisrael, ve-imru Amen.

תתכלי חרבא, וכפנא, ומותנא, ומרעין בישין, יעדי מננא ומנכון, ומעל עמה ישראל, ואמרו אמן:

Ye'he shelamah rabah min shemaya, chayyim ve-sava vishuah ve-nechamah ve-shezava ur-fuah ug-ulah us-lichah ve-chaparah, ve-revach ve-hatsalah lanu ul-chol amo Yisrael ve-imru Amen.

יהא שלמא רבא מן שמיא, חיים ושבע וישועה ונחמה ושזבא ורפואה וגאלה וסליחה וכפרה, ורוח והצלה לנו ולכל עמו ישראל ואמרו אמן.

Oseh shalom bim-ro-mav, hu be-rachamav ya-aseh shalom alenu ve-al kol amo Yisrael ve-imru Amen.

עשה שלום במרומיו הוא ברחמיו יעשה שלום עלינו ועל כל עמו ישראל, ואמרו אמן:

קדיש דרבנן

Yitgadal veyitkadash shmeh raba. Be'alma di bera chiruteh ve'yamlich Malchuteh Ve'yatzmach purkaneh, vikarev meshichah (amen) Be'cha-ye-chon uv-yo-me-chon uv-chayeh dechol bet Yisrael ba'agalah uvizman kariv ve-imru Amen.

יתגדל ויתקדש שמה רבא: אמן בעלמא די־ברא כרעותה, וימליך מלכותיה, ויצמח פרקנה, ויקרב משיחה: אמן בחייכוון וביומיכון, ובחיי דכל בית ישראל, בעגלא ובזמן קריב, ואמרו אמן: אמן

Ye'he she-meh rabah mevarach le-alam U'l-almeh almaya yitbarach, ve-yish-ta-bach, ve-yit-pa-ar, ve-yitromam ve-yitnaseh ve-yit-hadar ve-yit-aleh, ve-yit-halal shemeh de-kud-shah berich hu. (amen) Le-ela min kol birchata shirata tush-be-cha-ta ve-ne-cha-ma-ta, da'amiran be'alma ve'imru Amen.

יהא שמה רבה מברך, לעלם ולעלמי עלמיא יתברך, וישתבח, ויתפאר, ויתרומם, ויתנשא, ויתהדר, ויתעלה, ויתהלל, שמה דקדשא בריך הוא: אמן לעלא מן כל ברכתא, שירתא, תשבחתא ונחמתא, דאמירן בעלמא, ואמרו אמן: אמן

Al Yisrael ve'al Rabbanan ve'al Talmidehon ve'al kol talmideh talmidehon, de'askin be'orayta kadishta, di'batra hadin, ve'di bechol atar ve'atar. Ye'he lana u'lhon, u'lchon china, ve'chisda ve'rachamei min kadam mareh shemaya ve'ara ve'imru Amen

על ישראל, ועל רבנן, ועל תלמידיהון, ועל כל תלמידי תלמידיהון, דעסקין באוריתא קדשתא, די באתרא הדין, ודי בכל אתר ואתר, יהא לנא, ולהון, ולכון חנא, וחסדא, ורחמי, מן קדם מרא שמיא וארעא, ואמרו אמן: אמן

Yehe shelamah rabah min shemaya, chayyim ve-sava vishuah ve-nechamah ve-shezava ur-fuah ug-ulah us-lichah ve'chaparah, ve-revah ve'hatsalah lanu ul-chol amo Yisrael ve-imru Amen.

יהא שלמא רבא מן שמיא, חיים, ושבע, וישועה, ונחמה, ושיזבא, ורפואה, וגאלה, וסליחה, וכפרה, ורוח, והצלה, לנו ולכל עמו ישראל, ואמרו אמן: אמן

Oseh shalom bim-ro-mav, hu be-rachamav ya-aseh shalom alenu ve-al kol amo Yisrael ve-imru Amen.

עשה שלום במרומיו הוא ברחמיו יעשה שלום עלינו ועל כל עמו ישראל, ואמרו אמן:

Memorial Prayers – Hashkavot השכבות

השכבה לאיש

If the deceased is a scholar the following is introduction is recited:

וְהַחָכְמָה מֵאַיִן תִּמָּצֵא וְאֵיזֶה מְקוֹם בִּינָה: אַשְׁרֵי אָדָם מָצָא חָכְמָה וְאָדָם יָפִיק
תְּבוּנָה: מָה רַב טוּבְךָ אֲשֶׁר־צָפַנְתָּ לִּירֵאֶיךָ פָּעַלְתָּ לַחוֹסִים בָּךְ נֶגֶד בְּנֵי אָדָם:
מַה־יָּקָר חַסְדְּךָ אֱלֹהִים וּבְנֵי אָדָם בְּצֵל כְּנָפֶיךָ יֶחֱסָיוּן: יִרְוְיֻן מִדֶּשֶׁן בֵּיתֶךָ וְנַחַל
עֲדָנֶיךָ תַשְׁקֵם: טוֹב שֵׁם מִשֶּׁמֶן טוֹב וְיוֹם הַמָּוֶת מִיּוֹם הִוָּלְדוֹ: סוֹף דָּבָר הַכֹּל
נִשְׁמָע אֶת־הָאֱלֹהִים יְרָא וְאֶת־מִצְוֹתָיו שְׁמוֹר כִּי־זֶה כָּל־הָאָדָם: יַעְלְזוּ חֲסִידִים
בְּכָבוֹד יְרַנְּנוּ עַל מִשְׁכְּבוֹתָם:

(Male)

מְנוּחָה נְכוֹנָה. בִּישִׁיבָה עֶלְיוֹנָה. בְּמַעֲלַת קְדוֹשִׁים וּטְהוֹרִים. כְּזֹהַר הָרָקִיעַ
מְאִירִים וּמַזְהִירִים. וְחִלּוּץ עֲצָמִים. וְכַפָּרַת אֲשָׁמִים. וְהַרְחָקַת פֶּשַׁע. וְהַקְרָבַת
יֶשַׁע. וְחֶמְלָה וַחֲנִינָה. מִלִּפְנֵי מְעוֹנָה. וְחוּלָקָא טָבָא. לְחַיֵּי הָעוֹלָם הַבָּא. שָׁם
תְּהֵא מְנַת וּמְחִיצַת וִישִׁיבַת נֶפֶשׁ הַשֵּׁם הַטּוֹב (שם הנפטר) רוּחַ יְהֹוָה תַּנִיחֶנּוּ בְּגַן
עֵדֶן. דְּאִתְפְּטַר מִן עַלְמָא הָדֵין כִּרְעוּת אֱלָהָא מָארֵיהּ שְׁמַיָּא וְאַרְעָא. מֶלֶךְ מַלְכֵי
הַמְּלָכִים בְּרַחֲמָיו יְרַחֵם עָלָיו. וְיָחוֹס וְיַחְמוֹל עָלָיו. מֶלֶךְ מַלְכֵי הַמְּלָכִים בְּרַחֲמָיו
יַסְתִּירֵהוּ בְּצֵל כְּנָפָיו וּבְסֵתֶר אָהֳלוֹ לַחֲזוֹת בְּנֹעַם יְהֹוָה וּלְבַקֵּר בְּהֵיכָלוֹ. וּלְקֵץ
הַיָּמִין יַעֲמִידֵהוּ. וּמִנַּחַל עֲדָנָיו יַשְׁקֵהוּ. וְיִצְרוֹר בִּצְרוֹר הַחַיִּים נִשְׁמָתוֹ. וְיָשִׂים
כָּבוֹד מְנוּחָתוֹ. יְהֹוָה הוּא נַחֲלָתוֹ. וְיִלָּוֶה אֵלָיו הַשָּׁלוֹם וְעַל מִשְׁכָּבוֹ יִהְיֶה שָׁלוֹם.
כְּדִכְתִיב יָבֹא שָׁלוֹם יָנוּחוּ עַל מִשְׁכְּבוֹתָם הוֹלֵךְ נְכוֹחוֹ. הוּא וְכָל בְּנֵי יִשְׂרָאֵל
הַשּׁוֹכְבִים עִמּוֹ בִּכְלַל הָרַחֲמִים וְהַסְּלִיחוֹת וְכֵן יְהִי רָצוֹן וְנֹאמַר אָמֵן:

השכבה לאישה

(Female)

אֵשֶׁת־חַיִל מִי יִמְצָא וְרָחֹק מִפְּנִינִים מִכְרָהּ: שֶׁקֶר הַחֵן וְהֶבֶל הַיֹּפִי. אִשָּׁה יִרְאַת־
יְהֹוָה הִיא תִתְהַלָּל: תְּנוּ־לָהּ מִפְּרִי יָדֶיהָ וִיהַלְלוּהָ בַשְּׁעָרִים מַעֲשֶׂיהָ: רַחֲמָנָא
דְּרַחֲמָנוּתָא דִּי לֵיהּ הִיא וּבְמֵימְרֵיהּ אִתְבְּרִיאוּ עָלְמַיָּא עַלְמָא הָדֵין וְעַלְמָא דְּאָתֵי
וּגְנַז בֵּיהּ צִדְקָנִיּוֹת וְחַסְדָּנִיּוֹת דְּעַבְדָן רְעוּתֵיהּ וּבְמֵימְרֵיהּ וּבִיקָרֵיהּ וּבְתוּקְפֵיהּ
יֵאמַר לְמֵיעַל קֳדָמוֹהִי דּוּכְרָן נֶפֶשׁ הָאִשָּׁה הַכְּבוּדָה וְהַצְּנוּעָה וְהַנִּכְבֶּדֶת מָרַת
(שם הנפטרת) רוּחַ יְהֹוָה תַּנִיחֶנָּה בְּגַן עֵדֶן. דְּאִתְפְּטָרַת מִן עַלְמָא הָדֵין כִּרְעוּת

אֱלָהָא מָרֵיהּ שְׁמַיָּא וְאַרְעָא. הַמֶּלֶךְ בְּרַחֲמָיו יָחוּס וְיַחְמוֹל עָלֶיהָ. וִילַוֶּה עָלֶיהָ
הַשָּׁלוֹם וְעַל מִשְׁכָּבָהּ יִהְיֶה שָׁלוֹם. כְּדִכְתִיב יָבֹא שָׁלוֹם יָנוּחוּ עַל מִשְׁכְּבוֹתָם
הוֹלֵךְ נְכוֹחוֹ. הִיא וְכָל בְּנוֹת יִשְׂרָאֵל הַשּׁוֹכְבוֹת עִמָּהּ בִּכְלַל הָרַחֲמִים וְהַסְּלִיחוֹת
וְכֵן יְהִי רָצוֹן וְנֹאמַר אָמֵן:

After the Hashkavah the following is recited: אחר ההשכבה אומרים:

בִּלַּע הַמָּוֶת לָנֶצַח וּמָחָה יְהוָֹה אֱלֹהִים דִּמְעָה מֵעַל כָּל פָּנִים וְחֶרְפַּת עַמּוֹ יָסִיר מֵעַל
כָּל הָאָרֶץ כִּי יְהוָֹה דִּבֵּר: יִחְיוּ מֵתֶיךָ נְבֵלָתִי יְקוּמוּן הָקִיצוּ וְרַנְּנוּ שׁוֹכְנֵי עָפָר כִּי
טַל אוֹרֹת טַלֶּךָ וָאָרֶץ רְפָאִים תַּפִּיל: וְהוּא רַחוּם יְכַפֵּר עָוֹן וְלֹא יַשְׁחִית וְהִרְבָּה
לְהָשִׁיב אַפּוֹ וְלֹא יָעִיר כָּל חֲמָתוֹ: יְהוָֹה הוֹשִׁיעָה הַמֶּלֶךְ יַעֲנֵנוּ בְיוֹם קָרְאֵנוּ:

Before leaving the grave site the following verses are recited. Some communities place their right hand on the edge of the grave and say:

וְנָחֲךָ יְהוָֹה תָּמִיד וְהִשְׂבִּיעַ בְּצַחְצָחוֹת נַפְשֶׁךָ וְעַצְמֹתֶיךָ יַחֲלִיץ וְהָיִיתָ כְּגַן רָוֶה
וּכְמוֹצָא מַיִם אֲשֶׁר לֹא־יְכַזְּבוּ מֵימָיו (ישעיהו נח, יא): אָז יִבָּקַע כַּשַּׁחַר אוֹרֶךָ
וַאֲרֻכָתְךָ מְהֵרָה תִצְמָח וְהָלַךְ לְפָנֶיךָ צִדְקֶךָ כְּבוֹד יְהוָֹה יַאַסְפֶךָ (ישעיהו נח, ח):

Prayers recited during Shivah
Tzidduk Hadin see page 167.

BIRKAT HAMAZON

נְבָרֵךְ מְנַחֵם אֲבֵלִים שֶׁאָכַלְנוּ מִשֶּׁלּוֹ:
בָּרוּךְ מְנַחֵם אֲבֵלִים שֶׁאָכַלְנוּ מִשֶּׁלּוֹ וּבְטוּבוֹ חָיִינוּ:

בָּרוּךְ אַתָּה יְהוָֹה אֱלֹהֵינוּ מֶלֶךְ הָעוֹלָם, הָאֵל הַזָּן אוֹתָנוּ וְאֶת הָעוֹלָם כֻּלּוֹ בְּטוּבוֹ,
בְּחֵן בְּחֶסֶד בְּרֶיוַח וּבְרַחֲמִים. נֹתֵן לֶחֶם לְכָל־בָּשָׂר, כִּי לְעוֹלָם חַסְדּוֹ. וּבְטוּבוֹ
הַגָּדוֹל תָּמִיד לֹא חָסַר לָנוּ וְאַל יֶחְסַר לָנוּ מָזוֹן תָּמִיד לְעוֹלָם וָעֶד, כִּי הוּא אֵל זָן
וּמְפַרְנֵס לַכֹּל וְשֻׁלְחָנוּ עָרוּךְ לַכֹּל, וְהִתְקִין מִחְיָה וּמָזוֹן לְכָל־בְּרִיּוֹתָיו אֲשֶׁר בָּרָא
בְּרַחֲמָיו וּבְרוֹב חֲסָדָיו, כָּאָמוּר: פּוֹתֵחַ אֶת־יָדֶךָ, וּמַשְׂבִּיעַ לְכָל־חַי רָצוֹן: בָּרוּךְ
אַתָּה יְהוָֹה הַזָּן אֶת הַכֹּל:

נוֹדֶה לְךָ יְהוָֹה אֱלֹהֵינוּ עַל שֶׁהִנְחַלְתָּ לַאֲבוֹתֵינוּ אֶרֶץ חֶמְדָּה טוֹבָה וּרְחָבָה, בְּרִית

וְתוֹרָה, חַיִּים וּמָזוֹן. עַל שֶׁהוֹצֵאתָנוּ מֵאֶרֶץ מִצְרַיִם, וּפְדִיתָנוּ מִבֵּית עֲבָדִים, וְעַל בְּרִיתְךָ שֶׁחָתַמְתָּ בִּבְשָׂרֵנוּ, וְעַל תּוֹרָתְךָ שֶׁלִּמַּדְתָּנוּ, וְעַל חֻקֵּי רְצוֹנְךָ שֶׁהוֹדַעְתָּנוּ, וְעַל חַיִּים וּמָזוֹן שֶׁאַתָּה זָן וּמְפַרְנֵס אוֹתָנוּ.

וְעַל הַכֹּל יְהֹוָה אֱלֹהֵינוּ, אֲנַחְנוּ מוֹדִים לָךְ, וּמְבָרְכִים אֶת שְׁמָךְ, כָּאָמוּר, וְאָכַלְתָּ וְשָׂבָעְתָּ, וּבֵרַכְתָּ אֶת־יְהֹוָה אֱלֹהֶיךָ עַל־הָאָרֶץ הַטֹּבָה אֲשֶׁר נָתַן־לָךְ: בָּרוּךְ אַתָּה יְהֹוָה עַל הָאָרֶץ וְעַל הַמָּזוֹן:

רַחֵם יְהֹוָה אֱלֹהֵינוּ עָלֵינוּ וְעַל יִשְׂרָאֵל עַמָּךְ, וְעַל־יְרוּשָׁלַיִם עִירָךְ, וְעַל הַר צִיּוֹן מִשְׁכַּן כְּבוֹדָךְ, וְעַל הֵיכָלָךְ, וְעַל מְעוֹנָךְ, וְעַל דְּבִירָךְ, וְעַל הַבַּיִת הַגָּדוֹל וְהַקָּדוֹשׁ שֶׁנִּקְרָא שִׁמְךָ עָלָיו, אָבִינוּ רְעֵנוּ, זוּנֵנוּ, פַּרְנְסֵנוּ, כַּלְכְּלֵנוּ, הַרְוִיחֵנוּ, הַרְוַח־לָנוּ מְהֵרָה מִכָּל צָרוֹתֵינוּ, וְנָא אַל־תַּצְרִיכֵנוּ יְהֹוָה אֱלֹהֵינוּ לִידֵי מַתְּנוֹת בָּשָׂר וָדָם, וְלֹא לִידֵי הַלְוָאָתָם, שֶׁמַּתְּנָתָם מְעוּטָה וְחֶרְפָּתָם מְרֻבָּה, אֶלָּא לְיָדְךָ הַמְּלֵאָה וְהָרְחָבָה, הָעֲשִׁירָה וְהַפְּתוּחָה, שֶׁלֹּא נֵבוֹשׁ בָּעוֹלָם הַזֶּה, וְלֹא נִכָּלֵם לְעוֹלָם הַבָּא, וּמַלְכוּת בֵּית דָּוִד מְשִׁיחֶךָ תַּחֲזִירֶנָּה לִמְקוֹמָהּ בִּמְהֵרָה בְיָמֵינוּ:

נַחֵם יְהֹוָה אֱלֹהֵינוּ אֶת אֲבֵלֵי צִיּוֹן וְאֶת אֲבֵלֵי יְרוּשָׁלַיִם וְאֶת הָאֲבֵלִים הַמִּתְאַבְּלִים בָּאֵבֶל הַזֶּה נַחֲמֵם מֵאָבְלָם וְשַׂמְּחֵם מִיגוֹנָם כָּאָמוּר כְּאִישׁ אֲשֶׁר אִמּוֹ תְּנַחֲמֶנּוּ כֵּן אָנֹכִי אֲנַחֶמְכֶם וּבִירוּשָׁלַיִם תְּנֻחָמוּ: בָּרוּךְ אַתָּה יְהֹוָה מְנַחֵם אֲבֵלִים וּבוֹנֵה יְרוּשָׁלַיִם בִּמְהֵרָה בְיָמֵינוּ אָמֵן:

בְּחַיֵּינוּ תִּבְנֶה עִיר צִיּוֹן וְתִכּוֹן הָעֲבוֹדָה בִּירוּשָׁלַיִם: בָּרוּךְ אַתָּה יְהֹוָה אֱלֹהֵינוּ מֶלֶךְ הָעוֹלָם הָאֵל אָבִינוּ מַלְכֵּנוּ אַדִּירֵנוּ גֹּאֲלֵנוּ קְדוֹשֵׁנוּ קְדוֹשׁ יַעֲקֹב. הַמֶּלֶךְ הַחַי הַטּוֹב וְהַמֵּטִיב אֵל אֱמֶת שׁוֹפֵט בְּצֶדֶק לוֹקֵחַ נְפָשׁוֹת שַׁלִּיט בְּעוֹלָמוֹ לַעֲשׂוֹת כִּרְצוֹנוֹ וַאֲנַחְנוּ עַמּוֹ וַעֲבָדָיו וְעַל הַכֹּל אֲנַחְנוּ חַיָּבִים לְהוֹדוֹת לוֹ וּלְבָרְכוֹ גּוֹדֵר פְּרָצוֹת הוּא יִגְדּוֹר אֶת הַפִּרְצָה הַזֹּאת מֵעָלֵינוּ וּמֵעַל עַמּוֹ יִשְׂרָאֵל בְּרַחֲמִים. עוֹשֶׂה שָׁלוֹם בִּמְרוֹמָיו הוּא בְּרַחֲמָיו יַעֲשֶׂה שָׁלוֹם עָלֵינוּ וְעַל כָּל עַמּוֹ יִשְׂרָאֵל וְאִמְרוּ אָמֵן:

On the final day of Shivah, say:

ביום האחרון של השבעה בצאתם מהאבלות אומרים:

לֹא יָבֹא עוֹד שִׁמְשֵׁךְ וִירֵחֵךְ לֹא יֵאָסֵף כִּי יְהֹוָה יִהְיֶה לָּךְ לְאוֹר עוֹלָם וְשָׁלְמוּ יְמֵי אָבְלֵךְ: וּכְתִיב כְּאִישׁ אֲשֶׁר אִמּוֹ תְּנַחֲמֶנּוּ כֵּן אָנֹכִי אֲנַחֶמְכֶם וּבִירוּשָׁלַיִם תְּנֻחָמוּ:

When visiting the Grave the following Psalm is recited

Psalm 119　　　　　　　　　　　　　　　　　פרק קיט

אלף

א אַשְׁרֵי תְמִימֵי־דָרֶךְ הַהֹלְכִים בְּתוֹרַת יְהֹוָה: ב אַשְׁרֵי
נֹצְרֵי עֵדֹתָיו בְּכָל־לֵב יִדְרְשׁוּהוּ: ג אַף לֹא־פָעֲלוּ עַוְלָה
בִּדְרָכָיו הָלָכוּ: ד אַתָּה צִוִּיתָה פִקֻּדֶיךָ לִשְׁמֹר מְאֹד:
ה אַחֲלַי יִכֹּנוּ דְרָכָי לִשְׁמֹר חֻקֶּיךָ: ו אָז לֹא־אֵבוֹשׁ בְּהַבִּיטִי
אֶל־כָּל־מִצְוֹתֶיךָ: ז אוֹדְךָ בְּיֹשֶׁר לֵבָב בְּלָמְדִי מִשְׁפְּטֵי
צִדְקֶךָ: ח אֶת־חֻקֶּיךָ אֶשְׁמֹר אַל־תַּעַזְבֵנִי עַד־מְאֹד:

בית

ט בַּמֶּה יְזַכֶּה־נַּעַר אֶת־אָרְחוֹ לִשְׁמֹר כִּדְבָרֶךָ: י בְּכָל־לִבִּי
דְרַשְׁתִּיךָ אַל־תַּשְׁגֵּנִי מִמִּצְוֹתֶיךָ: יא בְּלִבִּי צָפַנְתִּי אִמְרָתֶךָ
לְמַעַן לֹא אֶחֱטָא־לָךְ: יב בָּרוּךְ אַתָּה יְהֹוָה לַמְּדֵנִי חֻקֶּיךָ:
יג בִּשְׂפָתַי סִפַּרְתִּי כֹּל מִשְׁפְּטֵי־פִיךָ: יד בְּדֶרֶךְ עֵדְוֹתֶיךָ
שַׂשְׂתִּי כְּעַל כָּל־הוֹן: טו בְּפִקֻּדֶיךָ אָשִׂיחָה וְאַבִּיטָה
אֹרְחֹתֶיךָ: טז בְּחֻקֹּתֶיךָ אֶשְׁתַּעֲשָׁע לֹא אֶשְׁכַּח דְּבָרֶךָ:

גמל

יז גְּמֹל עַל־עַבְדְּךָ אֶחְיֶה וְאֶשְׁמְרָה דְבָרֶךָ: יח גַּל־עֵינַי
וְאַבִּיטָה נִפְלָאוֹת מִתּוֹרָתֶךָ: יט גֵּר אָנֹכִי בָאָרֶץ אַל־תַּסְתֵּר
מִמֶּנִּי מִצְוֹתֶיךָ: כ גָּרְסָה נַפְשִׁי לְתַאֲבָה אֶל־מִשְׁפָּטֶיךָ
בְכָל־עֵת: כא גָּעַרְתָּ זֵדִים אֲרוּרִים הַשֹּׁגִים מִמִּצְוֹתֶיךָ:
כב גַּל מֵעָלַי חֶרְפָּה וָבוּז כִּי עֵדֹתֶיךָ נָצָרְתִּי: כג גַּם יָשְׁבוּ
שָׂרִים בִּי נִדְבָּרוּ עַבְדְּךָ יָשִׂיחַ בְּחֻקֶּיךָ: כד גַּם־עֵדֹתֶיךָ
שַׁעֲשֻׁעָי אַנְשֵׁי עֲצָתִי:

דלת

כה דָּבְקָה לֶעָפָר נַפְשִׁי חַיֵּנִי כִּדְבָרֶךָ: כו דְּרָכַי סִפַּרְתִּי וַתַּעֲנֵנִי לַמְּדֵנִי חֻקֶּיךָ: כז דֶּרֶךְ־פִּקּוּדֶיךָ הֲבִינֵנִי וְאָשִׂיחָה בְּנִפְלְאוֹתֶיךָ: כח דָּלְפָה נַפְשִׁי מִתּוּגָה קַיְּמֵנִי כִּדְבָרֶךָ: כט דֶּרֶךְ שֶׁקֶר הָסֵר מִמֶּנִּי וְתוֹרָתְךָ חָנֵּנִי: ל דֶּרֶךְ־אֱמוּנָה בָחָרְתִּי מִשְׁפָּטֶיךָ שִׁוִּיתִי: לא דָּבַקְתִּי בְעֵדְוֺתֶיךָ יְהֹוָה אַל־תְּבִישֵׁנִי: לב דֶּרֶךְ־מִצְוֺתֶיךָ אָרוּץ כִּי תַרְחִיב לִבִּי:

הא

לג הוֹרֵנִי יְהֹוָה דֶּרֶךְ חֻקֶּיךָ וְאֶצְּרֶנָּה עֵקֶב: לד הֲבִינֵנִי וְאֶצְּרָה תוֹרָתֶךָ וְאֶשְׁמְרֶנָּה בְכָל־לֵב: לה הַדְרִיכֵנִי בִּנְתִיב מִצְוֺתֶיךָ כִּי בוֹ חָפָצְתִּי: לו הַט־לִבִּי אֶל־עֵדְוֺתֶיךָ וְאַל אֶל־בָּצַע: לז הַעֲבֵר עֵינַי מֵרְאוֹת שָׁוְא בִּדְרָכֶךָ חַיֵּנִי: לח הָקֵם לְעַבְדְּךָ אִמְרָתֶךָ אֲשֶׁר לְיִרְאָתֶךָ: לט הַעֲבֵר חֶרְפָּתִי אֲשֶׁר יָגֹרְתִּי כִּי מִשְׁפָּטֶיךָ טוֹבִים: מ הִנֵּה תָּאַבְתִּי לְפִקֻּדֶיךָ בְּצִדְקָתְךָ חַיֵּנִי:

וו

מא וִיבֹאֻנִי חֲסָדֶךָ יְהֹוָה תְּשׁוּעָתְךָ כְּאִמְרָתֶךָ: מב וְאֶעֱנֶה חֹרְפִי דָבָר כִּי־בָטַחְתִּי בִּדְבָרֶךָ: מג וְאַל־תַּצֵּל מִפִּי דְבַר־אֱמֶת עַד־מְאֹד כִּי לְמִשְׁפָּטֶךָ יִחָלְתִּי: מד וְאֶשְׁמְרָה תוֹרָתְךָ תָמִיד לְעוֹלָם וָעֶד: מה וְאֶתְהַלְּכָה בָרְחָבָה כִּי פִקֻּדֶיךָ דָרָשְׁתִּי: מו וַאֲדַבְּרָה בְעֵדֹתֶיךָ נֶגֶד מְלָכִים וְלֹא אֵבוֹשׁ: מז וְאֶשְׁתַּעֲשַׁע בְּמִצְוֺתֶיךָ אֲשֶׁר אָהָבְתִּי: מח וְאֶשָּׂא כַפַּי אֶל־מִצְוֺתֶיךָ אֲשֶׁר אָהָבְתִּי וְאָשִׂיחָה בְחֻקֶּיךָ:

זין

מט זְכָר־דָּבָר לְעַבְדֶּךָ עַל אֲשֶׁר יִחַלְתָּנִי: נ זֹאת נֶחָמָתִי
בְעָנְיִי כִּי אִמְרָתְךָ חִיָּתְנִי: נא זֵדִים הֱלִיצֻנִי עַד־מְאֹד
מִתּוֹרָתְךָ לֹא נָטִיתִי: נב זָכַרְתִּי מִשְׁפָּטֶיךָ מֵעוֹלָם | יְהֹוָה
וָאֶתְנֶחָם: נג זַלְעָפָה אֲחָזַתְנִי מֵרְשָׁעִים עֹזְבֵי תּוֹרָתֶךָ:
נד זְמִרוֹת הָיוּ־לִי חֻקֶּיךָ בְּבֵית מְגוּרָי: נה זָכַרְתִּי בַלַּיְלָה
שִׁמְךָ יְהֹוָה וָאֶשְׁמְרָה תּוֹרָתֶךָ: נו זֹאת הָיְתָה־לִּי כִּי פִקֻּדֶיךָ
נָצָרְתִּי:

חית

נז חֶלְקִי יְהֹוָה אָמַרְתִּי לִשְׁמֹר דְּבָרֶיךָ: נח חִלִּיתִי פָנֶיךָ
בְכָל־לֵב חָנֵּנִי כְּאִמְרָתֶךָ: נט חִשַּׁבְתִּי דְרָכָי וָאָשִׁיבָה רַגְלַי
אֶל־עֵדֹתֶיךָ: ס חַשְׁתִּי וְלֹא הִתְמַהְמָהְתִּי לִשְׁמֹר מִצְוֹתֶיךָ:
סא חֶבְלֵי רְשָׁעִים עִוְּדֻנִי תּוֹרָתְךָ לֹא שָׁכָחְתִּי: סב חֲצוֹת־
לַיְלָה אָקוּם לְהוֹדוֹת לָךְ עַל מִשְׁפְּטֵי צִדְקֶךָ: סג חָבֵר אָנִי
לְכָל־אֲשֶׁר יְרֵאוּךָ וּלְשֹׁמְרֵי פִּקּוּדֶיךָ: סד חַסְדְּךָ יְהֹוָה
מָלְאָה הָאָרֶץ חֻקֶּיךָ לַמְּדֵנִי:

טית

סה טוֹב עָשִׂיתָ עִם־עַבְדְּךָ יְהֹוָה כִּדְבָרֶךָ: סו טוּב טַעַם
וָדַעַת לַמְּדֵנִי כִּי בְמִצְוֹתֶיךָ הֶאֱמָנְתִּי: סז טֶרֶם אֶעֱנֶה אֲנִי
שֹׁגֵג וְעַתָּה אִמְרָתְךָ שָׁמָרְתִּי: סח טוֹב־אַתָּה וּמֵטִיב
לַמְּדֵנִי חֻקֶּיךָ: סט טָפְלוּ עָלַי שֶׁקֶר זֵדִים אֲנִי בְּכָל־לֵב |
אֶצֹּר פִּקּוּדֶיךָ: ע טָפַשׁ כַּחֵלֶב לִבָּם אֲנִי תּוֹרָתְךָ שִׁעֲשָׁעְתִּי:
עא טוֹב־לִי כִי־עֻנֵּיתִי לְמַעַן אֶלְמַד חֻקֶּיךָ: עב טוֹב־לִי
תוֹרַת־פִּיךָ מֵאַלְפֵי זָהָב וָכָסֶף:

יוד

עג יָדֶיךָ עָשׂוּנִי וַיְכוֹנְנוּנִי הֲבִינֵנִי וְאֶלְמְדָה מִצְוֹתֶיךָ: עד יְרֵאֶיךָ יִרְאוּנִי וְיִשְׂמָחוּ כִּי לִדְבָרְךָ יִחָלְתִּי: עה יָדַעְתִּי יְהוָה כִּי־צֶדֶק מִשְׁפָּטֶיךָ וֶאֱמוּנָה עִנִּיתָנִי: עו יְהִי־נָא חַסְדְּךָ לְנַחֲמֵנִי כְּאִמְרָתְךָ לְעַבְדֶּךָ: עז יְבֹאוּנִי רַחֲמֶיךָ וְאֶחְיֶה כִּי תוֹרָתְךָ שַׁעֲשֻׁעָי: עח יֵבֹשׁוּ זֵדִים כִּי־שֶׁקֶר עִוְּתוּנִי אֲנִי אָשִׂיחַ בְּפִקּוּדֶיךָ: עט יָשׁוּבוּ־לִי יְרֵאֶיךָ וְיֹדְעֵי [וְיֹדְעֵי] עֵדֹתֶיךָ: פ יְהִי־לִבִּי תָמִים בְּחֻקֶּיךָ לְמַעַן לֹא אֵבוֹשׁ:

כף

פא כָּלְתָה לִתְשׁוּעָתְךָ נַפְשִׁי לִדְבָרְךָ יִחָלְתִּי: פב כָּלוּ עֵינַי לְאִמְרָתֶךָ לֵאמֹר מָתַי תְּנַחֲמֵנִי: פג כִּי־הָיִיתִי כְּנֹאד בְּקִיטוֹר חֻקֶּיךָ לֹא שָׁכָחְתִּי: פד כַּמָּה יְמֵי עַבְדֶּךָ מָתַי תַּעֲשֶׂה בְרֹדְפַי מִשְׁפָּט: פה כָּרוּ־לִי זֵדִים שִׁיחוֹת אֲשֶׁר לֹא כְתוֹרָתֶךָ: פו כָּל־מִצְוֹתֶיךָ אֱמוּנָה שֶׁקֶר רְדָפוּנִי עָזְרֵנִי: פז כִּמְעַט כִּלּוּנִי בָאָרֶץ וַאֲנִי לֹא־עָזַבְתִּי פִקּוּדֶיךָ: פח כְּחַסְדְּךָ חַיֵּנִי וְאֶשְׁמְרָה עֵדוּת פִּיךָ:

למד

פט לְעוֹלָם יְהוָה דְּבָרְךָ נִצָּב בַּשָּׁמָיִם: צ לְדֹר וָדֹר אֱמוּנָתֶךָ כּוֹנַנְתָּ אֶרֶץ וַתַּעֲמֹד: צא לְמִשְׁפָּטֶיךָ עָמְדוּ הַיּוֹם כִּי הַכֹּל עֲבָדֶיךָ: צב לוּלֵי תוֹרָתְךָ שַׁעֲשֻׁעָי אָז אָבַדְתִּי בְעָנְיִי: צג לְעוֹלָם לֹא־אֶשְׁכַּח פִּקּוּדֶיךָ כִּי־בָם חִיִּיתָנִי: צד לְךָ־אֲנִי הוֹשִׁיעֵנִי כִּי פִקּוּדֶיךָ דָרָשְׁתִּי: צה לִי קִוּוּ רְשָׁעִים לְאַבְּדֵנִי עֵדֹתֶיךָ אֶתְבּוֹנָן: צו לְכָל תִּכְלָה רָאִיתִי קֵץ רְחָבָה מִצְוָתְךָ מְאֹד:

מם

צז מָה־אָהַבְתִּי תוֹרָתֶךָ כָּל־הַיּוֹם הִיא שִׂיחָתִי: צח מֵאֹיְבַי
תְּחַכְּמֵנִי מִצְוֺתֶךָ כִּי לְעוֹלָם הִיא־לִי: צט מִכָּל־מְלַמְּדַי
הִשְׂכַּלְתִּי כִּי עֵדְוֺתֶיךָ שִׂיחָה לִי: ק מִזְּקֵנִים אֶתְבּוֹנָן כִּי
פִקּוּדֶיךָ נָצָרְתִּי: קא מִכָּל־אֹרַח רָע כָּלִאתִי רַגְלָי לְמַעַן
אֶשְׁמֹר דְּבָרֶךָ: קב מִמִּשְׁפָּטֶיךָ לֹא־סָרְתִּי כִּי־אַתָּה הוֹרֵתָנִי:
קג מַה־נִּמְלְצוּ לְחִכִּי אִמְרָתֶךָ מִדְּבַשׁ לְפִי: קד מִפִּקּוּדֶיךָ
אֶתְבּוֹנָן עַל־כֵּן שָׂנֵאתִי ׀ כָּל־אֹרַח שָׁקֶר:

נון

קה נֵר־לְרַגְלִי דְבָרֶךָ וְאוֹר לִנְתִיבָתִי: קו נִשְׁבַּעְתִּי
וָאֲקַיֵּמָה לִשְׁמֹר מִשְׁפְּטֵי צִדְקֶךָ: קז נַעֲנֵיתִי עַד־מְאֹד יְהֹוָה
חַיֵּנִי כִדְבָרֶךָ: קח נִדְבוֹת פִּי רְצֵה־נָא יְהֹוָה וּמִשְׁפָּטֶיךָ
לַמְּדֵנִי: קט נַפְשִׁי בְכַפִּי תָמִיד וְתוֹרָתְךָ לֹא שָׁכָחְתִּי:
קי נָתְנוּ רְשָׁעִים פַּח לִי וּמִפִּקּוּדֶיךָ לֹא תָעִיתִי: קיא נָחַלְתִּי
עֵדְוֺתֶיךָ לְעוֹלָם כִּי־שְׂשׂוֹן לִבִּי הֵמָּה: קיב נָטִיתִי לִבִּי
לַעֲשׂוֹת חֻקֶּיךָ לְעוֹלָם עֵקֶב:

סמך

קיג סֵעֲפִים שָׂנֵאתִי וְתוֹרָתְךָ אָהָבְתִּי: קיד סִתְרִי וּמָגִנִּי
אָתָּה לִדְבָרְךָ יִחָלְתִּי: קטו סוּרוּ מִמֶּנִּי מְרֵעִים וְאֶצְּרָה
מִצְוֺת אֱלֹהָי: קטז סָמְכֵנִי כְאִמְרָתְךָ וְאֶחְיֶה וְאַל־תְּבִישֵׁנִי
מִשִּׂבְרִי: קיז סְעָדֵנִי וְאִוָּשֵׁעָה וְאֶשְׁעָה בְחֻקֶּיךָ תָמִיד:
קיח סָלִיתָ כָּל־שׁוֹגִים מֵחֻקֶּיךָ כִּי־שֶׁקֶר תַּרְמִיתָם:
קיט סִגִים הִשְׁבַּתָּ כָל־רִשְׁעֵי־אָרֶץ לָכֵן אָהַבְתִּי עֵדֹתֶיךָ:
קכ סָמַר מִפַּחְדְּךָ בְשָׂרִי וּמִמִּשְׁפָּטֶיךָ יָרֵאתִי:

עין

קכא עָשִׂיתִי מִשְׁפָּט וָצֶדֶק בַּל־תַּנִּיחֵנִי לְעֹשְׁקָי: קכב עֲרֹב
עַבְדְּךָ לְטוֹב אַל־יַעַשְׁקֻנִי זֵדִים: קכג עֵינַי כָּלוּ לִישׁוּעָתֶךָ
וּלְאִמְרַת צִדְקֶךָ: קכד עֲשֵׂה עִם־עַבְדְּךָ כְחַסְדֶּךָ וְחֻקֶּיךָ
לַמְּדֵנִי: קכה עַבְדְּךָ־אָנִי הֲבִינֵנִי וְאֵדְעָה עֵדֹתֶיךָ: קכו עֵת
לַעֲשׂוֹת לַיהוָה הֵפֵרוּ תּוֹרָתֶךָ: קכז עַל־כֵּן אָהַבְתִּי
מִצְוֹתֶיךָ מִזָּהָב וּמִפָּז: קכח עַל־כֵּן ׀ כָּל־פִּקּוּדֵי כֹל יִשָּׁרְתִּי
כָּל־אֹרַח שֶׁקֶר שָׂנֵאתִי:

פה

קכט פְּלָאוֹת עֵדְוֹתֶיךָ עַל־כֵּן נְצָרָתַם נַפְשִׁי: קל פֵּתַח
דְּבָרֶיךָ יָאִיר מֵבִין פְּתָיִים: קלא פִּי־פָעַרְתִּי וָאֶשְׁאָפָה כִּי
לְמִצְוֹתֶיךָ יָאָבְתִּי: קלב פְּנֵה־אֵלַי וְחָנֵּנִי כְּמִשְׁפָּט לְאֹהֲבֵי
שְׁמֶךָ: קלג פְּעָמַי הָכֵן בְּאִמְרָתֶךָ וְאַל־תַּשְׁלֶט־בִּי כָל־אָוֶן:
קלד פְּדֵנִי מֵעֹשֶׁק אָדָם וְאֶשְׁמְרָה פִּקּוּדֶיךָ: קלה פָּנֶיךָ הָאֵר
בְּעַבְדֶּךָ וְלַמְּדֵנִי אֶת־חֻקֶּיךָ: קלו פַּלְגֵי־מַיִם יָרְדוּ עֵינָי עַל
לֹא־שָׁמְרוּ תוֹרָתֶךָ:

צדיק

קלז צַדִּיק אַתָּה יְהוָה וְיָשָׁר מִשְׁפָּטֶיךָ: קלח צִוִּיתָ צֶדֶק
עֵדֹתֶיךָ וֶאֱמוּנָה מְאֹד: קלט צִמְּתַתְנִי קִנְאָתִי כִּי־שָׁכְחוּ
דְבָרֶיךָ צָרָי: קמ צְרוּפָה אִמְרָתְךָ מְאֹד וְעַבְדְּךָ אֲהֵבָהּ:
קמא צָעִיר אָנֹכִי וְנִבְזֶה פִּקֻּדֶיךָ לֹא שָׁכָחְתִּי: קמב צִדְקָתְךָ
צֶדֶק לְעוֹלָם וְתוֹרָתְךָ אֱמֶת: קמג צַר־וּמָצוֹק מְצָאוּנִי
מִצְוֹתֶיךָ שַׁעֲשֻׁעָי: קמד צֶדֶק עֵדְוֹתֶיךָ לְעוֹלָם הֲבִינֵנִי
וְאֶחְיֶה:

קוף

קמה קָרָאתִי בְכָל־לֵב עֲנֵנִי יְהוָה חֻקֶּיךָ אֶצֹּרָה׃
קמו קְרָאתִיךָ הוֹשִׁיעֵנִי וְאֶשְׁמְרָה עֵדֹתֶיךָ׃ קמז קִדַּמְתִּי
בַנֶּשֶׁף וָאֲשַׁוֵּעָה לִדְבָרְךָ [לִדְבָרֶיךָ] יִחָלְתִּי׃ קמח קִדְּמוּ
עֵינַי אַשְׁמֻרוֹת לָשִׂיחַ בְּאִמְרָתֶךָ׃ קמט קוֹלִי שִׁמְעָה
כְחַסְדֶּךָ יְהוָה כְּמִשְׁפָּטֶךָ חַיֵּנִי׃ קנ קָרְבוּ רֹדְפֵי זִמָּה
מִתּוֹרָתְךָ רָחָקוּ׃ קנא קָרוֹב אַתָּה יְהוָה וְכָל־מִצְוֺתֶיךָ
אֱמֶת׃ קנב קֶדֶם יָדַעְתִּי מֵעֵדֹתֶיךָ כִּי לְעוֹלָם יְסַדְתָּם׃

ריש

קנג רְאֵה־עָנְיִי וְחַלְּצֵנִי כִּי־תוֹרָתְךָ לֹא שָׁכָחְתִּי׃ קנד רִיבָה
רִיבִי וּגְאָלֵנִי לְאִמְרָתְךָ חַיֵּנִי׃ קנה רָחוֹק מֵרְשָׁעִים יְשׁוּעָה
כִּי־חֻקֶּיךָ לֹא דָרָשׁוּ׃ קנו רַחֲמֶיךָ רַבִּים ׀ יְהוָה כְּמִשְׁפָּטֶיךָ
חַיֵּנִי׃ קנז רַבִּים רֹדְפַי וְצָרָי מֵעֵדְוֺתֶיךָ לֹא נָטִיתִי׃
קנח רָאִיתִי בֹגְדִים וָאֶתְקוֹטָטָה אֲשֶׁר אִמְרָתְךָ לֹא שָׁמָרוּ׃
קנט רְאֵה כִּי־פִקּוּדֶיךָ אָהָבְתִּי יְהוָה כְּחַסְדְּךָ חַיֵּנִי׃
קס רֹאשׁ־דְּבָרְךָ אֱמֶת וּלְעוֹלָם כָּל־מִשְׁפַּט צִדְקֶךָ׃

שין

קסא שָׂרִים רְדָפוּנִי חִנָּם וּמִדְּבָרְךָ [וּמִדְּבָרֶיךָ] פָּחַד לִבִּי׃
קסב שָׂשׂ אָנֹכִי עַל־אִמְרָתֶךָ כְּמוֹצֵא שָׁלָל רָב׃ קסג שֶׁקֶר
שָׂנֵאתִי וָאֲתַעֵבָה תּוֹרָתְךָ אָהָבְתִּי׃ קסד שֶׁבַע בַּיּוֹם
הִלַּלְתִּיךָ עַל מִשְׁפְּטֵי צִדְקֶךָ׃ קסה שָׁלוֹם רָב לְאֹהֲבֵי
תוֹרָתֶךָ וְאֵין לָמוֹ מִכְשׁוֹל׃ קסו שִׂבַּרְתִּי לִישׁוּעָתְךָ יְהוָה
וּמִצְוֺתֶיךָ עָשִׂיתִי׃ קסז שָׁמְרָה נַפְשִׁי עֵדֹתֶיךָ וָאֹהֲבֵם מְאֹד׃
קסח שָׁמַרְתִּי פִקּוּדֶיךָ וְעֵדֹתֶיךָ כִּי כָל־דְּרָכַי נֶגְדֶּךָ׃

תף

קסט תִּקְרַב רִנָּתִי לְפָנֶיךָ יְהֹוָה כִּדְבָרְךָ הֲבִינֵנִי: קע תָּבוֹא
תְחִנָּתִי לְפָנֶיךָ כְּאִמְרָתְךָ הַצִּילֵנִי: קעא תַּבַּעְנָה שְׂפָתַי
תְּהִלָּה כִּי תְלַמְּדֵנִי חֻקֶּיךָ: קעב תַּעַן לְשׁוֹנִי אִמְרָתֶךָ כִּי
כָל־מִצְוֹתֶיךָ צֶּדֶק: קעג תְּהִי־יָדְךָ לְעָזְרֵנִי כִּי פִקּוּדֶיךָ
בָחָרְתִּי: קעד תָּאַבְתִּי לִישׁוּעָתְךָ יְהֹוָה וְתוֹרָתְךָ שַׁעֲשֻׁעָי:
קעה תְּחִי־נַפְשִׁי וּתְהַלְלֶךָּ וּמִשְׁפָּטֶךָ יַעְזְרֻנִי: קעו תָּעִיתִי
כְּשֶׂה אֹבֵד בַּקֵּשׁ עַבְדֶּךָ כִּי מִצְוֹתֶיךָ לֹא שָׁכָחְתִּי:

1. Fortunate are they who are wholehearted in their way [of life], who walk in the Torah of Adonay.

2. Fortunate are they that keep His testimonies, with their whole heart, they seek Him.

3. Not only do they refrain from wrongdoings [but they] walk in His ways [and do good].

4. You have commanded Your precepts that we should preserve them diligently.

5. This is my fervent wish – may my ways be firmly established – to preserve Your statutes.

6. Then I will not be ashamed when I behold [i.e., understand] all Your commandments.

7. I will [be able to] give thanks to You with an upright heart, when I learn Your righteous mandates.

8. Your statutes I will preserve, do not forsake me, entirely.

9. How can a young man keep pure his way? By preserving it according to Your word.

10. With my whole heart, I have sought You, let me not err from Your commandments.

11. In my heart, I have treasured Your word, that I might not sin against You.

12. Blessed are You, Adonay, teach me Your statutes.

13. With my lips I have recounted [taught] all the mandates of Your mouth.
14. [Walking] in the way of Your testimonies, I have been gladdened as much as over all riches.
15. In Your precepts I will meditate, and [thereby] look upon [understand] Your ways.
16. In Your statutes, I will be engrossed, [therefore] I will not forget Your word.
17. Deal kindly with Your servant, that I may live and preserve Your word.
18. Unveil my eyes that I may behold [understand] the wonders of Your Torah.
19. I am a stranger upon the earth, do not conceal from me Your commandments.
20. My soul is crushed from its longing to [study] Your mandates at all times.
21. You have rebuked the insolent, accursed sinners, who err [stray] from Your commandments.
22. Remove from me humiliation and contempt, for I have kept Your testimonies.
23. Even though princes sit and talk against me, Your servant meditates in Your statutes.
24. Indeed, in Your testimonies I am engrossed, they are my counselors.
25. My soul clings to the dust; sustain me in life according to Your word.
26. My ways [needs] have I recounted, and You answered me; teach me Your statutes.
27. The way of Your precepts let me understand, and I will [be able to] speak of Your wonders.
28. My soul is diminished from grief, sustain me according to Your word.
29. The way of falsehood, remove from me, and with your Torah, be gracious to me.
30. The way of trust, I have chosen, Your mandates I have set before me.

31. I have attached myself to Your testimonies, Adonay, do not cause me to be ashamed.
32. In the way of Your commandments I will run, for You have expanded my heart.
33. Teach me, Adonay, the way of Your statutes, and I will keep Your Torah, and preserve it with my whole heart.
34. Give me understanding and I will keep Your Torah, and preserve it with my whole heart.
35. Guide me in the path of Your commandments, for therein is my desire.
36. Incline my heart to Your testimonies, and not to [selfish] gain.
37. Turn away my eyes from beholding vanity; in Your ways give me life.
38. Fulfill for Your servant, Your word [promise] that You gave [to me] who fears You.
39. Turn away my humiliation which I dread, because Your mandates are good.
40. Behold, I long [to fulfill] Your precepts, in Your righteousness give me life.
41. May Your kindness come to me, Adonay. Your deliverance, according to Your word [promise].
42. That I may answer him who taunts me, for I have trusted in Your word.
43. Take not from my mouth, the word of truth to the full, for in Your mandates I have hoped.
44. And [then] I will preserve Your Torah constantly, forever and ever.
45. And I will walk in widely accepted ways, for Your precepts, have I sought.
46. And I will speak of Your testimonies in the presence of kings, and I will not be ashamed.
47. And I will be engrossed in Your commandments which I have loved.
48. And I will lift my hands to Your commandments which I have loved, and I will meditate in Your statutes.
49. Remember [Your] word to Your servant, through which You have given me cause to hope.

50. This is my consolation in my affliction, for Your word [promise] has given me life.
51. Insolent sinners have derided me greatly, [but] from Your Torah I have not turned.
52. I remembered Your mandates of old, Adonay, and I found myself consoled.
53. Burning indignation gripped me because of the wicked who forsake Your Torah.
54. Your statutes have been my songs in the house of my wanderings.
55. I remembered in the night, Your name, Adonay, and I have preserved Your Torah.
56. This [crown of royalty] has been mine, because Your precepts I have kept.
57. My portion is [in] Adonay; I have said, "I will preserve Your word."
58. I have entreated the favor of Your countenance with my whole heart; be gracious unto me according to Your promise.
59. I considered my ways [my opinions], and I turned my feet to Your testimonies.
60. I hurried and did not delay to preserve Your commandments.
61. Bands of wicked [men] have robbed me, but Your Torah I have not forgotten.
62. At midnight I rise to thank You for your righteous mandates.
63. I am a companion to all who fear You, and to those who preserve Your precepts.
64. Your kindness, Adonay, fills the earth, teach me Your statues.
65. You have done good with your servant, Adonay, according to Your word.
66. Good [Torah] reasoning and knowledge, teach me, for in Your commandments I have believed.
67. Before I afflicted myself [in Torah study] I erred [in the performance of commandments], but afterwards I was able to preserve Your word.
68. You are good, and You do good, teach me Your statutes.
69. They have slandered me falsely, the insolent [ones], but with my whole heart I will keep Your precepts.
70. Thick like fat is their heart, but I am engrossed in your Torah.

71. It is good for me to have been afflicted in order that I learn Your statutes [see verse 67].
72. It is better for me, the teachings of Your mouth, than thousands of gold and silver.
73. Your hands have made me and established me; give me understanding and I will learn Your commandments.
74. Those who fear You will see me [in my glory], and they will rejoice because [they know] that in Your work I hoped.
75. I know, Adonay, that Your mandates are just, and I believe that you have afflicted me [justly].
76. Please! May your kindness console me, according to Your promise to Your servant.
77. May Your compassion come to me that I might live, for in your Torah I am engrossed.
78. Let the insolent sinners be ashamed, for falsely have they distorted my sins, but I will [continue] to meditate in Your precepts.
79. Let them return to me, those who fear You, and those who know Your testimonies.
80. May my heart be whole in Your statutes in order that I may not be ashamed.
81. My soul yearns for Your deliverance, in Your word I have hoped.
82. My eyes yearn [to see the fulfillment] of Your promise, saying, When will You console me?.
83. For I have become [dry] like a leather skin in the smoke, [yet] Your statutes I have not forgotten.
84. How many are the days of Your servant – when will You judge those who pursue me?
85. Insolent sinners have dug pits for me, because [they say]: I am not fit according to Your Torah.
86. All Your commandments are faithful; with falsehood they pursue me, help me.
87. They have almost destroyed me on earth, and [yet] I have not forsaken Your precepts
88. According to Your kindness, give me life, and I will preserve [the testimony] of Your mouth.

89. [You] are forever, Adonay, Your word stands [eternal as] the heavens.

90. From generation to generation is Your faithfulness, You established the earth and it endures.

91. [To carry out] Your judgments, they [the heavenly hosts] stand ready this day, for they are all Your servants.

92. Were it not for Your Torah in which I was [constantly] engrossed, I would have perished in my affliction.

93. I will never forget Your precepts, for with them You have given me life.

94. I am Yours; deliver me, for Your precepts I have sought [to fulfill].

95. The wicked have hoped to destroy me, but Your testimonies I strive to understand.

96. To every purpose I have seen an end: Your commandment, however, is exceedingly broad.

97. How much have I loved Your Torah! All the day it is my meditation.

98. Your commands make me wiser than my enemies, for they are always with me.

99. From all my teachers I have learned understanding, for Your testimonies are my meditation.

100. I understand more than my elders, for I have kept Your precepts [from my youth].

101. From every evil path I have restrained my feet, in order to preserve Your word.

102. From your mandates I have not turned away, for You have instructed me.

103. How sweet to my palate are Your words! [They are] sweeter than honey to my mouth!

104. From Your precepts I acquire understanding, therefore I hate every path of falsehood.

105. A lamp for my feet is Your word and a light for my path.

106. I have sworn and I have fulfilled [my oath] to preserve Your righteous mandates.

107. I am afflicted greatly, Adonay, give me life according to Your word.

108. [With] the offerings of my mouth be pleased, I beseech You, Adonay, and Your mandates teach me.

109. My soul is in my hand constantly, yet Your Torah I have not forgotten.
110. The wicked have laid a snare for me, yet from your precepts I have not strayed.
111. Your testimonies are my heritage forever, for they are the gladness of my heart.
112. I have inclined my heart to do [fulfill] Your statutes, forever, at every step.
113. Those who think evil thoughts I hate, and Your Torah I love.
114. You are my hidden fortress and shield, [only] in Your word do I hope.
115. Depart from me [you] evildoers, and I will keep the commandments of my God.
116. Assist me according to Your word [promise] and I will live, and do not shame me in my hope.
117. Support me and I will be delivered, and I will be engrossed in Your statutes always.
118. You trample all who [say they] erred in Your statutes, for false is their deceitful claim.
119. Like ashes have You nullified all the wicked of the earth, therefore I love Your Torah.
120. My flesh shuddered for dread of You and of Your judgments, I was afraid.
121. I have done justice and righteousness, do not leave me to my oppressors.
122. Be surety for Your servant for good. Let me not be oppressed by insolent sinners.
123. My eyes yearn to [see] Your deliverance, and [the fulfillment of] Your righteous word.
124. Do with Your servant according to Your kindness, and Your statutes, teach them to me.
125. I am your servant; give me understanding and I will know Your testimonies.
126. It is a time to act for Adonay, they have made void Your Torah.
127. Therefore I have loved Your commandments more than gold and even refined gold.

128. Therefore all [Your] precepts regarding all things; I consider [them] upright; every path of falsehood I hate.

129. Wonderfully concealed are [the rewards of] Your testimonies, therefore my soul has treasured [all of] them.

130. Your opening words give light, they give understanding to the simple.

131. I opened my mouth and eagerly swallowed them, because for Your commandments I yearned.

132. Turn to me and be gracious to me, as is Your custom with those who love Your Name.

133. Train my steps by Your word, and may I not be dominated by any iniquity

134. Redeem me from the oppression of man, and I will preserve Your precepts.

135. Your face – make it shine upon Your servant, and teach me Your statutes.

136. Rivers of water [tears] stream from my eyes because they have not preserved Your Torah.

137. Righteous are You, Adonay, and upright are Your mandates.

138. You have commanded the righteousness of Your testimonies, and they are exceedingly faithful.

139. I am ruined by my zealousness [that] my adversaries have forgotten Your words.

140. Your word is refined to the utmost, and Your servant loves it.

141. I am young and despised [by my enemies], yet Your precepts I have not forgotten.

142. Your righteousness is righteousness everlasting, and Your Torah is truth.

143. Distress and anguish have found me, [yet in] Your commandments I am engrossed

144. Righteous are your testimonies forever, let me understand [them] and I will live.

145. I have called with my whole heart, answer me Adonay; Your statutes I will treasure.

146. I have called You – deliver me, and I will preserve Your testimonies

147. I rose before dawn, and cried; in Your word I hoped.
148. My eyes were [opened] early [even] before the [last two] night watches to meditate in Your word.
149. Hear my voice according to Your kindness, Adonay; as is Your custom, give me life.
150. They draw near, those who pursue lewdness, [but] from Your Torah, they remain far.
151. You are near, Adonay, [to those who repent,] and all Your commandments are true.
152. From the beginning I have known [wisdom] from Your testimonies, because You have established them forever.
153. See my affliction and free me from it, for Your Torah I have not forgotten.
154. Defend my cause and redeem me; for the sake of Your word, give me life.
155. Far removed from the wicked is deliverance, for Your statutes they have not sought.
156. Your mercies are great, Adonay; as is Your custom, give me life.
157. Many are my pursuers and adversaries, yet from Your testimonies I have not turned.
158. I have seen men without faith [in Torah] and I quarreled with them, for Your word they did not preserve.
159. See how I loved Your precepts; Adonay, according to Your kindness, give me life.
160. The beginning of Your word is truth, and forever are all Your righteous mandates.
161. Princes have pursued me without cause, but only of Your words am I in awe.
162. I am happy with Your word like one who finds great gain.
163. Falsehood I hate, and it is despicable: Your Torah do I love.
164. Seven [i.e., many] times a day I praise You because of Your righteous mandates.
165. Great is the peace of those who love Your Torah, and there is no stumbling for them.
166. I have hoped for Your deliverance, Adonay, and Your commandments I have done.

167. My soul has preserved Your testimonies, and I love them greatly.

168. I have preserved Your precepts and Your testimonies; [You know this] because all my ways are before You.

169. May my song of prayer come near before You, Adonay; according to Your word, give me understanding.

170. May my supplication come before You; according to Your word [promise], save me.

171. My lips will utter praise, when You have taught me Your statutes.

172. My tongue will give voice to Your word, for all Your commandments are righteous.

173. May Your hand [be ready to] help me, for Your precepts I have chosen.

174. I have yearned for Your deliverance, Adonay, and in Your Torah I am engrossed.

175. May my soul live that it might praise You, and may Your judgments help me.

176. I have strayed like a lost sheep; seek Your servant [bring him back to You], for Your commandments I have not forgotten.

COMMENTARY

Psalm 119 is referred to by several names, including *Alfa Beta* and *Temania Apei Be'alef* ("The Eight Facets of the *Alef Bet*"). These names reflect the fact that the structure of the psalm is based on the Hebrew alphabet. Each paragraph consists of eight verses, each of which begins with a letter of the alphabet in order. The alefbet is therefore repeated eight times. In Jewish mysticism, as is well known, the number seven represents the physical world, and eight represents the transcendent world, the world beyond the physical plane.

In this psalm, we are given a glimpse into the inner life of one who endeavors to attain understanding and moral perfection according to the spirit of Judaism. The primary theme of the psalm is the message that understanding and fulfilling the divine law are the supreme concern of the righteous.

The afterlife is described as a reunion, and all of life is a preparation for it. Our sages compare this world to a wedding. Said Rabbi Bunam: "If a man makes every preparation for the wedding feast but forgets to purchase a wedding ring, the marriage cannot take place."[2] Similarly, we may labor all our lives, but if we forget to attain the means to acquire the ring, that is to say, the instrument of sanctifying ourselves to God, we will not be able to enter the life eternal.

Nothing else is important but the fulfillment of God's word. It is the Torah that is man's delight; it constitutes our yearning, our desire, our love, our most precious treasure, the theme of all our supplications, our sole purpose. All of our spiritual growth and development is based upon the Torah. The psalmist writes: "How I love Your Torah, It is my mediation all the day." All of our experiences in life, our entire pilgrimage on earth, serve to add understanding to God's word.

Reflections and Meditations

I.

"You protect my head on the day of *neshek* [kissing]" (Psalm 140:8). The day when the two worlds kiss each other [is] the day a man leaves this world and enters the world-to-come.[3]

II.

Rav had a favorite saying: "The world-to-come is not like this world. In the world-to-come, there is no eating, no drinking, no procreation, no commerce, no envy, no hatred, no rivalry; the righteous sit with crowns on their heads and enjoy the radiance of the Divine Presence."[4]

III.

Rabbi Joseph son of Rabbi Joshua ben Levi became ill, and his spirit flew away. After his spirit returned to him, his father asked him, "What did you see?" He replied, "I saw a world turned upside down – the people high up here were moved down, and the lowly were moved up." Rabbi Joshua said, "My son, you saw a world in which right is made clear. But what of you and me, where were we placed?" "Just as we are esteemed here, so were we esteemed there. I also heard them say, 'Happy is he who comes with his learning in hand.' I also heard them say, 'They who were martyred by the [Roman] government, no man is allowed to stand within their compartment.'"[5]

IV.

All Israel have a portion in the world-to-come, as it is said: "Thy people are all righteous. They shall inherit the world that is forever: The branch of My planting, the work of My hands, wherein I glory" (Isaiah 60:21).[6]

V.

We have been taught: For twelve months the human body remains in existence while the soul ascends and descends [to join the body]. After twelve months the body ceases to exist, and the soul ascends to the treasury of souls and descends no more.[7]

VI.

"They are new every morning; great is Thy faithfulness" (Lamentations 3:23). Rabbi Alexandri said: "Because You renew our spirits each and every morning [as we awaken], we are certain that in Your faithfulness You will restore our spirits to us at the resurrection."[8]

VII.

We have been taught that Rabbi Simeon ben Eleazar said: "He who stands by a dying man at the moment of the soul's departure is obligated to rend his garment [even on Shabbat]. To what may the moment of a soul's departure be likened? To the moment when a Torah scroll is consumed by fire."[9]

VIII.

Commenting on the verse in Ecclesiastes [7:1] "the day of death is better than the day of birth," Rabbi Levi explained: "This can be compared to two ocean-going ships, one leaving the harbor and the other entering. Everybody is celebrating the departing ship, but only a few are rejoicing at the ship that is arriving. A wise man seeing this said, 'I see here an irony. People should not celebrate the departing ship, since they have no way of knowing what conditions she will meet, what seas she will encounter, and what winds she will have to face. People should rejoice, rather, over the ship that is entering the harbor, because it has safely returned from its voyage.'"[10]

IX.

On the day that Rabbi Judah was dying, the rabbis declared a public fast, and offered prayers that God have mercy and spare him…. Rabbi Judah's maid went up to the roof of his house and offered this prayer: "The angels in heaven desire Rabbi Judah to join them, and the mortals on earth desire him to remain with them. May it be the will of God that the mortals overpower the angels." However, when she saw how much Rabbi Judah was suffering, she offered a second prayer: "May it be the will of God that the angels overpower the mortals." As the rabbis continued their incessant prayers, she took a jar and threw it down from the roof. It made a great noise; for a moment the rabbis ceased praying and the soul of Rabbi Judah departed.[11]

X.

When Rabbi Yohanan ben Zakkai's son died, his disciples came to comfort him. Rabbi Eliezer entered, sat down before him, and said to him, "Master, with your permission may I say something to you?"

"Speak," he replied.

Rabbi Eliezer said, "Adam had a son who died, yet he allowed himself to be comforted concerning him. And how do we know that he allowed himself to be comforted? For it is said: 'And Adam knew his wife again' [and they had another son] (Genesis 4:25). You too, let yourself be comforted."

Said Rabbi Yohanan to him, "It is not enough that I grieve over my own son that you remind me of the grief of Adam?"

[The process continued: Rabbi Joshua entered and asked him to be comforted as was Job. Rabbi Yohanan responded, "Is it not enough that I grieve over my own son, that you remind me of the grief of Job?" Rabbi Yose reminded him that Aaron allowed himself to be comforted over the death of his two sons, and Rabbi Simeon mentioned how David was comforted when his son died.]

Rabbi Elazar ben Arakh entered. As soon as Rabbi Yohanan saw him, he said to his servants, "Take my clothing and follow me to the bathhouse, for he is a great man and I shall be unable to resist him."

Rabbi Elazar entered and sat down before him, and said to him, "I shall tell you a parable. To what may your situation be compared? To a man whom the king entrusted an object to be carefully guarded. Every day the man would weep and cry out, 'Woe is me! When shall I be freed from this trust and again be at peace? You too, master. You had a son; he studied the Torah, the Prophets, the Holy Writings, he studied Mishnah, Halakhah, Aggadah, and he left this world without sin. Now that you have returned that which was entrusted to you, it is appropriate for you to be comforted."

Said Rabbi Yohanan to him, "Rabbi Elazar, my son, you have comforted me the way people ought to give comfort."[12]

XI.

It happened that while Rabbi Meir was expounding in the house of study on a Sabbath afternoon, his two sons died. What did their mother do? She put them both on a couch and spread a sheet over them.

At the end of the Sabbath, R. Meir returned home from the house of study and asked, "Where are my two sons?" She replied, "They went to the house of study." R. Meir: "I looked for them there but did not see them."

Then she gave him the cup for *Havdalah*, and he pronounced the blessing. Again he asked, "Where are my two sons?" She replied, "They went to such-and-such a place and will be back soon." Then she brought food for him. After he had eaten, she said, "My teacher, I have a question." R. Meir: "Ask your question." She: "My teacher, a while ago a man came and deposited something in my keeping. Now he has come back to claim what he left. Shall I return it to him or not?" R. Meir: "My daughter, is not one who holds a deposit required to return it to its owner?" She: "Still, without your opinion, I would not have returned it."

Then what did she do? She took R. Meir by his hand, led him up to the chamber, and brought him near the couch. Then she pulled off the sheet that covered them, and he saw that both children lying on the couch were dead. He began to weep and said, "My sons, my sons, my teachers, my teachers. My sons in the way of the world, but my teachers because they illumined my eyes with their understanding of Torah."

Then she came out with: "My teacher, did you not say to me that we are required to restore to the owner what is left with us in trust? 'The Lord gave, the Lord took. May the Name of the Lord be blessed' (Job 1:21)."[13]

XII.

Our rabbis taught: When Rabbi Yose ben Kisma fell ill, Rabbi Hanina ben Teradion went to visit him.

Rabbi Yose said to him: "Hanina, my brother, don't you know that heaven has ordained this [Roman] nation to reign? Even though she [Rome] has laid waste to [God's] House, burned His Temple, killed His pious ones, and caused His best ones to perish, she continues to stand! Yet what is this I hear about you? That [even though you know it is forbidden], you are gathering large crowds in public to teach them with a Torah scroll in your lap." Hanina answered, "Let the heavens have mercy."

Rabbi Yose replied, "I speak to you words that make sense, and you say, let the heavens have mercy? I wouldn't be surprised if they burn both you and your Torah at the stake." …

It wasn't long before Rabbi Yose ben Kisma died and the Romans eulogized him with great fanfare. When they [the Romans] returned from the funeral, they found Rabbi Hanina teaching Torah to the multitudes with a Torah scroll in his lap. They tied him together with his Torah and surrounded Hanina with kindling wood. The executioner took sponges of wool, soaked them in water, and placed them on Hanina's heart so he would not die quickly. The executioner lit the fire, and Hanina's daughter cried, "Father, is this what you deserve?" Hanina answered, "This might be difficult if I were being burned alone, but the one who would disgrace the Torah may as well disgrace me."

His students asked, "Rebbe, what do you see?" He answered, "The parchments are burning, but the letters are flying free." They replied, "You too, open your mouth and let the flames take you." Hanina answered, "Let the one who gave me life take it away, and let me not harm myself."

The executioner then said to him, "Rabbi, if I raise the flame and remove the woolen sponges from over your heart, will you bring me to [your] *olam haba* (world-to-come)?"

"Yes," Rabbi Hanina replied.

"Swear to me." Rabbi Hanina swore to him. So he increased the flames and removed the wool from Hanina's heart, and Hanina expired quickly. Then, suddenly, the executioner himself jumped into the flames and died.

A *bat-kol* (voice from heaven) exclaimed: "Rabbi Hanina ben Teradion and the executioner have been welcomed in the world-to-come."

[Upon witnessing this] Rebbe [Rabbi Judah the Prince, the leader of the Jewish community] wept and said: "There are those who earn their world-to-come in a single moment, and those for whom it takes many years."[14]

XIII.

I hold it true, whate'er befall;
I feel it, when I sorrow most;
'Tis better to have loved and lost
Than never to have loved at all.[15]

XIV.

Rachel weeps for her children, she refuses to be comforted.[16]

XV.

Moses said: "God is great, mighty, and awesome." Jeremiah said: "Gentiles are trampling in His temple"; where is His awesomeness? He would no longer say "awesome." Daniel said: "Gentiles have enslaved His children"; where is His might? He would no longer say "mighty." They [the Men of the Great Assembly] came and said, "On the contrary! It is the culmination of His might that He represses His inclination to act and is long-suffering toward the wicked. And if He were not awesome, how could one nation [the Jews] endure among the nations of the world?"[17]

Endnotes

1. The word *mikhtam* or *ketem,* when used as a noun, denotes a superior kind of gold. It occurs in the verbal form in Jeremiah 2:22, *nikhtam avonha,* where it denotes an indelible stain. In rabbinic literature *ketamim* are stains.
2. Heard orally, source unknown.
3. TY Yevamot 15:2.
4. TB Berakhot 17a.
5. TB Pesahim 50a.
6. TB Sanhedrin 90a.
7. TB Shabbat 152b–153a.
8. Genesis Rabbah 78:1.
9. TB Shabbat 105b.
10. Exodus Rabbah 48:1.
11. TB Ketubot 104a.
12. Avot deRabbi Natan 14:6.
13. Midrash on Proverbs 31:10, ed. Buber, pp. 108–109.
14. TB Avodah Zarah 18a.
15. Alfred, Lord Tennyson, *In Memoriam.*
16. Jeremiah 31:15.
17. TB Yoma 69b.